Percy Bysshe Shelley, Harry Buxton Forman

Works in Verse and Prose

Now First Brought Together With Many Pieces Not Published Before. Vol. 7

Percy Bysshe Shelley, Harry Buxton Forman

Works in Verse and Prose
Now First Brought Together With Many Pieces Not Published Before. Vol. 7

ISBN/EAN: 9783744685955

Printed in Europe, USA, Canada, Australia, Japan

Cover: Foto ©Thomas Meinert / pixelio.de

More available books at **www.hansebooks.com**

THE WORKS

OF

PERCY BYSSHE SHELLEY

IN VERSE AND PROSE

NOW FIRST BROUGHT TOGETHER

WITH MANY PIECES NOT BEFORE PUBLISHED

EDITED

With Prefaces Notes and Appendices

BY

HARRY BUXTON FORMAN

IN EIGHT VOLUMES

SEVENTH VOLUME—PROSE III

LONDON
REEVES AND TURNER 196 STRAND
1880

CONTENTS.

ILLUSTRATION TO VOL. III.

REMARKS ON "MANDEVILLE" AND MR. GODWIN.

[This composition was published in *The Athenæum* for the 27th of October, 1832, and afterwards in *The Shelley Papers;* but not in Mrs. Shelley's editions of the *Essays* &c. Mr. Rossetti in the Memoir prefixed to his 1878 edition of Shelley's Poetical Works (Vol. I, page 150) assigns the composition to the year 1816. The first edition of *Mandeville* bears the date 1817 : still it is possible that it was issued late in 1816, and in Shelley's hands in time to admit of his having reviewed it before the turn of the year. This seems like a review meant for contemporary issue ; but I do not know of its having appeared before 1832.—H. B. F.]

REMARKS ON "MANDEVILLE" AND MR. GODWIN.

THE author of "Mandeville" is one of the most illustrious examples of intellectual power of the present age. He has exhibited that variety and universality of talent which distinguishes him who is destined to inherit lasting renown, from the possessors of temporary celebrity. If his claims were to be measured solely by the accuracy of his researches into ethical and political science, still it would be difficult to name a contemporary competitor. Let us make a deduction of all those parts of his moral system which are liable to any possible controversy, and consider simply those which only to allege is to establish, and which belong to that most important class of truths which he that announces to mankind seems less to teach than to recall.

"Political Justice" is the first moral system explicitly founded upon the doctrine of the negativeness of rights and the positiveness of duties,—an obscure feeling of which has been the basis of all the political liberty and private virtue in the world. But he is also the author of "Caleb Williams"; and if we had no record of a mind, but simply some fragment containing the conception of the character of Falkland, doubtless we should say, "This is an extraordinary mind, and undoubtedly was capable of the very sublimest enterprises of thought."

St. Leon and Fleetwood are moulded with somewhat inferior distinctness, in the same character of a union of delicacy and power. The Essay on Sepulchres has all the solemnity and depth of passion which belong to a mind that sympathizes, as one man with his friend, in the interest of future ages, in the concerns of the vanished generations of mankind.

It may be said with truth, that Godwin has been treated unjustly by those of his countrymen, upon whose favour temporary distinction depends. If he had devoted his high accomplishments to flatter the selfishness of the rich, or enforced those doctrines on which the powerful depend for power, they would, no doubt, have rewarded him with their countenance, and he might have been more fortunate in that sunshine than Mr. Malthus or Dr. Paley. But the difference would have been as wide as that which must for ever divide notoriety from fame. Godwin has been to the present age in moral philosophy what Wordsworth is in poetry. The personal interest of the latter would probably have suffered from his pursuit of the true principles of taste in poetry, as much as all that is temporary in the fame of Godwin has suffered from his daring to announce the true foundations of minds, if servility, and dependence, and superstition, had not been too easily reconcileable with his species of dissent from the opinions of the great and the prevailing.[1] It is singular that the other nations of Europe should have anticipated, in this respect, the judgment of posterity; and that the name of Godwin and that of his late illustrious and admirable wife, should be pronounced, even by those who know but little of English literature, with reverence and admiration; and that the writings of Mary Wollstonecraft should have been translated, and universally read, in France and Germany, long after the bigotry of faction has stifled them in our own country.

"Mandeville" is Godwin's last production. In interest it is perhaps inferior to "Caleb Williams." There is no character like Falkland, whom the author, with that sublime casuistry which is the parent of toleration and forbearance, persuades us personally to love, whilst his actions must for ever remain the theme of our astonishment and abhorrence. Mandeville challenges our compassion, and no more. His errors arise from an immutable necessity of internal nature, and from much constitutional antipathy and suspicion, which soon spring up into hatred and contempt, and barren misanthropy, which, as it has no root in genius or virtue, produces no fruit uncongenial with the soil wherein it grew. Those of Falkland sprang from a high, though perverted conception of human nature, from a powerful sympathy with his species, and from a temper which led him to believe that the very reputation of excellence should walk among mankind unquestioned and unassailed. So far as it was a defect to link the interest of the tale with anything

[1] This passage may be usefully compared with the Sonnet to Wordsworth (Poetical Works, Vol. I, p. 55) and with various passages in *Peter Bell the Third*. See also the foot-note at the end of that poem (*Ib.*, Vol. III, p. 224).

inferior to Falkland, so is "Mandeville" defective. But the varieties of human character, the depth and complexity of human motive,—those sources of the union of strength and weakness—those powerful sources of pleading for universal kindness and toleration,—are just subjects for illustration and developement in a work of fiction; as such, "Mandeville" yields in interest and importance to none of the productions of the author. The events of the tale flow like the stream of fate, regular and irresistible, growing at once darker and swifter in their progress: there is no surprise, no shock: we are prepared for the worst from the very opening of the scene, though we wonder whence the author drew the shadows which render the moral darkness, every instant more fearful, at last so appalling and so complete. The interest is awfully deep and rapid. To struggle with it, would be the gossamer attempting to bear up against the tempest. In this respect it is more powerful than "Caleb Williams": the interest of "Caleb Williams" being as rapid, but not so profound, as that of "Mandeville." It is a wind that tears up the deepest waters of the ocean of mind.

The language is more rich and various, and the expressions more eloquently sweet, without losing that energy and distinctness which characterize "Political Justice" and "Caleb Williams." The moral speculations have a strength, and consistency, and boldness, which has been less clearly aimed at in his other works of fiction. The pleadings of Henrietta to Mandeville, after his recovery from madness, in favour of virtue and of benevolent energy, compose, in every respect, the most perfect and beautiful piece of writing of modern times. It is the genuine doctrine of "Political Justice," presented in one perspicacious and impressive river, and clothed in such enchanting melody of language, as seems, not less than the writings of Plato, to realize those lines of Milton:

> How charming is divine Philosophy!
> Not harsh and crabbed . . .
> But musical as is Apollo's lute, . . .

Clifford's talk, too, about wealth, has a beautiful, and readily to be disentangled intermixture of truth and error. Clifford is a person, who, without those characteristics which usually constitute the sublime, is sublime from the mere excess of loveliness and innocence. Henrietta's first appearance to Mandeville, at Mandeville House, is an occurrence resplendent with the sunrise of life: it recalls to the memory many a vision—or perhaps but one—which the delusive exhalations of unbaffled hope have invested with a rose-like lustre as of morning, yet unlike morning—a light which, once extinguished, never can return. Henrietta seems at first to be all that a susceptible heart imagines in the object of its earliest passion. We scarcely can see her, she is so beautiful. There is a mist of dazzling loveliness which encircles her, and shuts out from the sight all that is mortal in her transcendent charms. But the veil is gradually undrawn, and she "fades into the light of common day." Her actions, and even her sentiments, do not correspond to the elevation of her speculative opinions, and the fearless sincerity which should be the accompaniment of truth and virtue. But she has a divided affection, and she is faithful there only where infidelity would have been self-sacrifice. Could the spotless Henrietta have subjected her love to Clifford, to the vain and insulting accident of wealth and reputation, and the babbling of a miserable old woman, and yet have proceeded unshrinking to her nuptial feast from the expostulations of Mandeville's impassioned and pathetic madness? It might be well in the author to show the foundations of human hope thus overthrown, for his picture might otherwise have been illumined with one gleam of light. It was his skill to enforce the moral, "that all things are vanity," and "that the house of mourning is better than the house of feasting"; and we are indebted to those who make us feel the instability of our nature, that we may lay the knowledge (which is its foundation) deep, and make the affections (which are its cement) strong. But one regrets that Henrietta,—who soared far beyond her contemporaries in her opinions, who was so beautiful that she seemed a spirit among mankind,—should act and feel no otherwise than the least exalted of her sex; and still more, that the author, capable of conceiving something so admirable and lovely, should have been withheld, by the tenour of the fiction which he chose, from executing[1] it in its full extent. It almost seems in the original conception of the character of Henrietta, that something was imagined too vast and too uncommon to be realized; and the feeling weighs like disappointment on the mind. But these objections, considered with reference to the close of the story, are extrinsical.

The reader's mind is hurried on as he approaches the end with breathless and accelerated impulse. The noun *smorfia* comes at last, and touches some nerve which jars the inmost soul, and grates, as it were, along the blood; and we can scarcely believe that that grin which must accompany Mandeville to his grave, is not stamped upon our own visage.

[1] In *The Athenæum* and *The Shelley Papers* we read *execrating*, an obvious error of transcription or of the press.

ON "FRANKENSTEIN."

[These remarks on Mrs. Shelley's Novel *Frankenstein* appeared in *The Athenæum* for the 10th of November, 1832, and in *The Shelley Papers*; but Mrs. Shelley, for obvious reasons, did not include the essay when publishing her husband's prose writings. Mr. Rossetti (*Poetical Works*, Vol. I, page 150) assigns the composition to the year 1817. The first edition of *Frankenstein* is dated 1818; but of course Shelley had plenty of opportunities of seeing it while in progress.—H. B. F.]

ON "FRANKENSTEIN."

THE novel of "Frankenstein, or The Modern Prometheus," is undoubtedly, as a mere story, one of the most original and complete productions of the day. We debate with ourselves in wonder, as we read it, what could have been the series of thoughts—what could have been the peculiar experiences that awakened them—which conduced, in the author's mind, to the astonishing combinations of motives and incidents, and the startling catastrophe, which compose this tale. There are, perhaps, some points of subordinate importance, which prove that it is the author's first attempt. But in this judgment, which requires a very nice discrimination, we may be mistaken; for it is conducted throughout with a firm and steady hand. The interest gradually accumulates and advances towards the conclusion with the accelerated rapidity of a rock rolled down a mountain. We are led breathless with suspense and sympathy, and the heaping up of incident on incident, and the working of passion out of passion. We cry "hold, hold! enough!"—but there is yet something to come; and, like the victim whose history it relates, we think we can bear no more, and yet more is to be borne. Pelion is heaped on Ossa, and Ossa on Olympus. We climb Alp after Alp, until the horizon is seen blank, vacant, and limitless; and the head turns giddy, and the ground seems to fail under our feet.

This novel rests its claim on being a source of powerful and profound emotion. The elementary feelings of the human mind are exposed to view; and those who are accustomed to reason deeply on their origin and tendency will, perhaps, be the only persons who can sympathize, to the full extent, in the interest of the actions which are their result. But, founded on nature as they are, there is perhaps no reader, who can endure anything beside a new love-story, who will not feel a responsive string touched in his inmost soul. The sentiments are so affectionate and so innocent—the characters of the subordinate agents in this strange drama are clothed in the light of such a mild and gentle mind—the pictures of domestic manners are of the most simple and attaching character: the pathos[1] is irresistible and deep. Nor are the crimes and malevolence of the single Being, though indeed withering and tremendous, the offspring of any unaccountable propensity to evil, but flow irresistibly from certain causes fully adequate to their production. They are the children, as it were, of Necessity and Human Nature. In this the direct moral of the book consists; and it is perhaps the most important, and of the most universal application, of any moral that can be enforced

[1] In *The Athenæum* and *The Shelley Papers* the word *father's* occurs here instead of *pathos*. As *father's* barely makes sense, and *pathos* is unquestionably the right word, there need be no hesitation in crediting Medwin with an error of transcription.

by example. Treat a person ill, and he will become wicked. Requite affection with scorn;—let one being be selected, for whatever cause, as the refuse of his kind—divide him, a social being, from society, and you impose upon him the irresistible obligations—malevolence and selfishness. It is thus that, too often in society, those who are best qualified to be its benefactors and its ornaments, are branded by some accident with scorn, and changed, by neglect and solitude of heart, into a scourge and a curse.

The Being in "Frankenstein" is, no doubt, a tremendous creature. It was impossible that he should not have received among men that treatment which led to the consequences of his being a social nature. He was an abortion and an anomaly; and though his mind was such as its first impressions framed it, affectionate and full of moral sensibility, yet the circumstances of his existence are so monstrous and uncommon, that, when the consequences of them became developed in action, his original goodness was gradually turned into inextinguishable misanthropy and revenge. The scene between the Being and the blind De Lacey in the cottage, is one of the most profound and extraordinary instances of pathos that we ever recollect. It is impossible to read this dialogue,—and indeed many others of a somewhat similar character,—without feeling the heart suspend its pulsations with wonder, and the "tears stream down the cheeks." The encounter and argument between Frankenstein and the Being on the sea of ice, almost approaches, in effect, to the expostulation of Caleb Williams with Falkland. It reminds us, indeed, somewhat of the style and character of that admirable writer, to whom the author has dedicated his work, and whose productions he seems to have studied.

There is only one instance, however, in which we detect the least approach to imitation; and that is the conduct of the incident of Frankenstein's landing in Ireland. The general character of the tale, indeed, resembles nothing that ever preceded it. After the death of Elizabeth, the story, like a stream which grows at once more rapid and profound as it proceeds, assumes an irresistible solemnity, and the magnificent energy and swiftness of a tempest.

The churchyard scene, in which Frankenstein visits the tombs of his family, his quitting Geneva, and his journey through Tartary to the shores of the Frozen Ocean, resemble at once the terrible reanimation of a corpse and the supernatural career of a spirit. The scene in the cabin of Walton's ship—the more than mortal enthusiasm and grandeur of the Being's speech over the dead body of his victim—is an exhibition of intellectual and imaginative power, which we think the reader will acknowledge has seldom been surpassed.

ON PEACOCK'S "RHODODAPHNE."

[In writing to Peacock on the 20th of April, 1818, Shelley says, "You tell me nothing of Rhododaphne, a book from which, I confess, I expected extraordinary success." Mr. Rossetti (Poetical Works, 1878, Vol. I, page 150) mentions as a minor work of 1818 "now perhaps lost," a criticism by Shelley of that poem; and I presume it was written in the early part of the year. It seems to have been meant for a newspaper or magazine article, and sent to Leigh Hunt, among whose papers it was found by Mr. Townshend Mayer—not, unfortunately, quite complete. It was either dictated to or transcribed by Mrs. Shelley; but the MS., mainly in her writing, has been carefully revised and interpolated by Shelley. It is headed, in review fashion, *Rhododaphne, or the Thessalian Spell: a Poem—Hookhams.* The book, though published anonymously in 1818, is acknowledged in the Collected Works of Thomas Love Peacock, published in 1875, in three volumes, by Messrs. R. Bentley & Sons.—H. B. F.]

ON "RHODODAPHNE,

OR

THE THESSALIAN SPELL,"

A POEM BY THOMAS LOVE PEACOCK.

RHODODAPHNE is a poem of the most remarkable character, and the nature of the subject no less than the spirit in which it is written forbid us to range it under any of the classes of modern literature.[1] It is a Greek and Pagan poem. In sentiment and scenery it is essentially antique. There is a strong *religio loci* throughout which almost compels us to believe that the author wrote from the dictation of a voice heard from some Pythian cavern in the solitudes where Delphi stood. We are transported to the banks of the Peneus and linger under the crags of Tempe, and see the water lilies floating on

[1] Shelley is not the only poet who has thought well of *Rhododaphne*. Edgar Allan Poe in his *Marginalia* (Mr. J. H. Ingram's edition, Edinburgh, 1874-5, Vol. III, p. 443) has this laconic criticism :—

"'Rhododaphne' (who wrote it?) is brimful of music :—e.g.

By living streams, in sylvan shades,
Where wind and wave symphonious make
Rich melody, the youths and maids
No more with choral music wake
Lone echo from her tangled brake."

In these lines, the opening of Canto III, the right reading is *winds and waves* in line 2, and *Sweet* for *Rich* in line 3.

the stream. We sit with Plato by old Ilissus under the sacred Plane tree among the sweet scent of flowering sallows; and above there is the nightingale of Sophocles in the ivy of the pine, who is watching the sunset so that it may dare to sing; it is the radiant evening of a burning day, and the smooth hollow whirlpools of the river are overflowing with the aërial gold of the level sunlight. We stand in the marble temples of the Gods, and see their sculptured forms gazing and almost breathing around. We are led forth from the frequent pomp of sacrifice into the solitude of mountains and forests where Pan, "the life, the intellectual soul of grove and stream,"[1] yet lives and yet is worshipped. We visit the solitudes of Thessalian magic, and tremble with new wonder to hear statues speak and move and to see the shaggy changelings minister to their witch queen with the shape of beasts and the reason of men, and move among the animated statues[2] who people her inchanted palaces and gardens. That wonderful overflowing of fancy the *Syria Dea* of Lucian, and the impassioned and elegant pantomime of Apuleius, have contributed to this portion of the poem. There is here, as in the songs of ancient times, music and dancing and the luxury of voluptuous delight. The Bacchanalians toss on high their leaf-inwoven hair, and the tumult and fervour of the chase is depicted; we hear its clamour gathering among the woods, and she who impels it is so graceful and so fearless that we are charmed—and it needs no feeble spell to see nothing of the agony and blood of that royal sport.

[1] These words are quoted, not quite accurately, from Canto III of *Rhododaphne*, pp. 48—9:

The streams no sedge-crowned Genii roll
From bounteous urn: great Pan is dead
The life, the intellectual soul
Of vale, and grove, and stream, has fled
For ever with the creed sublime
That nursed the Muse of earlier time.

[2] Cancelled MS. reading, *forms* for *statues*.

This it is to be a scholar; this it is to have read Homer and Sophocles and Plato.

Such is the scenery and the spirit of the tale. The story itself presents a more modern aspect, being made up of combinations of human passion which seem to have been developed since the Pagan system has been outworn. The poem opens in a strain of elegant but less powerful versification than that which follows. It is descriptive of the annual festival of Love[1] at his temple in Thespia. Anthemion is among the crowd of votaries; a youth from the banks of Arcadian Ladon:

> The flower of all Arcadia's youth
> Was he: such form and face, in truth,
> As thoughts of gentlest maidens seek
> In their day-dreams: soft glossy hair
> Shadowed his forehead, snowy-fair,
> With many a hyacinthine cluster:
> Lips, that in silence seemed to speak,
> Were his, and eyes of mild blue lustre:
> And even the paleness of his cheek,
> The passing trace of tender care,
> Still shewed how beautiful it were
> If its own natural bloom were there.—CANTO I, p. 11.

He comes to offer his vows at the shrine for the recovery of his mistress Calliroë, who is suffering under some strange, and as we are led to infer, magical disease. As he presents his wreath of flowers at the altar they are suddenly withered up. He looks and there is standing near him a woman of exquisite beauty who gives him another wreath which he places on the altar and it does not wither. She turns to him and bids him wear a

[1] The word *Uranian* before *Love* stands cancelled in the MS.

flower which she presents, saying, with other sweet words—

Some meet for once and part for aye,
Like thee and me, and scarce a day
Shall each by each remembered be:
But take the flower I give to thee,
And till it fades remember me.—CANTO I, p. 22.

As Anthemion passes from the temple among the sports and dances of the festival "with vacant eye"

——— the trains
Of youthful dancers round him float,
As the musing bard from his sylvan seat
Looks on the dance of the noontide heat,
Or the play of the watery flowers, that quiver
In the eddies of a lowland river.—CANTO II, p. 29.

He there meets an old man who tells him that the flower he wears is the profane laurel-rose which grows in Larissa's unholy gardens, that it is impious to wear it in the temple of Love, and that he, who has suffered evils which he dares not tell from Thessalian inchantments, knows that the gift of this flower is a spell only to be dissolved by invoking his natal genius and casting the flower into some stream with the caution of not looking upon it after he has thrown it away. Anthemion obeys his direction, but so soon as he has . . . .[1]

*　　*　　*　　*　　*　　*

[1] A portion of the MS. is here wanting. Probably it contained little more than an abstract of the movement of the third and fourth Cantos, illustrated by extracts, as the next fragment begins with a quotation from the fifth Canto. It will be useful to supply here the thread of the story. As soon as Anthemion has thrown the flower into the water he hears a sudden cry, Calliroë's voice:

He turned to plunge into the tide,
But all again was still:
The sun upon the surface bright
Poured his last line of crimson light,
Half-sunk behind the hill;
But through the solemn plane-trees past
The pinions of a mightier blast,
And in its many-sounding sweep,
Among the foliage broad and deep,
Aërial voices seemed to sigh,
As if the spirits of the grove
Mourned in prophetic sympathy
With some disastrous love.—
CANTO II, pp. 43–4.

Canto III shews Anthemion, on his way back to Thespia, repelled by sounds of revelry, and seeking solitude by "Aganippe's fountain-wave." Musing on Calliroë, he hears music, prelusive to the appearance of the "radiant maid" whom he had met in the Thespian temple: he learns that her name is

— round his neck
Are closely twined the silken rings
Of Rhododaphne's glittering hair,
And round him her bright arms she flings,
And cinctured thus in loveliest bands
The charmed waves in safety bear
The youth and the enchantress fair
And leave them on the golden sands.—

CANTO V, pp. 110—11.

They now find themselves on a lonely moor on which stands a solitary cottage—ruined and waste; this scene is transformed by Thessalian magic to a palace surrounded by magnificent gardens. Anthemion enters the hall of the palace where, surrounded by sculptures of divine workmanship, he sees the earthly image of Uranian Love.

Rhododaphne, and receives her declarations of love. She utters the words

These lips are mine; the spells have won them,
Which round and round thy soul I twine;
And be the kiss I print upon them
Poison to all lips but mine!—

CANTO III, pp. 66—7.

Stung by the thought of Calliroë, he escapes this time from the encircling arms of Rhododaphne. The fourth Canto sets forth that "magic and mystery" have been chased away by Reason; but the poet adds

Yet deem not so. The Power of Spells
Still lingers on the earth, but dwells
In deeper folds of close disguise,
That baffle Reason's searching eyes:
Nor shall that mystic Power resign
To Truth's cold sway his webs of guile,
Till woman's eyes have ceased to shine,
And woman's lips have ceased to smile,
And woman's voice has ceased to be
The earthly soul of melody.—

CANTO IV pp. 72—3.

This is introductory to the working of the spell. Seeking Calliroë, he finds her recovered, rejoices with her one evening, kisses her, and sees her fade and at once become as one dead. Fleeing along the shore, he is seized by pirates (Canto V), on board whose ship he is set beside a maiden similarly snatched away, who turns out to be Rhododaphne. By her incantations she raises a storm; the boat is wrecked, and Anthemion is borne to shore by the magic of Rhododaphne. Such is the portion of the poem that the missing leaves of the MS. doubtless epitomize. Shelley would scarcely have failed to quote the following description of Rhododaphne preparing for the storm:

She rose, and loosed her radiant hair,
And raised her golden lyre in air.
The lyre, beneath the breeze's wings,
As if a spirit swept the strings,
Breathed airy music, sweet and strange,
In many a wild phantastic change.
Most like a daughter of the Sun
She stood: her eyes all radiant shone
With beams unutterably bright;
And her long tresses, loose and light,
As on the playful breeze they rolled,
Flamed with rays of burning gold.—

CANTO V, p. 105.

The extract with which the next leaf of the MS. opens is the conclusion of Canto V; and the paragraph beginning with *They now find themselves* epitomizes Canto VI. At the opening of the paragraph there is a cancelled reading, *The scene in which they now find themselves is then described.*

Plato says, with profound allegory, that Love is not itself beautiful, but seeks the possession of beauty; this idea seems embodied in the deformed dwarf who bids, with a voice as from a trumpet, Anthemion enter. After feast and music the natural result of the situation of the lovers[1] is related by the poet to have place.

The last Canto relates the enjoyments and occupations of the lovers; and we are astonished to discover that any thing can be added to the gardens of Armida and Alcína, and the Bower of Bliss: the following description among many of a Bacchanalian dance is a remarkable instance of a fertile and elegant imagination.[2]

Oft, 'mid those palace-gardens fair,
The beauteous nymph (her radiant hair
With mingled oak and vine-leaves crowned)
Would grasp the thyrsus ivy-bound,
And fold, her festal vest around,
The Bacchic nebris, leading thus
The swift and dizzy thiasus:
And as she moves, in all her charms,
With springing feet and flowing arms,
'Tis strange in one fair shape to see
How many forms of grace can be.
The youths and maids, her beauteous train,
Follow fast in sportive ring,
Some the torch and mystic cane,
Some the vine-bough, brandishing;
Some, in giddy circlets fleeting,
The Corybantic timbrel beating:
Maids, with silver flasks advancing,
Pour the wine's red-sparkling tide,
Which youths, with heads recumbent dancing,
Catch in goblets as they glide:

[1] Cancelled reading, *their situation.*

[2] Cancelled reading, *is worthy remark.*

All upon the odorous air
Lightly toss their leafy hair,
Ever singing, as they move,
— "Io Bacchus! son of Jove!"[1]—

CANTO VII, pp. 148—50.

[1] There must have been another leaf or two of the MS. The last leaf I have ends without completing the extract; and I have added the final couplet. Doubtless Shelley followed his friend's narrative to the catastrophe,—the slaying of Rhododaphne by Uranian Love, who, as he sends his shaft into her breast, exclaims

With impious spells hast thou profaned
My altars; and all-ruling Jove,
Though late, yet certain, has unchained
The vengeance of Uranian Love!—

CANTO VII, p. 159.

How Anthemion finds himself with the dead Rhododaphne near Calliroë's door, how Calliroë comes out, the spell of her trance being broken, to greet her lover, Shelley doubtless told in few words, and perhaps concluded with verses that must have commended themselves to him—

But when the maid Anthemion led
To where her beauteous rival slept
The long last sleep, on earth dispread,
And told her tale, Calliroë wept
Sweet tears for Rhododaphne's doom;
For in her heart a voice was heard:
—"'Twas for Anthemion's love she erred!"—

CANTO VII, pp. 165—6.

THE COLISEUM,

A FRAGMENT OF A ROMANCE.

[A large portion of this fragment appeared in *The Athenæum* for the 1st of September, 1832, and was afterwards included in *The Shelley Papers*. Mrs. Shelley published the whole of what is here given in the *Essays* &c. (1840). Medwin's version, as far as it goes, has been collated with the more authoritative version of Mrs. Shelley here adopted; and all variations of the least importance are noted. After speaking of the fragment on Love, Mrs. Shelley says (Preface, page x) "'The Coliseum' is a continuation to a great degree of the same subject. Shelley had something of the idea of a story in this. The stranger was a Greek,—nurtured from infancy exclusively in the literature of his progenitors,—and brought up as a child of Pericles might have been; and the greater the resemblance, since Shelley conceived the idea of a woman, whom he named Diotima, who was his instructress and guide. In speaking of his plan, this was the sort of development he sketched; but no word more was written than appears in these pages." Mrs. Shelley adds that *The Assassins* (1814) was "composed many years before"; and Mr. Rossetti cannot be far wrong in assigning *The Coliseum* to the year 1819. Indeed Medwin assigns it to the winter of 1818—19, and (*Shelley Papers*, page 52) says, "Like Byron in 'Childe Harold,' or Madame de Staël, he meant to have idealized himself in the principal character. This exquisite fragment he allowed me to copy," &c. It would be rash to set down to the characteristic way in which this opportunity was embraced the whole of the variations of text. It seems probable that, in adding to the fragment, Shelley revised the part already copied out by Medwin.—H. B. F.]

THE COLISEUM,

A FRAGMENT OF A ROMANCE.

At the hour of noon, on the feast of the Passover, an old man accompanied by a girl, apparently his daughter, entered the Coliseum at Rome. They immediately passed through the Arena, and seeking a solitary chasm among the arches of the southern part of the ruin, selected a fallen column for their seat, and clasping each other's hands, sate as[1] in silent contemplation of the scene. But the eyes of the girl were fixed upon her father's lips, and[2] his countenance, sublime and sweet, but motionless as some Praxitelean image of the greatest of poets, filled the silent air with smiles, not[3] reflected from external forms.

It was the great feast of the Resurrection, and the whole native population of Rome, together with all[4] the

[1] Medwin omits *as*.

[2] Medwin omits the word *and*, and makes this a new sentence.

[3] The sense is wholly subverted in *The Shelley Papers* by the omission of the word *not*.

[4] In this line Medwin leaves out the words *of Rome* and *all*.

foreigners who flock from all parts of the earth to contemplate its celebration, were assembled round the Vatican. The most awful religion of the world went forth surrounded by emblazonry of mortal greatness, and mankind had assembled to wonder at and worship the creations of their own power.[1] No straggler was to be met with in the streets and grassy lanes which led to the Coliseum. The father and daughter had sought this spot immediately on their arrival.[2]

A figure, only visible at Rome in night or solitude, and then only to be seen amid the desolated temples of the Forum, or gliding among the weed-grown[3] galleries of the Coliseum, crossed their path. His form, which, though emaciated, displayed the elementary outlines of exquisite grace, was enveloped in an ancient chlamys, which half concealed his face;[4] his snow-white feet were fitted with ivory sandals, delicately sculptured in the likeness of two female figures, whose wings met upon the heel, and whose eager and half-divided lips seemed quivering to meet. It was a face, once seen, never to be forgotten. The mouth[5] and the moulding of the chin resembled the eager and impassioned tenderness of the statues[6] of Antinous; but instead of the effeminate sullenness of the eye, and the narrow smoothness of the forehead, shone an expression of profound and piercing thought; the brow was clear and open, and his eyes deep, like two wells of crystalline

[1] In Medwin's version, *the creation of its own power.*

[2] According to Medwin, "No stranger was to be met with in the avenues that led to the Coliseum. Accident had conducted the father and daughter to the spot immediately on their arrival."

[3] Medwin omits *weed-grown*, and adds after *Coliseum* the words *or the ruined arches of the Baths of Caracalla.*

[4] Medwin omits the next sentence, down to *meet.*

[5] Medwin reads *lips.*

[6] Medwin reads *shapes.*

water which reflect the all-beholding heavens. Over all was spread a timid expression[1] of womanish tenderness and hesitation, which contrasted, yet intermingled strangely, with the abstracted and fearless character that predominated in his form and gestures.

He avoided, in an extraordinary degree, all communication with the Italians, whose language he seemed scarcely to understand,[2] but was occasionally seen to converse with some accomplished foreigner, whose gestures and[3] appearance might attract him amid his solemn haunts. He spoke Latin, and especially Greek, with fluency, and with[4] a peculiar but sweet accent; he had apparently acquired a knowledge of the northern languages of Europe. There was no circumstance connected with him that gave the least intimation of his country, his origin, or his occupation. His dress was strange, but splendid and solemn.[5] He was for ever alone. The literati of Rome thought him a curiosity, but there was something in his manner unintelligible but impressive, which awed their obtrusions into distance and silence. The countrymen, whose path he rarely crossed, returning by starlight from their market at Campo Vaccino, called him, with that strange mixture of religious and historical ideas so common in Italy, *Il Diavolo di Bruto.*

Such was the figure which interrupted the contem-

[1] Medwin, after *expression,* reads *of diffidence and retirement, which intermingled strangely with the abstract,* &c.; and, in a foot-note he says of this passage, "There never was drawn a more perfect portrait of Shelley himself."

[2] Medwin, after *degree,* reads *what is called society, but was,* &c.

[3] Medwin omits *gestures and.*

[4] According to Medwin, *He spoke Italian with fluency, though with* &c.; and he omits the next sentence, down to *Europe.*

[5] Medwin omits this sentence, and, after *He was for ever alone,* he leaves out the rest of this paragraph, down to *Bruto.*

plations, if they were so engaged, of the strangers, by addressing them[1] in the clear, and exact, but unidiomatic phrases of their native language :—

"Strangers, you are two; behold the third in this great city, to whom alone the spectacle of these mighty[2] ruins is more delightful than the mockeries of a superstition which destroyed them."

"I see nothing," said the old man.

"What do you here,[3] then ?"

"I listen to the sweet singing of the birds, and the sound of my daughter's breathing composes me like the soft murmur of water—and I feel the sun-warm wind—and this is pleasant to me."[4]

"Wretched old man, know you not that these are the ruins of the Coliseum ?"—

"Alas! stranger," said the girl, in a voice like mournful music, "speak not so—he[5] is blind."—

The stranger's eyes were[6] suddenly filled with tears, and the lines of his countenance became relaxed.

[1] Medwin omits *by addressing them*, and reads *phrase* for *phrases* in the next line, which is very likely right.

[2] Medwin reads *great* for *mighty*, and tones down the end of the speech thus,—*than the pageantry of religion.*

[3] Medwin reads *hear.*

[4] According to Medwin, "I listen to the sweet singing of the birds, the humming of the bees, which, and the sound of my daughter's breathing, compose me like the soft murmur of waters; and this sun-warm wind is pleasant to me."

[5] Medwin reads *my father* for *he.*

[6] Medwin substitutes *now* for *were.*

"Blind!" he exclaimed, in a tone of suffering, which was more than an apology; and seated himself apart on a flight of shattered and mossy stairs[1] which wound up among the labyrinths of the ruin.

"My sweet Helen," said the old man, "you did not tell me that this was the Coliseum."

"How should I tell you, dearest father, what I knew not? I was on the point of inquiring the way to that building, when we entered this circle of ruins,[2] and, until the stranger accosted us, I remained silent, subdued by the greatness of what I see."[3]

"It is your custom, sweetest child[4], to describe to me the objects that give you delight. You array them in the soft radiance of your words, and whilst you speak I only feel the infirmity which holds me in such dear dependence,[5] as a blessing. Why have you been silent now?"[6]

"I know not—first the wonder and pleasure of the sight, then the words of the stranger, and then thinking on what he had said, and how he had[7] looked—and now, beloved father, your own words."

"Well, tell me now,[8] what do you see?"

"I see a great circle of arches built upon arches, and

[1] According to Medwin, *shallow and mossy steps.*

[2] According to Medwin, *the circle of the ruins.*

[3] Medwin reads *saw.*

[4] Medwin reads *'Tis* for *It is* and *girl* for *child.*

[5] In Medwin's version, *diffidence.*

[6] Medwin reads *so long silent.*

[7] Medwin omits *had*, and inserts *on* before *your own words.*

[8] Medwin reads *Well, dearest* for *Well, tell me now.*

shattered stones lie around, that once made a part of the solid wall.[1] In the crevices, and on the vaulted roofs, grow a multitude of shrubs, the wild olive and the myrtle —and intricate brambles, and entangled weeds and plants I never saw before.[2] The stones are immensely massive, and they jut out one from the other.[3] There are terrible rifts in the wall,[4] and broad windows through which you see the blue heaven. There seems to be more than a thousand arches, some ruined, some entire, and they are all immensely high and wide. Some are shattered,[5] and stand forth in great heaps, and the underwood is tufted on their crumbling summits.[6] Around us lie enormous columns, shattered and shapeless—and fragments of capitals and cornice, fretted with delicate sculptures."—

"It is open to the blue[7] sky?" said the old man.

"Yes. We see the liquid depth of heaven above through the rifts and the windows; and the flowers, and the weeds, and the grass and creeping moss, are nourished by its unforbidden rain. The blue sky is above—the wide, bright, blue sky—it flows through the great rents[8] on high, and through the bare boughs of the marble-rooted fig-tree, and through the leaves and flowers of the weeds,

[1] According to Medwin's version, "I see a vast circle of arches built upon arches, and stones like shattered crags, so vast are they, and walls giddily hanging—totteringly—on walls."

[2] Medwin reads, "the wild olive, the myrtle, and the jasmine, and intricate brambles, and entangled weeds, and strange feathery plants like dishevelled hair, such as I never saw before."

[3] Medwin reads *jut out from each other like mountain cliffs.*

[4] Medwin reads *walls and high windows through which is seen the light of the blue heavens. There seem to me*, &c.

[5] Medwin reads *broken.*

[6] In Medwin's version, *tufted in their crumbling fragments;* and the next sentence stands thus—"Around us lie enormous collections of shattered and shapeless capitals and cornices, loaded with delicate sculpture."

[7] Medwin omits *blue*, the note of interrogation, and the word *Yes* at the beginning of the next speech.

[8] Medwin reads *rifts.*

even to the dark arcades beneath. I see—I feel its[1] clear and piercing beams fill the universe, and impregnate the joy-inspiring wind with life and light, and casting the veil of its splendour over all things—even me.[2] Yes, and through the highest rift the noonday waning moon is hanging, as it were, out of the solid sky, and this shows that the atmosphere has all[3] the clearness which it rejoices me that you feel."

"What else see you?"[4]

"Nothing."

"Nothing?"

"Only the bright green mossy ground, speckled by[5] tufts of dewy clover-grass that run into the interstices of the shattered arches, and round the isolated pinnacles of the ruin.[6]"

"Like the lawny dells of soft short grass which wind among the pine[7] forests and precipices in the Alps of Savoy?"

"Indeed, father, your eye has a vision more serene than mine."

"And the great wrecked arches, the shattered masses

[1] In Medwin's version, *I feel, I see it—its* &c.

[2] Medwin reads *with warmth and light and life, and interpenetrate all things, even me, father;* and again omits the initial *Yes.*

[3] Medwin omits *all* and reads *I feel* for *you feel.*

[4] According to Medwin, *Dearest child, what else see you?*

[5] Medwin reads *interspersed with* instead of *speckled by.*

[6] In Medwin's version, *ruins.*

[7] Medwin has *high* for *pine.*

of precipitous ruin, overgrown with the younglings of the forest, and more like chasms rent by an earthquake[1] among the mountains, than like the vestige of what was human workmanship—what are they?"

"Things awe-inspiring and wonderful."

"Are they not caverns such as the untamed elephant[2] might choose, amid the Indian wilderness, wherein to hide her cubs; such as, were the sea to overflow the earth, the mightiest[3] monsters of the deep would change into their spacious chambers?"

"Father, your words image forth what I would have expressed, but, alas![4] could not."

"I hear the rustling of leaves, and the sound of waters,—but it does not rain,—like the faint[5] drops of a fountain among woods."

"It falls from among the heaps of ruin over our heads—it is, I suppose, the water collected in the rifts by[6] the showers."

"A nursling of man's art, abandoned by his care, and transformed by the enchantment of Nature into a likeness of her own creations, and destined to partake their

[1] Medwin reads *earthquakes* for *an earthquake*, omits *like* in the next line, gives *what are they* as a separate speech of the daughter, and makes the daughter's next speech the opening of the father's.

[2] In Medwin's version the words *and tigress* are here inserted, and *wildernesses* is substituted for *wilderness*, the next clause being *where to hide their cubs*.

[3] Medwin reads *mighty*, and *vast* for *spacious* in the next line.

[4] Medwin omits *alas!*

[5] Mrs. Shelley has *fast*, but Medwin's reading, *faint*, must be right.

[6] Medwin reads *from*, and in the next line *A nursling of man now* &c.

immortality! Changed into a mountain cloven with[1] woody dells, which overhang its labyrinthine glades, and shattered into toppling precipices, even[2] the clouds, intercepted by its craggy summits,[3] feed its eternal fountains with their rain. By the column on which I[4] sit, I should judge that it had once been crowned by a temple or a theatre, and that on sacred days the multitude wound up its craggy path to the[5] spectacle or the sacrifice——It was such itself!* Helen, what sound of wings is that?"

"It is[6] the wild pigeons returning to their young. Do you not hear the murmur of those that are brooding in their nests?"

* Nor does a recollection of the use to which it may have been destined interfere with these emotions. Time has thrown its purple shadow athwart this scene, and no more is visible than the broad and everlasting character of human strength and genius, that pledge of all that is to be admirable and lovely in ages yet to come. Solemn temples, where the senate of the world assembled, palaces, triumphal arches, and cloud-surrounded columns, loaded with the sculptured annals of conquest and domination—what actions and deliberations have they been destined to enclose and commemorate? Superstitious rites, which in their mildest form, outrage reason, and obscure the moral sense of mankind; schemes for wide-extended murder, and devastation, and misrule, and servitude; and, lastly, these schemes brought to their tremendous consummations, and a human being returning in the midst of festival and solemn joy, with thousands and thousands of his enslaved and desolated species chained behind his chariot, exhibiting, as titles to renown, the labour of ages, and the admired creations of genius, overthrown by the brutal force, which was placed as a sword within his hand, and,—contemplation fearful and abhorred!—he himself a being capable of the gentlest and best emotions, inspired with the persuasion that he has done a virtuous deed! We do not forget these things. * * [SHELLEY'S NOTE.]

[1] Medwin reads *to a mountain cloven into.*

[2] Mrs. Shelley sets a full stop at precipices and begins a fresh sentence with *Even.* The version of the text is Medwin's.

[3] This word is singular in Mrs. Shelley's version, plural in that of Medwin, who reads *supply* for *feed its.*

[4] Medwin, who gives this passage, as far as *sacrifice,* to the daughter, reads *we* for *I*, and lets the father take up the word again with *It was such.*

[5] Mrs. Shelley omits *the.*

[6] Medwin here inserts *of.*

"Ay, it is the language of their happiness.[1] They are as happy as we are, child, but in a different manner. They know not the sensations which this ruin excites within us. Yet it is pleasure to them to inhabit it; and the succession of its forms as they pass, is connected with associations in their minds, sacred to them as these to us. The internal nature of each being is surrounded by a circle, not to be surmounted by his fellows; and it is this repulsion which constitutes the misfortune of the condition of life. But there is a circle which comprehends, as well as one which mutually excludes, all things which feel. And, with respect to man, his public and his private happiness consists in diminishing the circumference which includes those resembling himself, until they become one with him, and he with them. It is because we enter into the meditations, designs and destinies of something beyond ourselves, that the contemplation of the ruins of human power excites an elevating sense of awfulness and beauty. It is therefore, that the ocean, the glacier, the cataract, the tempest, the volcano, have each a spirit which animates the extremities of our frame with tingling joy. It is therefore that the singing of birds, and the motion of leaves, the sensation of the odorous earth beneath, and the freshness of the living wind around, is sweet. And this is Love. This is the religion of eternity, whose votaries have been exiled from among the multitude of mankind. O Power!" cried the old man, lifting his sightless eyes towards the undazzling sun, "thou which interpenetratest all things, and without which this glorious world were a blind and formless chaos, Love, Author of Good, God, King, Father! Friend of these thy worshippers! Two

[1] Medwin, omitting the word *Ay*, ended here, and did not give the foot-note to the words *It was such itself* in the last paragraph but one.

solitary hearts invoke thee, may they be divided never! If the contentions of mankind have been their misery; if to give and seek that happiness which thou art, has been their choice and destiny; if, in the contemplation of these majestic records of the power of their kind, they see the shadow and the prophecy of that which thou mayst have decreed that he should become; if the justice, the liberty, the loveliness, the truth, which are thy footsteps, have been sought by them, divide them not! It is thine to unite, to eternize; to make outlive the limits of the grave those who have left among the living, memorials of thee. When this frame shall be senseless dust, may the hopes, and the desires, and the delights which animate it now, never be extinguished in my child; even as, if she were borne into the tomb, my memory would be the written monument of all her nameless excellences!"

The old man's countenance and gestures, radiant with the inspiration of his words, sunk, as he ceased, into more than its accustomed calmness, for he heard his daughter's sobs, and remembered that he had spoken of death.—"My father, how can I outlive you?" said Helen.

"Do not let us talk of death," said the old man, suddenly changing his tone. "Heraclitus, indeed, died at my age, and if I had so sour a disposition, there might be some danger. But Democritus reached a hundred and twenty, by the mere dint of a joyous and unconquerable mind. He only died at last, because he had no gentle and beloved ministering spirit, like my Helen, for whom it would have been his delight to live. You remember his gay old sister requested him to put off starving himself to death until she had returned from the festival of

Ceres; alleging, that it would spoil her holiday if he refused to comply, as it was not permitted to appear in the procession immediately after the death of a relation; and how good-temperedly the sage acceded to her request."

The old man could not see his daughter's grateful smile, but he felt the pressure of her hand by which it was expressed.—" In truth," he continued, "that mystery, death, is a change which neither for ourselves nor for others is the just object of hope or fear. We know not if it be good or evil, we only know, it is. The old, the young, may alike die; no time, no place, no age, no foresight, exempts us from death, and the chance of death. We have no knowledge, if death be a state of sensation, of any precaution that can make those sensations fortunate, if the existing series of events shall not produce that effect. Think not of death, or think of it as something common to us all. It has happened," said he, with a deep and suffering voice, "that men have buried their children."

"Alas! then, dearest father, how I pity you. Let us speak no more."

They arose to depart from the Coliseum, but the figure which had first accosted them interposed itself:—" Lady," he said, "if grief be an expiation of error, I have grieved deeply for the words which I spoke to your companion. The men who anciently inhabited this spot, and those from whom they learned their wisdom, respected infirmity and age. If I have rashly violated that venerable form, at once majestic and defenceless, may I be forgiven?"

"It gives me pain to see how much your mistake afflicts you," she said; "if you can forget, doubt not that we forgive."

"You thought me one of those who are blind in spirit," said the old man, "and who deserve, if any human being can deserve, contempt and blame. Assuredly, contemplating this monument as I do, though in the mirror of my daughter's mind, I am filled with astonishment and delight; the spirit of departed generations seems to animate my limbs, and circulate through all the fibres of my frame. Stranger, if I have expressed what you have ever felt, let us know each other more."

"The sound of your voice, and the harmony of your thoughts, are delightful to me," said the youth, "and it is a pleasure to see any form which expresses so much beauty and goodness as your daughter's; if you reward me for my rudeness, by allowing me to know you, my error is already expiated, and you remember my ill words no more. I live a solitary life, and it is rare that I encounter any stranger with whom it is pleasant to talk; besides, their meditations, even though they be learned, do not always agree with mine; and, though I can pardon this difference, they cannot. Nor have I ever explained the cause of the dress I wear, and the difference which I perceive between my language and manners, and those with whom I have intercourse. Not but that it is painful to me to live without communion with intelligent and affectionate beings. You are such, I feel."

NOTES ON SCULPTURES IN ROME AND FLORENCE.

[Of these Notes, though only eight were given in the *Essays* &c. (1840), eleven have already appeared in print. The rest are from a MS. Note-book, the order of which is here preserved in preference to that adopted by Medwin in *The Shelley Papers* and followed by Mrs. Shelley. In the preface to the 1840 collection, Mrs. Shelley says of certain of the Fragments, "Small portions of these and other Essays were published by Captain Medwin in a newspaper. Generally speaking, his extracts are incorrect and incomplete. I must except the Essay on Love, and Remarks on some of the Statues in the Gallery of Florence, however, as they appeared there, from the blame of these defects." My own impression is that the reason for this exception was negative, that Mrs. Shelley had not the original Note-books by her. Medwin was notoriously incapable of perfect accuracy; but beyond the results of that incapacity, we discern in the versions given by him, and generally adopted implicitly by Mrs. Shelley, signs of tampering, as any student of Shelley will judge by noting the variations given in the following pages. The variations between *The Shelley Papers* and the *Essays* in regard to the eight Notes printed in both, affect only five words and some dozen and a half stops, as far as I can find; and only one change is other than the printer would be likely to make. Medwin says (*Shelley Papers*, page 55), "Shelley, while at Florence, passed much of his time in the gallery, where, after his severe mental labours, his imagination reposed and luxuriated amid the divine creations of the Greeks. The Niobe, the Venus Anadyomine, the group of Bacchus and Ampelus, were the subjects of his inexhaustible and insatiable admiration. On these I have heard him expatiate with all the eloquence of poetic enthusiasm. He had made ample notes on the wonders of art in this gallery, from which, on my leaving Pisa, he allowed me to make extracts, far surpassing in eloquence anything Winkelman has left on this subject." In his life of Shelley (Vol. I, page 351), Medwin records that these notes were "thrown off in the gallery, in a burst of enthusiasm." He does not say that he made extracts from a similar Note-book on statues at Rome; but most likely he did; and the two books were probably continuous; as the Notes at the opening of the book in my possession are Roman, and those on the Arch of Titus and the Laocoön, given by Medwin, are of course also Roman. For convenience of identification, the particular printed sources are indicated in separate foot-notes in this edition. All the Notes on Sculpture not so distinguished are from the MS. book.—H. B. F.]

NOTES ON SCULPTURES IN ROME AND FLORENCE.

ROME.

I.

THE ARCH OF TITUS.[1]

On the inner compartment of the Arch of Titus, is sculptured, in deep relief, the desolation of a city. On one side, the walls of the Temple, split by the fury of conflagrations, hang tottering in the act of ruin. The accompaniments of a town taken by assault, matrons and virgins and children and old men gathered into groups, and the rapine and licence of a barbarous and enraged soldiery, are imaged in the distance. The

[1] *The Arch of Titus* appeared in *The Athenæum* for the 29th of September, 1832, and afterwards in *The Shelley Papers.* Mrs. Shelley reprinted it (*Essays* &c., 1840, Vol. II, p. 208), as a note to a passage about the same arch in a letter to Peacock. We may presume that this and the Laocoön Note were copied by Medwin from a Note-book which Shelley used in Rome; and they must of course have preceded the three Notes which in the book in my possession precede the Florentine series.

foreground is occupied by a procession of the victors, bearing in their profane hands the holy candlesticks and the tables of shewbread, and the sacred instruments of the eternal worship of the Jews. On the opposite side, the reverse of this sad picture, Titus is represented standing in a chariot drawn by four horses, crowned with laurel, and surrounded by the tumultuous numbers of his triumphant army, and the magistrates, and priests, and generals, and philosophers, dragged in chains beside his wheels. Behind him stands a Victory eagle-winged.

The arch is now mouldering into ruins, and the imagery almost erased by the lapse of fifty generations. Beyond this obscure monument of Hebrew desolation, is seen the tomb of the Destroyer's family, now a mountain of ruins.

The Flavian amphitheatre has become a habitation for owls and dragons. The power, of whose possession it was once the type, and of whose departure it is now the emblem, is become a dream and a memory. Rome is no more than Jerusalem.

II.

THE LAOCOÖN.[1]

The subject of the Laocoön is a disagreeable one, but whether we consider the grouping, or the execution,

[1] Surely Mrs. Shelley would have given this Note had the Roman Note-book of her husband not been lost or mislaid. We are indebted for it to Medwin, who printed it in Vol. I, pp. 352-4 of his Life of Shelley. It is essential to take Shelley's praises of this group literally and no more: it will then be observed that the excellences dwelt upon are mainly technical,—the "execution," the "grouping," the "anatomical fidelity and force." Note the significant qualification at p. 66, at the close of the Note on two Statues of Marsyas.

nothing that remains to us of antiquity can surpass it. It consists of a father and his two sons. Byron thinks that Laocoön's anguish is absorbed in that of his children, that a mortal's agony is blending with an immortal's patience. Not so. Intense physical suffering, against which he pleads with an upraised countenance of despair, and appeals with a sense of its injustice, seems the predominant and overwhelming emotion, and yet there is a nobleness in the expression, and a majesty that dignifies torture.

We now come to his children.[1] Their features and attitudes indicate the excess of the filial love and devotion that animates them, and swallows up all other feelings. In the elder of the two, this is particularly observable. His eyes are fixedly bent on Laocoön—his whole soul is with—is a part of that of his father. His arm extended towards him, not for protection, but from a wish as if instinctively to afford it, absolutely speaks. Nothing can be more exquisite than the contour of his form and face, and the moulding of his lips, that are half open, as if in the act of—not uttering any unbecoming complaint, or prayer or lamentation, which he is conscious are alike useless—but addressing words of consolatory tenderness to his unfortunate parent. The intensity of his bodily torments is only expressed by the uplifting of his right foot, which he is vainly and impotently attempting to extricate from the grasp of the mighty folds in which it is entangled.

In the younger child, surprise, pain, and grief seem to contend for mastery. He is not yet arrived at an age

[1] This mode of transition seems suspiciously unlike Shelley.

when his mind has sufficient self-possession, or fixedness of reason, to analyse the calamity that is overwhelming himself and all that is dear to him. He is sick with pain and horror. We almost seem to hear his shrieks. His left hand is on the head of the snake, that is burying its fangs in his side, and the vain and fruitless attempt he is making to disengage it, increases the effect. Every limb, every muscle, every vein of Laocoön expresses, with the fidelity of life, the working of the poison, and the strained girding round of the inextricable folds, whose tangling sinuosities are too numerous and complicated to be followed. No chisel has ever displayed with such anatomical fidelity and force, the projecting muscles of the arm, whose hand clenches the neck of the reptile, almost to strangulation, and the mouth of the enormous asp, and his terrible fangs widely displayed, in a moment to penetrate and meet within its victim's heart, make the spectator of this miracle of sculpture turn away with shuddering and awe, and doubt the reality of what he sees.

III.

VASA BORGHESE A PARIGI.

A Bronze cast of the Bas relief—a bacchanalian subject—a beautiful reference to Unity. Bacchus with a countenance of calm and majestic beauty surrounded by the tumultuous figures whom the whirlwinds of his Deity are tossing into all attitudes, like the sun in the midst of his planets; power calm amid confusion.—He leans on a Woman with a lyre within her arms, on whom he looks with grand yet gentle love. On one side is a Silenus who has let fall the cup and hangs heavily his vine-crowned head, supported by another Bacchanal. The contrast between the flowing robe which wraps the lower part of his form, and the soft but more defined outline of the leg of the Bacchanal who supports him, is in the true harmony of Art.

IV.

A BRONZE.

A child riding on a swan with a dart in his hand.

V.

A BACCHANAL

* * * * holding a lion's skin in one hand, and a flaming torch in the other, with his muscles starting through his skin, and his hair dishevelled.

VI.

AN ACCOUCHEMENT; A BAS RELIEF.[1]

[PROBABLY THE SIDES OF A SARCOPHAGUS.]

The lady is lying on a couch, supported by a young woman, and looking extremely exhausted and thin; her hair is flowing[2] about her shoulders, and she is half-covered with drapery which falls over the couch.

Her tunic is exactly like a shift, only the sleeves are longer, coming half way down the upper part of the arm. An old wrinkled woman, with a cloak over her head, and an enormously sagacious look, has a most professional

[1] So headed in the MS. note-book. Medwin and Mrs. Shelley headed it "A Bas-relief probably the Sides of a Sarcophagus"; and Medwin added a remark that "this bas-relief is not antique. It is of the Cinquecento." He first gave this Note in *The Athenæum* for the 22nd of September, 1832; and it was re-printed in *The Shelley Papers* and the *Essays, Letters* &c.

[2] In previous editions, *extremely exhausted; her dishevelled hair is floating;* in the next line *on* for *over;* and in the next but one *chemise* for *shift*.

appearance, and is taking hold of her arm gently with one hand, and with the other is supporting it. I think she is feeling her pulse. At the side of the couch sits a woman as in grief, holding her head in her hands. At the bottom of the bed is another old woman[1] tearing her hair, and in the act of screaming out most violently, which she seems, however, by the rest of her gestures, to do with the utmost deliberation, as having come to the conclusion[2] that it was a correct thing to do. Behind is another old woman of the most ludicrous ugliness, crying I suppose, with her hands crossed upon her neck. There is a young woman also lamenting. To the left of the couch a woman[3] is sitting on the ground, nursing the child, which is swaddled.[4] Behind her is a woman[5] who appears to be in the act of rushing in, with dishevelled hair and violent gestures, and in one hand either[6] a whip or a thunderbolt. She is probably some emblematic person, whose[7] personification would be a key to the whole. What they are all wailing at, I don't[8] know; whether the lady is dying, or the father has ordered[9] the child to be exposed: but if the mother be not dead, such a tumult would kill a woman in the straw in these days.

The other compartment or[10] second scene of the drama

[1] In previous editions, *matron*.

[2] Medwin and Mrs. Shelley read, *resolution that it was a correct thing to do so. Behind her is a gossip, of the most ludicrous ugliness, crying, I suppose, or praying, for her arms are crossed upon her neck. There is also a fifth setting up a wail.*

[3] In previous editions, *nurse*.

[4] In previous editions, *dandling the child in her arms, and wholly occupied in so doing. The infant is swaddled.*

[5] Medwin and Mrs. Shelley read *female*.

[6] Medwin and Mrs. Shelley read *brandishing* instead of *either*.

[7] In previous editions, *This is probably some emblematic person, the messenger of death, or a fury, whose* &c.

[8] In former editions, *I know not*.

[9] We read *directed* for *ordered* in other editions.

[10] Medwin and Mrs. Shelley printed *in the* instead of *or*.

tells the story of the presentation of the child to its father. An old nurse has it in her[1] arms, and with professional and mysterious officiousness is holding it out to the father.[2] The father, a middle-aged and very respectable-looking man, perhaps not married above nine months, is looking with the wonder of a bachelor upon the strange little being which once was himself; his hands are clasped, and his brow wrinkled up with a kind of inexperienced wonder, and he has gathered up between his arms the folds of his cloke, an emblem of the gathering up of all his faculties to understand so unusual a circumstance.

An old man is standing behind[3] him, probably his own father, with some curiosity and much tenderness in his looks, and around are collected a host of his relations, of whom the youngest seem the most unconcerned.[4] It is altogether an admirable piece quite in the spirit of the comedies of Terence,[5] though I confess I am totally at a loss to comprehend the cause of all that tumult visible in the first scene.

VII.

A MERCURY.

A bronze Mercury standing on the wind.

[1] In previous editions *An old man has it in his.*

[2] The rest of this paragraph varies considerably from the chastened text of Medwin: "The father, a middle-aged and very respectable-looking man, perhaps not long married, is looking with the admiration of a bachelor on his first child, and perhaps thinking, that he was once such a strange little creature himself. His hands are clasped, and he is gathering up between his arms the folds of his cloak; an emblem of his gathering up all his faculties to understand the tale the gossip is bringing."

[3] In former editions *beside.*

[4] Medwin and Mrs. Shelley here read *of whom the youngest, a handsome girl, seems the least concerned.*

[5] In previous editions the final confession is wanting.

VIII.

AN OX.

A most admirable ox in bronze.[1]

IX.

AN URN.

An urn whose ansæ are formed of the horned faces of Ammonian Jove, and oversculptured with labyrinth work of leaves and flowers and buds and strange looking insects, and a tablet with this inscription

ΤΩΝ ΑΓΑΘΩΝ Η ΜΝΗΜΗ ΑΕΙ ΘΑΛΗΣ.

"The memory of the good is ever green."

And art thou then forgotten?

X.

VIEW FROM THE PITTI GARDENS.[2]

You see below, Florence a smokeless city, its domes and spires occupying the vale; and beyond to the right the Apennines, whose base extends even to the walls,[3] and whose summits were intersected with ashen-coloured clouds. The green vallies of these mountains which gently unfold themselves upon the plain, and the interven-

[1] This note is followed in the MS. Note-book by one on the Demon of Socrates—a memorandum of a thought which would seem to have occurred to Shelley while in the Gallery among the statues. This will be found among the Platonic fragments.

[2] Not from the Boboli Gardens, as stated by Medwin in introducing this sketch (Life of Shelley, Vol. I, p. 314). His transcript appears to have been at least as careless as usual. I have only noted the more significant variations.

[3] Medwin omits the rest of this sentence, to *clouds*, and, further on, the words *now full with the winter rains*.

ing hills covered with vineyards and olive plantations are occupied by the villas which are as it were another city; a Babylon of palaces and gardens. In the midst of the picture rolls the Arno, now full with the winter rains, through woods, and bounded by the aerial snow and summits of the Lucchese Apennines. On the left[1] a magnificent buttress of lofty craggy hills, overgrown with wilderness, juts out in many shapes over a lovely vale, and approaches the walls of the city. Cascini and Ville[2] occupy the pinnacles and the abutments of those hills, over which is seen at intervals the ætherial mountain line[3] hoary with snow and intersected by clouds. The vale below is covered with cypress groves whose obeliskine forms of intense green pierce the grey shadow of the wintry hill that overhangs[4] them.—The cypresses too of the garden form a magnificent foreground of accumulated verdure; pyramids of dark leaves and shining cones[5] rising out of a mass, beneath which were cut like caverns recesses which conducted into walks.[6]—The Cathedral with its grey marble Campanile and the other domes and spires of Florence were at our feet.[7]

XI.

VICTORY.

Lips of wisdom and arch yet sublime tenderness, a simple yet profound expression of . . .

[1] In Medwin's version, *snowy heights of the Apennines. On the right* &c.

[2] Not *Cascini and other villages*, as in Medwin's book.

[3] Medwin gives *aerial mountains.*

[4] Not *overlooks*, as printed by Medwin.

[5] Medwin reads *pyramids of dark green* and omits *leaves and shining cones.*

[6] The final sentence is omitted in Medwin's version.

[7] Between this Note and the next in the MS. Note-book occur the following poetic jottings:—

His love and sympathy, his boyish love
His enmity with Life
His admiration of the hidden energies.

XII.

A BOY.[1]

A graceful boy with the skin of a wild beast hanging on his shoulders and a bunch of grapes in his hand. He is crowned with a vine wreath and buds and grapes: the legs are modern, and the face has not an antique but it expresses cheerful and earnest . . .

XIII.

A PRIESTESS.

The drapery beautifully expressed, the face bad.

XIV.

AN ATHLETE.

(Curse these fig leaves; why is a round tin thing more decent than a cylindrical marble one ?) An exceedingly fine statue—full of graceful strength; the countenance full of sweetness and strength. Its attitude with a staff lifted in one hand and some in the other, expresses serene dignity and power; a personification in the firmness and lightness of its form of that perfection of manhood when the will can be freely communicated to every fibre of the body. The muscles are represented how differently from a statue since anatomy has corrupted it.

XV.

A POMONA.

A woman in the act of lightly advancing—much care

[1] The word *Staircase* is written above this Note in the MS. Note-book: how far the description of the statues on the staircase extends, I do not know.

has been taken to render the effect of the drapery as thrown back by the wind of her motion.

XVI.

AN ATHLETE

in every respect different from and inferior to the first.

XVII.

AN URANIA

holding a globe in one hand and compasses in the other: her countenance though not of the highest beauty, is beautiful: her drapery drawn closely round shews the conformation of her left side and falls in graceful folds over the right arm.

XVIII.

A VESTAL.

Probably a portrait. This face, which represented a real person, denotes an admirable disposition and mind, and is not beautiful but wise and gentle although with some mixture of severity. Her office might have contributed to this expression.

XIX.

A VENUS GENITRIX.

Remarkable for the voluptuous effect of her finely proportioned form being seen through the folds of a drapery, the original of which must have been the "woven wind" of Chios. There is a softness in the attitude and upper part of the statue—the restoration of the arms and hand truly hideous.

XX.

A CALLIOPE.

Half modern—the drapery rather coarse.

XXI.

A HERCULES ON AN EMBLEMATIC BASE.

The arms probably restored, for the right hand especially is in villainous proportion.

XXII.

A MUSE.

A statue they call the Muse Polyhymnia—poor Muse—the head which may be a misapplication is of the family likeness of those shrewish and evil-minded Roman women of rank with the busts of whom the Capitol overflows. The form otherwise is too thin and spare for the ideal beauty in which the Muses were clothed. The drapery is very remarkable and very admirable; it is arranged in such large and unrestrained folds as the motions and the shape of a living form naturally forces a form into.

XXIII.

MERCURY.

Another glorious creature of the Greeks. His countenance expresses an imperturbable and god-like self-possession; he seems in the enjoyment of delight which nothing can destroy. His figure nervous yet light, expresses the animation of swiftness emblemed by the plumes of his sandalled feet. Every muscle and nerve of his frame has tranquil and energetic life.

XXIV.

A VENUS

with villanous modern arms—this figure is rather too slight and weak—the body is correctly but feebly expressed.

XXV.

ANOTHER VENUS.

A very insipid person in the usual insipid attitude of this lady. The body and hips and where the lines of the   fade into the thighs is exquisitely imagined and executed.

XXVI.

AN APOLLO[1]

with his serpent crawling round a trunk of laurel on which his quiver is suspended. It probably was, when complete, magnificently beautiful. The restorer of the head and arms following the indications[2] of the muscles of the right side, has lifted the right arm, as if

[1] The Note on an Apollo appeared in *The Athenæum* for the 22nd of September, 1832, and was reprinted in *The Shelley Papers* and in Mrs. Shelley's volumes of 1840. In all these cases it was unsuspectingly given with the following opening—*with serpents twining round a wreath of laurel on which the quiver is suspended.*

[2] In former editions, *indication.*

in triumph[1] at the success of an arrow; imagining to imitate the Lycian Apollo, or that[2] so finely described by Apollonius Rhodius when the dazzling radiance of his beautiful limbs suddenly[3] shone over the dark Euxine.

XXVII.

ANOTHER APOLLO.

In every respect a coarse statue, with a goose or swan who has got the end of his pallium in his bill. Seen on one side the intense energy and god-like animation of those limbs, the spirit which seems as if it would not be contained.

XXVIII.

A CUPID.

Apparently part of a group—as in laughing defiance of those which are lost. It seeks to express what cannot be expressed in sculpture—the coarser and more violent effects of comic feeling cannot be seized by this art. Tenderness, sensibility, enthusiasm, terror, poetic inspiration, the profound, the beautiful, Yes.

XXIX.

BACCHUS AND AMPELUS.[4]

Less beautiful than that in the royal collection of

[1] In former editions, *the arm, as in triumph*.

[2] Not *in that*, as printed by Medwin and Mrs. Shelley.

[3] Medwin and Mrs. Shelley omit *suddenly*, and add after *Euxine* what seems a revised transfer from the next note: *The action, energy, and godlike animation of those limbs speak a spirit which seems as if it could not be consumed.* The intention was apparently to contrast the coarse statue with the great work seen beside it.

[4] This Note also would hardly have been omitted by Mrs. Shelley had it been at hand. Medwin gave it, not in *The Shelley Papers*, but in the Life (Vol. I, pp. 355-6). His version is apparently much manipulated. The opening comparison is omitted, and he starts with the improbable form of words, *Look! the figures are walking* &c.

Naples and yet infinitely lovely. The figures are walking as it were with a sauntering and idle pace, and talking to each other as they walk, and this is expressed in the motions of their delicate and flowing[1] forms. One arm of Bacchus rests on the shoulder of Ampelus, and the other, the fingers being gently curved as with the burning[2] spirit which animates their flexible joints, is gracefully thrown forward corresponding with the advance of the opposite leg. He has sandals and buskins clasped with two serpent heads, and his leg is cinctured with their skins. He is crowned with vine leaves laden with their crude fruit, and the crisp leaves fall as with the inertness of a lithe and faded leaf over his rich and over-hanging hair,[3] which gracefully divided on his forehead falls in delicate wreaths upon his neck and breast.[4] Ampelus with a beast skin[5] over his shoulder holds a cup in his right hand, and with his left half embraces the waist of Bacchus.[6] Just as you may have seen (yet how seldom from their dissevering and tyrannical institutions do you see) a younger and an elder boy at school walking in some remote grassy spot of their play-ground with that tender friendship towards each other which has so much of love.[7]—The countenance of Bacchus is sublimely sweet and lovely, taking a shade of gentle and playful tenderness from the arch looks of Ampelus, whose cheerful face turned towards him, expresses the suggestions of some droll and merry device. It has a divine and

[1] Not *glowing* as in Medwin's version.

[2] Not *living* as printed by Medwin.

[3] Medwin reads *hang with the inertness of a faded leaf over his neck and massy, profuse, down-hanging hair.*

[4] In Medwin's version, *wreaths on each side his neck, and curls upon the breast.*

[5] Medwin reads *a young lion's or lynx's skin.*

[6] Medwin reads *encircles Bacchus*, and omits the interesting parenthesis just below.

[7] Medwin reads *for the other that the age inspires.* I notice he constantly has *that* for Shelley's *which.*

supernatural beauty, as one who walks through the world untouched by its corruptions,[1] its corrupting cares; it looks like one who unconsciously yet with delight confers pleasure and peace.[2] The flowing fulness and roundness of the breast and belly, whose lines fading into each other, are continued with a gentle motion as it were to the utmost extremity of his limbs. Like some fine strain of harmony which flows round the soul and enfolds it, and leaves it in the soft astonishment of a satisfaction, like the pleasure of love with one whom we most love, which having taken away desire, leaves pleasure, sweet pleasure. The countenance of the Ampelus is in every respect inferior; it has a rugged and unreproved appearance; but the Bacchus is immortal beauty.

XXX.

A BACCHANTE WITH A LYNX.

The effect of the wind partially developing her young and delicate form upon the light and floating drapery, and the aerial motion of the lower part of her limbs are finely imagined. But the inanimate expression of her countenance and the position of her arms are at enmity with these indications.

XXXI.

APOLLO WITH A SWAN.

The arms restored. The same expression of passionate

[1] Medwin omits *its corruptions*, and *yet with delight* in the next line.

[2] Instead of the remainder of this Note, Medwin has the following:

"The countenance of Ampelus is in some respects boyish and inferior, that of Bacchus expresses an imperturbable and god-like self-possession—he seems in the enjoyment of a calm delight, that nothing can destroy. His is immortal beauty."

and enthusiastic tenderness seems to have created the intense and sickening beauty, by which it is expressed, the same radiance of beauty, arising from lines only less soft and more sublimely flowing than those of Bacchus. This has some resemblance with the Apollo of the Capitol.

XXXII.

LEDA.

A dull thing.

XXXIII.

VENUS ANADYOMENE.[1]

She seems to have just issued from the bath, and yet to be animated[2] with the enjoyment of it. She seems all soft and mild enjoyment, and the curved lines of her fine limbs flow into each other with never-ending continuity[3] of sweetness. Her face expresses a breathless yet passive and innocent voluptuousness without affectation, without doubt;[4] it is at once desire and enjoyment and the pleasure arising from both.—Her lips which are without the sublimity of lofty and impetuous passion like or[5] the grandeur of enthusiastic imagination like the Apollo of the Capitol, or an union[6] of both like the

[1] So headed in the Note-book, not *On the Venus, called Anadyomene* as in former editions. This Note appeared in *The Athenæum* for the 22nd of September 1832, before being printed in *The Shelley Papers* and the *Essays, Letters* &c.

[2] In former editions *has issued* and *is animated.*

[3] Medwin and Mrs. Shelley read *sinuosity.*

[4] Instead of the words *without affectation, without doubt,* and the whole of the sentence following, Medwin and Mrs. Shelley have simply *free from affectation.*

[5] Medwin and Mrs. Shelley disguise the incompleteness by eliminating *like* and *or.*

[6] Not *the union* as in previous editions.

Apollo Belvedere, have the tenderness of arch yet pure and affectionate desire, and the mode in which the ends are drawn in yet opened by the smile which for ever circles round them, and the tremulous curve into which they are wrought by inextinguishable desire, and the tongue lying against the lower lip as in the listlessness of passive joy, express love, still love.

Her eyes seem heavy and swimming with pleasure, and her small forehead fades on both sides into that sweet swelling and then[1] declension of the bone over the eye, and prolongs itself to the cheek in that mode which expresses simple and tender feelings.

The neck is full and swollen as with the respiration[2] of delight, and flows with gentle curves into her perfect form.

Her form is indeed perfect. She is half sitting on and half rising from a shell, and the fulness of her limbs, and their complete roundness and perfection, do not diminish the vital energy with which they seem to be embued.[3] The mode in which the lines of the curved back flow into and around the thighs, and the wrinkled muscles of the belly, wrinkled by the attitude, is truly astonishing. The attitude of her arms which are lovely beyond imagination, is natural, unaffected and unforced.[4] This perhaps is the finest personification of Venus, the

[1] Medwin and Mrs. Shelley read *thin* for *then*, and, after *eye*, omit *and prolongs itself to the cheek*, substituting *in the mode* for *in that mode*.

[2] Not *panting as with the aspiration*, as in former editions.

[3] Medwin and Mrs. Shelley read *animated* for *embued*, omit the whole of the next sentence, down to *astonishing*, and open the sentence after with *The position of the arms*.

[4] In previous editions, *easy*.

Deity of superficial desire, in all antique statuary. Her[1] pointed and pear-like bosom ever virgin—the virgin Mary might have this beauty, but alas ! * * * * * * * * * *

THIRD DAY.[2]

XXXIV.

A STATUE OF MINERVA.

The arm restored. The head is of the very highest beauty. It has a close helmet, from which the hair delicately parted on the forehead, half escapes. The face uplifted[3] gives entire effect to the perfect form of the neck, and to that full and beautiful moulding of the lower part of the face and the jaw,[4] which is, in living beings, the seat of the expression of a simplicity and integrity of nature. Her face uplifted[5] to Heaven is animated with a profound, sweet and impassioned melancholy, with an earnest, fervid and disinterested pleading against some vast and inevitable wrong : it is the joy and the poetry of sorrow, making grief beautiful, and giving to that nameless feeling which from the imperfection of language we call pain, but which is not all pain, those feelings which make[6] not only the possessor but the

[1] Instead of this closing sentence Medwin and Mrs. Shelley have "Her pointed and pear-like person, ever virgin, and her attitude modesty itself."

[2] So in the Note-book, where however, there is nothing to shew the division between first day and second day. Medwin and Mrs. Shelley head this Note *The Minerva* and omit *The arm restored*. The Note appeared in *The Athenæum* for the 22nd of September, 1832, before its issue in *The Shelley Papers* and the *Essays* &c.

[3] Medwin and Mrs. Shelley read *attitude* for *face uplifted*.

[4] In previous editions *mouth* for *the jaw*.

[5] In previous editions, *up-raised*.

[6] Not *through a feeling which makes*, as in former editions : that must surely be Medwin's way of perfecting Shelley's work.

spectator of it prefer it to what is called pleasure, in which all is not pleasure. It is difficult to think that the head, though of the highest ideal beauty, is the head of Minerva, although the attributes and attitude of the lower part of the statue, certainly suggest that idea. The Greeks rarely in their representations of the Divinities[1] (unless we call the poetic enthusiasm of Apollo, a mortal passion) expressed the disturbance of human feeling; and here is deep and impassioned grief, animating a divine countenance. It is indeed divine, as Wisdom which as Minerva it may be supposed to emblem, pleading[2] earnestly with Power, and invested with the expression of that grief because it must ever plead so vainly. An owl is sitting at her feet.[3] The drapery of the statue, the gentle beauty of the feet and the grace of the attitude are what may be seen in many other statues belonging to that astonishing era which produced it;—such a countenance is seen in few.

This statue happens to be placed on an altar, the subject of the reliefs of which are[4] in a spirit wholly the reverse. It was probably an altar to Bacchus, possibly a funerary urn. It has this inscription: D. M. M. ULPIUS. TERPNUS. FECIT. SIBI ET ULPIÆ SECUNDILLÆ LIBERTÆ. B. M.[5] Under the festoons of fruits and flowers at the corners of the altar with the skulls of goats and in the middle with an inverted flower suspended from a

[1] Medwin and Mrs. Shelley have instead of *Divinities*, the words *characters of their Gods*.

[2] In former editions we read *It is, indeed, divine. Wisdom (which Minerva may be supposed to emblem,) is pleading* &c.

[3] This sentence was not given by Medwin and Mrs. Shelley.

[4] In previous editions, *a pedestal, the subject of whose reliefs is*.

[5] The sentence with the inscription was not given by Medwin and Mrs Shelley.

twisted stem are sculptured in moderate relief four[1] figures of Mænads under the inspiration of the God. Nothing can be imagined[2] more wild and terrible than their gestures, touching as they do upon the verge of distortion, in which their fine limbs and lovely forms are thrown. There is nothing however that exceeds the possibility of Nature, although it borders on its utmost line.

The tremendous spirit of superstition aided by drunkenness and producing something beyond insanity, seems to have caught them in its whirlwinds, and to bear them over the earth as the rapid volutions of a tempest bear[3] the ever-changing trunk of a water-spout, as the torrent of a mountain river whirls the leaves in[4] its full eddies. Their hair loose and floating seems caught in the tempest of their own tumultuous motion, their heads are thrown back leaning with a strange inanity[5] upon their necks, and looking up to Heaven, while they totter and stumble even in the energy of their tempestuous dance. One—perhaps Agave[6] with the head of Pentheus, has a human head in one hand and in the other a great knife; another[7] has a spear with its pine cone, which was their thyrsus; another dances with mad voluptuousness; the fourth is dancing to a kind of tambourine.

[1] In previous editions *flowers that grace the pedestal, the corners of which are ornamented with the skulls of goats, are sculptured some figures* &c. The filling of the blank with *grace the pedestal* is little calculated to inspire confidence in the genuineness of the text of Medwin.

[2] In former editions, *conceived.*

[3] Not *have*, as given by Medwin and Mrs. Shelley.

[4] In former editions, *whirls the autumnal leaves resistlessly along in* &c.

[5] Medwin and Mrs. Shelley read *delirium* instead of *inanity.*

[6] In previous editions we read, *One represents Agave with the head of Pentheus*, and the words *has a human head* are left out.

[7] In former editions, *a second;* in the next line, *the Thyrsus;* and in the next but one *beating* for *dancing to.*

This was indeed a monstrous superstition only capable of existing in Greece because there alone[1] capable of combining ideal beauty and poetical and abstract enthusiasm with the wild errors from which it sprung. In Rome it had a more familiar, wicked and dry appearance—it was not suited to the severe and exact apprehensions of the Romans, and their strict morals once violated by it, sustained[2] a deep injury little analogous to its effects upon the Greeks who turned all things, superstition, prejudice, murder, madness—to Beauty.

XXXV.

A TRIPOD.

Said to be dedicated to Mars—three winged figures with emblematic instruments.

XXXVI.

A FAUN.

A pretty thing but little remarkable. A lynx is slily peeping round the stem covered with vines on which he leans and gnawing the grapes.

XXXVII.

A GANYMEDE.

A statue of surpassing beauty. One of the Eagle's wings is half-enfolded round him and one of his arms is

[1] In previous editions we read, *a monstrous superstition, even in Greece, where it was alone,* &c.

[2] In Medwin's and Mrs. Shelley's editions, *were violated by it, and sustained* &c.

placed round the Eagle and his delicate hand lightly touches the wing; the other holds what I imagine to be a representation of the thunder. These hands and fingers are so delicate and light that it seems as if the spirit of pleasure, of light, life and beauty that lives in them half lifted them, and deprived them of the natural weight of mortal flesh. The roundness and fulness of the flowing perfection of his form is strange and rare. The attitude and form of the legs and the relation borne to each other by his light and delicate feet is peculiarly beautiful. The calves of the legs almost touching each other, one foot is placed on the ground, a little advanced before the other which is raised, the knee being a little bent as those who are slightly, but slightly fatigued with standing. The face though innocent and pretty has no ideal beauty. It expresses inexperience and gentleness and innocent wonder, such as might be imagined in a rude and lovely shepherd-boy and no more.

XXXVIII.

A VENUS.

A beautiful Venus, sculptured with great accuracy but without the feeling and the soft and flowing proportions of the Anadyomene. It has great perfection and beauty of form; it is a most admirable piece of sculpture, but hard, angular and with little of the lithe suppleness or light of life.

XXXIX.

A TORSO OF FAUNUS.

(Why I don't know.) The sculpture remarkably good.

XL.

TWO STATUES OF MARSYAS.

Two of those hideous St. Sebastians[1] of Antiquity opposite each other,—Marsyas: one looks as if he had been flayed, and the other as if he was going to be flayed. This is one of the few abominations of the Greek religion. This is as bad as the everlasting damnation and hacking and hewing between them of Joshua and Jehovah. And is it possible that there existed in the same imagination the idea of that tender and sublime and poetic and life-giving Apollo, and of the author of this deed as the same person?[2] It would be worse than confounding Jehovah and Jesus in the same Trinity, which to those who believe in the divinity of the latter is a pretty piece of blasphemy in any intelligible sense of the word. As to the sculpture of these pieces, it is energetic, especially that of the one already flayed, and moderate. If he knew as much as the moderns about anatomy, which I hope to God he did not, he, at least, abstained from taking advantage of his subject for making the same absurd display of it. These great artists abstained from overstepping in this particular, except in some cases, as perhaps in the Laocoön, what Shakespeare calls the modesty of nature.

[1] Shelley was not, it would seem, as familiar with the history of the Christian Martyrs as with the mythology of the Greeks, or he would of course have written "Two of those hideous St. Bartholomews." One would think, however, that he must have seen so many pictures in Italy of both martyrdoms that, even if he did not, as he would not, study them much, the slip in this case could scarcely be other than a slip of the pen.

[2] Students of mythology will doubtless answer No. This variable and contradictory creation was the offspring of many imaginations; and no single imagination worth the name mixed up these two particular conceptions as an article of religious belief.

XLI.

THETIS.

Thetis on a sea-horse—the face far from idealism seems to be a real face of much énergy and goodness. She sits on the curved back of the monster, and holds in one hand something like a sponge, in the other the ears of the head of the sharp beast.[1]

XLII.

HYGIEIA.

An Hygieia with a serpent. A resemblance of the famous Dis—a copy. The forms are soft and flowing but not the most perfect proportion. The head and countenance is of great beauty. There is the serene sweetness of expectation, the gathered firm and yet the calm and gentle lip.

XLIII.

JUPITER.

A Jupiter in every respect of a very ordinary character.

XLIV.

A MINERVA.

Evidently a production of very great antiquity.

[1] It was doubtless intended to erase some words here.

XLV.

A JUNO.[1]

A statue of great merit. The countenance expresses a stern and unquestioned severity of dominion, with a certain sadness. The lips are beautiful—susceptible of expressing scorn—but not without sweetness in their beauty.[2] Fine lips are never wholly bad, and never belong to the expression of emotions completely[3] selfish—lips being the seat of imagination. The drapery is finely conceived, and the manner in which the act of throwing back one leg is expressed in the diverging folds of the drapery of the left breast, fading in bold yet graduated lines into a skirt of it which descends from the right[4] shoulder is admirably imagined.

XLVI.

A WOUNDED SOLDIER.

An unknown figure. His arms are folded within his mantle.—His countenance which may be a portrait is sad but gentle.

XLVII.

A YOUTH.

A youth playing on a lyre—one arm and leg is a restoration and there is no appearance of the head or arm belonging to it. The body and the right leg are of the most consummate beauty. It may or may not be an Apollo.

[1] Medwin first gave this Note in *The Athenæum* for the 22nd of September, 1832. Like the others so given, it was reprinted in *The Shelley Papers* and *Essays, Letters &c.*

[2] Medwin and Mrs. Shelley omit *in their beauty*, and begin the next sentence thus—*With fine lips a person is.*

[3] In previous editions, *wholly.*

[4] Medwin and Mrs. Shelley read, *a skirt, as it descends from the left shoulder.*

XLVIII.

THE FIGURE OF A YOUTH SAID TO BE APOLLO.

It was difficult to conceive anything more delicately beautiful than the Ganymede; but the spirit-like lightness, the softness, the flowing perfection of these forms, surpass it. The countenance though exquisite lovely and gentle is not divine. There is a womanish vivacity of winning yet passive happiness and yet a boyish inexperience exceedingly delightful. Through the limbs there seems to flow a spirit of life which gives them lightness. Nothing can be more perfectly lovely than the legs and the union of the feet with the ancles, and the fading away of the lines of the feet to the delicate extremities. It is like a spirit even in dreams. The neck is long yet full and sustains the head with its profuse and knotted hair as if it needed no sustaining.

XLIX.

AN ÆSCULAPIUS.

A Statue of Æsculapius—the same as in the Borghese Gardens in the temple there.

L.

AN ÆSCULAPIUS.

A Statue of Æsculapius far superior. It is leaning forward upon a knotty staff imbarked and circled by a viper,—with a bundle of plants in one hand and the other with the forefinger in an attitude of instruction. The majestic head, its thick beard and profuse hair bound by a fillet leans forward, and the gentle smile of its benevolent lips seems a commentary on his instructions. The upper part of the figure with the exception of the right shoulder is naked, but the rest to the feet is involved in drapery, whose folds flow from the point where the staff confines them sustaining the left arm.

LI.

OLINTHUS

(as they call a youth seated). Another of those sweet and gentle figures of adolescent youth in which the Greeks delighted.

LII.

MARCUS AURELIUS.

A Statue of Marcus Aurelius which is rather without faults than with beauties.

LIII.

BACCHUS AND AMPELUS.

A lovely group.

LIV.

LEDA.

Leda with a very ugly face. I should be a long time before I should make love with her.

LV.

A MUSE.

A most hideous thing they call a Muse—evidently the production of some barbarian and of a barbarous age.

LVI.

AN OLD CUIRASS

with all the frogs and fringe complete—a fine piece of antique dandyism.

LVII.

A BACCHUS BY MICHAEL ANGELO.[1]

The countenance of this figure is the most revolting mistake of the spirit and meaning of Bacchus. It looks drunken, brutal, and narrow-minded, and has an expression of dissoluteness the most revolting. The lower part of the figure is stiff, and the manner in which the shoulders are united to the breast, and the neck to the head, abundantly inharmonious. It is altogether without unity, as was the idea of the Deity of Bacchus in the conception of a Catholic. On the other hand, considered merely[2] as a piece of workmanship, it has great merits. The arms are executed in the most perfect[3] and manly beauty; the body is conceived with great energy,[4] and the lines which describe

[1] So headed in the Note-book, but *Michael Angelo's Bacchus* in former editions.

[2] In former editions, *only*.

[3] Not *in a style of the most perfect*, &c., as in previous editions.

[4] In Medwin's and Mrs. Shelley's editions we read from here as follows—*and the manner in which the lines mingle into each other, of the highest boldness and truth. It wants unity as a work of art—as a representation of Bacchus it wants everything.*

the sides and thighs, and the manner in which they mingle into one another are of the highest order of boldness and beauty. It wants as a work of art unity and simplicity; as a representation of the Greek Deity of Bacchus it wants every thing.

LVIII.

SLEEP.

A remarkable figure of Sleep as a winged child supine on a lion's skin, sleeping on its great half unfolded wing of black *obsidian* stone. One hand is lightly placed on a horn, with which it might be supposed to call together its wandering dreams, the horn of dreams, and in the other a seedy poppy. The hardness of the stone does not permit the arriving at any great expression.

LIX.

COPY OF THE LAOCOÖN.

An admirable copy of the Laocoön in which is expressed with fidelity the agony of the poison and the straining round of the angry serpents. The left hand child seems sick with agony and horror, and the vain and feeble attempt he makes to disentangle himself from its grasp increases the effect. (See Rome.[1])

[1] This is of course a reference to the missing Note-book from which Medwin seems to have copied the remarks on the Laocoön standing second in this series. See pp. 42 and 44.

LX.

THE NIOBE.[1]

This figure is probably the most consummate personification of loveliness with regard to its countenance, as that of the Apollo of the Vatican is with regard to its entire form, that remains to us of Greek Antiquity. It is a colossal figure; the size of a work of art rather adds to its beauty, because it allows the spectator the choice of a greater number of points of view, in which to catch a greater number of the infinite modes of expression of which any form approaching ideal beauty is necessarily composed, of a mother in the act of sheltering from some divine and inevitable peril, the last, we will[2] imagine, of her surviving children.

The child[3] terrified we may conceive at the strange destruction of all its kindred, has fled to its mother, and[4] hiding its head in the folds of her robe and casting up[5]

[1] The Note on the Niobe appeared in *The Athenæum* for the 15th of September, 1832, and afterwards in *The Shelley Papers* and Mrs. Shelley's volumes of 1840. It seems to have been very considerably edited by Medwin, the opening being rendered thus:

"Of all that remains to us of Greek antiquity, this figure is perhaps the most consummate personification of loveliness, with regard to its countenance, as that of the Venus of the Tribune is with regard to its entire form of woman. It is colossal: the size adds to its value;"

and after the words *points of view*, we read *and affords him a more analytical one*. Further on there is, in Medwin's text, a period after *composed;* and a new sentence is begun with the words, *It is the figure*. In fact we are to read *It is a colossal figure ... of a mother in the act* &c., the remarks on size in sculpture being parenthetic. Had Shelley used his rough note for one of the noble letters to Peacock, or for any literary purpose, he would doubtless have made it read more smoothly; but his roughest work never fails to convey a perfectly clear sense, and is of course preferable to Medwin's smoothest.

[2] In former editions, *may*.

[3] Medwin and Mrs. Shelley put *little creature* for *child*.

[4] Medwin and Mrs. Shelley alter the construction by inserting *is* here.

[5] In previous editions, *back* instead of *up*.

one arm as in a passionate appeal for defence from her,[1] where it never before could have been sought in vain, seems in the marble to have scarcely suspended the motion of her terror; as though conceived to be yet in the act of arrival. The child[2] is clothed in a thin tunic of delicatest woof, and her hair is gathered[3] on her head into a knot, probably by that mother whose care will never gather it again. Niobe is enveloped in profuse drapery, a portion of which the left hand has gathered up and is in the act of extending it over the child in the instinct of defending[4] her from what reason knows, to be inevitable. The right[5]—as the restorer of it has rightly comprehended, is gathering up her child to her and with a like instinctive gesture is encouraging by its gentle pressure the child to believe that it can give security.—The countenance which is the consummation of feminine majesty and loveliness, beyond which the imagination scarcely doubts that it can conceive anything, that[6] master-piece of the poetic harmony of marble, expresses other feelings. There is embodied a sense of the inevitable and rapid destiny which is consummating around her as if it were already over. It seems

[1] Former editions omit *from her*, and the sentence ends with a period at *vain*, the subtle passage from *seems in the marble* to *arrival* being left out.

[2] Medwin and Mrs. Shelley have *She* for *The child*.

[3] In former editions, *fastened* for *gathered*, and *fasten* in the next line instead of *gather*. As an utterance contemporary with *The Cenci* this passage is peculiarly interesting. (Compare Act V, Scene IV (Vol. II, p. 131 of my edition):

> Here, mother, tie
> My girdle for me, and bind up this hair
> In any simple knot; aye, that does well.
> And yours I see is coming down. How often
> Have we done this for one another; now
> We shall not do it any more. My Lord,
> We are quite ready. Well, 'tis very well.

Even the tragic resignation of the close corresponds with Shelley's piercing criticism of this group.

[4] In former editions, *shielding*.

[5] This passage is rendered thus by Medwin and Mrs. Shelley:

> "The right (as the restorer has properly imagined), is drawing up her daughter to her; and with that instinctive gesture, and by its gentle pressure, is encouraging the child to believe that it can give security. The countenance of Niobe is, &c."

[6] This is not a fresh sentence as in former editions.

as if despair and beauty had combined and produced nothing but the sublime loveliness[1] of grief. As the motions of the form expressed the instinctive sense of the possibility of protecting the child, and the accustomed and affectionate assurance that she would find protection[2] within her arms, so reason and imagination speak in the countenance the certainty that no mortal defence is of avail.

There is no terror in the countenance—only grief—deep[3] grief.—There is no anger—of what avail is indignation against what is known to be omnipotent? There is no selfish shrinking from personal pain; there is no panic at supernatural agency—there is no adverting to herself as herself—the calamity is mightier than to leave scope for such emotion.[4]

Every thing is swallowed up in sorrow.—Her countenance in assured expectation of the arrow piercing its victim[5] in her embrace, is fixed on her omnipotent enemy. The[6] pathetic beauty of the mere expression of her tender and serene despair, which is yet so profound and so incapable of being ever worn away, is beyond any effect of sculpture.—As soon as the arrow shall have pierced her

[1] Medwin and Mrs. Shelley read *sublimity* instead of *sublime loveliness*.

[2] In previous editions, *an asylum*.

[3] The additional word *remediless* is here inserted in previous editions.

[4] Not *emotions*, as given by Medwin and Mrs. Shelley, who insert after *sorrow* in the next line, *she is all tears*.

[5] In previous editions, *its last victim*.

[6] This sentence is replaced in *The Athenæum* and *The Shelley Papers* by the following:

"The pathetic beauty of the expression of her tender, and inexhaustible, and unquenchable despair, is beyond the effect of sculpture."

Mrs. Shelley followed this, merely inserting *any other* before *sculpture*,—conjecturally, I presume, for the words are not in the Note-book.

last child, the fable that she was dissolved[1] into a fountain of tears, will be but a feeble emblem of the sadness of despair,[2] in which the years of her remaining life, we feel, must flow away.

It is difficult to speak of the beauty of her countenance, or to make intelligible in words the forms from which[3] such astonishing loveliness results. The head, resting somewhat backward, upon the full and flowing contour of the neck, is in the act of watching an event momently to arrive. The hair is delicately divided on the forehead, and a gentle beauty gleams from the broad and clear forehead, over which its strings are drawn. The face is altogether broad[4] and the features conceived with the daring harmony[5] of a sense of power. In this respect it resembles the careless majesty which Nature stamps upon those rare master-pieces of her creation, harmonizing them as it were from the harmony of the spirit within. Yet all this not only consists with but is the cause of the subtlest delicacy of that clear and tender beauty which is the expression at once of innocence and sublimity of soul, of purity and strength, of all that which touches the most removed and divine of the strings[6] of that which makes music within my thoughts, and which

[1] In previous editions, *shall pierce her last tie upon earth, that fable that she was turned into stone, or dissolved* &c.

[2] Medwin and Mrs. Shelley read *hopelessness* for *despair* and insert *few and evil* before *years*.

[3] Previous editions read *from what* instead of *the forms from which*.

[4] In former editions, *of an oval fulness*.

[5] Medwin and Mrs. Shelley omit the word *harmony*.

[6] Instead of *the strings* &c. as in the text, former editions have *the chords that make music in our thoughts, of that which shakes with astonishment even the most superficial*. The final sentence is omitted.

shakes with astonishment my most superficial faculties. Compare for this effect the countenance as seen in front and as seen from under the left arm, moving to the right and towards the statue, until the line of the forehead shall coincide with that of the wrist.

NOTE

ON

THE HUNDRED AND ELEVENTH SONNET OF SHAKESPEARE.[1]

THAT famous passage in that pathetic sonnet in which, addressing a dear friend, he complains of his own situation as an actor, and says that his nature is (I quote from memory)

> "Subdued
> To what it works in, like the dyer's hand."

Observe these images, how simple they are, and yet animated with what intense poetry and passion.

[1] This note from the *Relics of Shelley* has already been reprinted in a foot-note in Vol. II of the Poetical Works, as Mr. Garnett informs us that it is written upon the original MS. of the Preface to *The Cenci*. It is not certain that it is a cancelled passage of that Preface, and it may suitably be set among the prose fragments of Shelley, with the sonnet to which it refers :—

O for my sake do you with fortune chide,
The guilty goddess of my harmful deeds,
That did not better for my life provide,
Than public means which public manners breeds.
Thence comes it that my name receives a brand,
And almost thence my nature is subdued
To what it works in, like the Dyer's hand:
Pity me then, and wish I were renewed,
Whilst like a willing patient I will drink
Potions of Eysel 'gainst my strong infection,
No bitterness that I will bitter think,
Nor double penance to correct correction.
Pity me then dear friend, and I assure ye,
Even that your pity is enough to cure me.

"TRUE KNOWLEDGE LEADS TO LOVE."[1]

TRUE knowledge leads to love. The meanest of our fellow beings containes qualities which, if developed, we must admire and adore. The selfish, the hollow and the base, alone despise and hate. To them I have erred much.

[1] This characteristic jotting is from the Note-book containing the Notes on Sculpture. Shelley seems to have blended into one text the words from Wordsworth's *Lines left upon a Seat in a Yew-tree,* which stand at the head of this note, and the expression "the meanest thing that feels" in that beautiful quatrain which he extracted from *Hart-Leap Well,* and commended to the author's notice in *Peter Bell the Third.* See Poetical Works, Vol. III, p. 215.

FRAGMENT

OF A

LETTER TO THE EDITOR OF THE QUARTERLY REVIEW.[1]

SIR,—I observe in the Sept. No. of the *Review*, which . . . .

the author of that article, after depreciating the merits of a poem written by me, asserts that what "he now knows to the disadvantage of my personal character affords an unanswerable comment on the text either of his review or my poem." I hereby call upon the author of that article, or you as the responsible agent, publicly to produce your proofs, or, as you have thrust yourself forward to deserve the character of a slanderer, to acquiesce also in . . . .

[1] This fragment of a draft letter (for I have no ground for supposing such a letter to have been actually finished and sent) is from Mr. Garnett's *Relics of Shelley*, where it is assigned to the year 1819. Leigh Hunt appears to have taken up the matter referred to in this fragment, and to have noticed in *The Examiner* (October 10, 1819) the attack of the *Quarterly*. Shelley's letter to Hunt adverting to this subject will be found in its place in Vol. IV of this edition. Its date is the 2nd of November, 1819.

UNA FAVOLA.

[The following Fable, affording one of the few extant examples of Shelley's fluency in the composition of Italian, is from the *Relics of Shelley*, wherein Mr. Garnett assigns it to the year 1820.—H. B. F.]

UNA FAVOLA.

C'ERA un giovane il quale viaggiava per paesi lontani, cercando per il mondo una donna, della quale esso fu innamorato. E chi fu quella donna, e come questo giovane s'innamorò di lei, e come e perchè gli cessò l'amore tanto forte che aveva, sono cose degne d'essere conosciute da ogni gentil cuore.

Al spuntare della decima quinta primavera della sua vita, uno chiamandosi Amore gli destava, dicendo che una chi egli aveva molte volte veduto nei sogni gli stava aspettando. Quello fu accompagnato d'una schiera immensa di persone, tutte velate in bianchi veli, e coronate di lauro, ellera e mirto inghirlandite ed intrecciate di viole, rose, e fiordilisi. Cantavano si dolcemente che forse l'armonia delle sfere alla quale le stelle ballano, e meno soave. E le maniere e le parole loro erano cosi lusinghevoli, che il giovane fu allettato, e levandosi del letto, si fece pronto di fare tutto il volere di quello che si chiamava Amore, al di cui cenno lo seguitava per solinghe vie ed eremi e caverne, fino chè tutta la schiera arrivò ad un bosco solitario in una cupa valle per due altissime montagne, il quale fu piantato a guisa di laberinto di pini, cipressi, cedari e tassi, le ombre dei quali destavano un misto di diletto e malinconia. Ed in questo bosco il giovane seguitava per un anno intero i passi incerti di questo compagno e duce suo, come la luna segue la terra; non però tramutandosi come essa. E fu egli nutrito delle fruttà d'un certo albero che crebbe nel mezzo del laberinto, un cibo insieme dolce ed amaro, il quale essendo freddo come ghiaccio sulle labbre, pareva fuoco nelle vene. Le forme velate sempre gli furono intorno, erano servi e ministri, ubbedienti al menomo cenno, e corrieri per lui ed Amore quando per affari suoi l'Amore un poco lo lascierebbe. Ma queste forme, eseguendo ogni altra ordine sua prestamente, mai non vollero svelarsi a lui quantunque le pregasse sollecitamente; eccettuato una, che aveva nome la Vita, ed aveva riputazione di incantatrice gagliarda. Era essa grande di persona e bella, allegra e sciolta, ed ornata riccamente, e, siccome pareva dal suo pronto svelarsi, voleva bene a questo giovane. Ma ben presto la riconobbe d'essere piu finta che alcuna Sirena, poichè per consiglio suo, Amore gli lasciò in questo selvaggio luogo, colla sola compagnia di queste velate, le quali per il loro ostinato celarsi sempre gli avevano fatte qualche paura. E, sé quelle forme erano i spettri dei suoi proprii morti pensieri, ovvero le ombre dei vivi pensieri dell' Amore, nessuno può schiarire. La Vita, vergognandosi forse della sua fraude, si celò allora dentro alla spelonca d'una sua sorella abitando colá; ed Amore se ne tornò, sospirando, alla sua terza sfera.

Appena fu partito Amore, quando le mascherate forme, solute della sua legge, si svelarono davanti all' attonito giovane. E per molti giorni le sopradette figure ballavano intorno di lui dovunque andasse—ora motteggiando ed ora minacciandolo, e la notte quando riposava sfilavano in lunga e lenta processione davanti al suo letto, ognuna più schifosa e terribile che l'altra. Il loro orribile aspetto e ria figura gli ingombrava tanto il cuore di tristezza, che il bel cielo, coperto di quella ombra, si vestì di nuvoloso tutto agli occhi suoi; e tanto pianse, che le erbe del suo cammino pasciate di lagrime in vece di rugiada, diventarono come lui, pallide e chinate. Stanco alfine di questo soffrire, veniva alla grotta della Sorella della Vita, incantatrice anch'ella e la trovò seduta davanti un pallido fuoco di odorose legna, cantando lai soavemente dolorosi, e tessendo una bianca mortaia, sopra la quale suo nome era a mezzo intessato, con qualche altro nome oscuro ed imperfetto; ed egli la pregò di dirlo suo nome, ed ella disse con voce fiocca ma dolce—"La Morte;" ed il giovane disse—"O bella Morte, ti prego di aiutarmi contre di queste noiose immagini, compagni della tua sorella, le quali mi tormentano tutta-via." E la Morte lo rassicurò, gli prese la mano, ridendo, e gli baciò la fronte e le guancie, sicchè tremava ogni vena di gioia e di paura; e gli fece stare presso di se, in una camera della sua grotta, dove, disse, fu contro al destino che le rie forme, compagne della Vita, venissero. Il giovane continuamente praticandosi colla Morte, ed ella, coll' animo di sorella, carezzandolo e facendo ogni cortesia di atto e di parola, ben presto s'innamorò di lei; e la Vita stessa, non che alcuna della sua schiera, non gli pareva bella. E tanto lo vinse la passione, che sul ginocchio pregò la Morte di amarlo come egli amava lei, e di voler fare il suo piacere. Ma la Morte disse, "Ardito che tu siei, al desir del quale mai ha la Morte corrisposta? Si tu non mi amasti, io forse ti amerei, amandomi io ti odio, e fuggo." Cosi dicendo, uscì della spelonca, e la sua oscura ed eterea figura fu presto persa fra gli intrecciati rami della selva.

Da quel punto il giovane seguiva le orme della Morte, e si forte fu l' amore chi lo menava, che aveva circuito l' orbe, ed indagato ogni sua regione; e molti anni erano già spenti, ma le soffranze più che gli anni avevano imbiancita la chioma ed appassito il fiore della forma, quando si trovò sui confini della stessa selva della quale aveva cominciato il suo misero errare. E si gittò sull' erba, e per molte ore pianse; e le lagrime l'accecavano tanto, che per molto tempo non se n' avvidde, che tutte quelle che bagnavano il viso e il petto, non furono sue proprie; ma che una donna chinata dietro di lui pianse per pietà del suo pianto. E levando gli occhi la vidde; e mai gli pareva d' aver veduto una visione si gloriosa: e dubitava forte si fosse cosa umana. Sue amore per la Morte fu improvvisamente cangiato in odio e sospetto, perche questo nuovo amore fu si forte che vinse ogni altro pensiero. E quella pietosa donna primo gli amava per pietà sola, ma tosto colla compassione crebbe l'amore; e gl' amava schiettamente, non avendo più uopo d'essere compatito alcuno amato da quella. Fu questa la donna, in traccia della quale Amore aveva menato il giovane per quel oscuro laberinto, e fatto tanto errare e soffrire; forse che lo giudicava indegno ancora di tanta gloria, e che lo vedeva debole per tolerare si immensa gioia. Dopo avere un poco asciugato il pianto, quei due passeggiavano insieme in questa stessa selva, fin chè la Morte si mise avanti e disse, "Mentre che, o giovane, mi amasti, io ti odiava, ed ora che tu mi odiasti, ti amo, e voglio tanto bene a te ed alla tua sposa che nel mio regno, che tu puoi chiamare Paradiso, ho serbato un eletto luogo, dove voi potete securamente compire i vostri felici amori." E la donna sdegnata, o forse un poco ingelosita per cagione dell' amore passato dello suo sposo, tornò il dosso sopra la Morte, dicendo fra se stesso, "Che vuol questa amante del mio sposo che viene qui turbarci?" e chiamò "Vita, Vita!" e la Vita venne col viso allegro, coronata d'una iride, e vestita in versicolore manto di pelle di cameleone, e la Morte se ni andò piangendo, e partendo disse dolcemente, "Voi mi sospettate, ma io vi lo perdono, e vi aspetto dove bisogna che passiate, perchè io abito coll' Amore e coll' Eternità, con quelle e forza che praticassero quelle anime che eternamente amano. Voi vedrete allora se io ho meritata i vostri dubbj. Intanto vi raccomando alla Vita, e, sorella mia, ti prego per amore di quella Morte della quella tu sei la gemella, di non adoperare contra di questi amanti le tue solite arti, che ti basti il tribute già pagato di sospiri e di lagrime, che sono le ricchezze tue." Il giovane, rammentandosi di quanti mali gli aveva recati in quel bosco, se disfidava della Vita; ma la donna, quantunque in sospetto, essendo pure gelosa della Morte, . . .

A FABLE.

[TRANSLATION OF THE FOREGOING.]

[In the *Relics of Shelley* this admirable translation immediately follows the foregoing Fable in Italian; and I believe it has been usually accepted as Shelley's own translation. It is in fact by Mr. Garnett, and bears unmistakeable traces of the fine enthusiasm which carried him through the difficult task of digging out from Shelley's rough note-books and fragmentary papers the main contents of the beautiful little volume of "Relics."—H. B. F.]

A FABLE.

THERE was a youth who travelled through distant lands, seeking throughout the world a lady of whom he was enamoured. And who this lady was, and how this youth became enamoured of her, and how and why the great love he bore her forsook him, are things worthy to be known by every gentle heart.

At the dawn of the fifteenth spring of his life, a certain one calling himself Love awoke him, saying that one whom he had ofttimes beheld in his dreams abode awaiting him. This Love was accompanied by a great troop of female forms, all veiled in white, and crowned with laurel, ivy, and myrtle, garlanded and interwreathed with violets, roses, and lilies. They sang with such sweetness that perhaps the harmony of the spheres, to which the stars dance, is not so sweet. And their manners and words were so alluring, that the youth was enticed, and, arising from his couch, made himself ready to do all the pleasure of him who called himself Love; at whose behest he followed him by lonely ways and deserts and caverns, until the whole troop arrived at a solitary wood, in a gloomy valley between two most lofty mountains, which valley was planted in the manner of a labyrinth, with pines, cypresses, cedars, and yews, whose shadows begot a mixture of delight and sadness. And in this wood the youth for a whole year followed the uncertain footsteps of this his companion and guide, as the moon follows the earth, save that there was no change in him, and nourished by the fruit of a certain tree which grew in the midst of the labyrinth—a food sweet and bitter at once, which being cold as ice to the lips, appeared fire in the veins. The veiled figures were continually around him, ministers and attendants obedient to his least gesture, and messengers between him and Love, when Love might leave him for a little on his other errands. But these figures, albeit executing his every other command with swiftness, never would unveil themselves to him, although he anxiously besought them; one only excepted, whose name was Life, and who had the fame of a potent inchantress. She was tall of person and beautiful, cheerful and easy in her manners, and richly adorned, and, as it seemed from her ready unveiling of herself, she wished well to this youth. But he soon perceived that she was more false than any Siren, for by her counsel Love abandoned him in this savage place, with only the company of these shrouded figures, who, by their obstinately remaining veiled, had always wrought him dread. And none can expound whether these figures were the spectres of his own dead thoughts, or the shadows of the living thoughts of Love. Then Life, haply ashamed of her deceit, concealed herself within the cavern of a certain sister of hers dwelling there; and Love, sighing, returned to his third heaven.

Scarcely had Love departed, when the masked forms, released from his government, unveiled themselves before the astonished youth. And for many days these figures danced around him whithersoever he went, alternately mocking and threatening him; and in the night while he reposed they defiled in long and slow procession before his couch, each more hideous and terrible than the other. Their horrible aspect and loathsome figure so overcame his heart with sadness that the fair heaven, covered with that shadow, clothed itself in clouds before his eyes; and he wept so much that the herbs upon his path, fed with tears instead of dew, became pale and bowed like himself. Weary at length of this suffering, he came to the grot of the Sister of Life, herself also an enchantress, and found her sitting before a pale fire of perfumed wood, singing laments sweet in their melancholy, and weaving a white shroud, upon which his name was half wrought, with the obscure and imperfect beginning of a certain other name; and he besought her to tell him her own, and she said, with a faint but sweet voice, "Death." And the youth said, "O lovely Death, I pray thee to aid me against these hateful phantoms, companions of thy sister, which cease not to torment me." And Death comforted him, and took his hand with a smile, and kissed his brow and cheek, so that every vein thrilled with joy and fear, and made him abide with her in a chamber of her cavern, whither, she said, it was against Destiny that the wicked companions of Life should ever come. The youth continually conversing with Death, and she, like-minded to a sister, caressing him and showing him every courtesy both in deed and word, he quickly became enamoured of her, and Life herself, far less any of her troop, seemed fair to him no longer: and his passion so overcame him, that upon his knees he prayed Death to love him as he loved her, and consent to do his pleasure. But Death said, "Audacious that thou art, with whose desire has Death ever complied? If thou lovedst me not, perchance I might love thee—beloved by thee, I hate thee and I fly thee." Thus saying, she went forth from the cavern, and her dusky and ætherial form was soon lost amid the interwoven boughs of the forest.

From that moment the youth pursued the track of Death; and so mighty was the love that led him, that he had encircled the world and searched through all its regions, and many years were already spent, but sorrows rather than years had blanched his locks and withered the flower of his beauty, when he found himself upon the confines of the very forest from which his wretched wanderings had begun. He cast himself upon the grass and wept for many hours, so blinded by his tears that for much time he did not perceive that not all that bathed his face and his bosom were his own, but that a lady bowed behind him wept for pity of his weeping. And lifting up his eyes he saw her, and it seemed to him never to have beheld so glorious a vision, and he doubted much whether she were a human creature. And his love of Death was suddenly changed into hate and suspicion, for this new love was so potent that it overcame every other thought. This compassionate lady at first loved him for mere pity; but love grew up swiftly with compassion, and she loved for Love's own sake, no one beloved by her having need of pity any more. This was the lady in whose quest Love had led the youth through that gloomy labyrinth of error and suffering, haply for that he esteemed him unworthy of so much glory, and perceived him too weak to support such exceeding joy. After having somewhat dried their tears, the twain walked together in that same forest, until Death stood before them, and said, "Whilst, O youth, thou didst love me, I hated thee, and now that thou hatest me, I love thee, and wish so well to thee and thy bride that in my kingdom, which thou mayest call Paradise, I have set apart a chosen spot, where ye may securely fulfil your happy loves." And the lady, offended, and perchance somewhat jealous by reason of the past love of her spouse, turned her back upon Death, saying within herself, "What would this lover of my husband who comes here to trouble us?" and cried, "Life! Life!" and Life came, with a gay visage, crowned with a rainbow, and clad in a various mantle of chameleon skin; and Death went away weeping, and departing said with a sweet voice, "Ye mistrust me, but I forgive ye, and await ye where ye needs must come, for I dwell with Love and Eternity, with whom the souls whose love is everlasting must hold communion; then will ye perceive whether I have deserved your distrust. Meanwhile I commend ye to Life; and, sister mine, I beseech thee, by the love of that Death with whom thou wert twin born, not to employ thy customary arts against these lovers, but content thee with the tribute thou hast already received of sighs and tears, which are thy wealth." The youth, mindful of how great evil she had wrought him in that wood, mistrusted Life; but the lady, although she doubted, yet being jealous of Death, . . .

A DEFENCE OF POETRY.

[*A Defence of Poetry* is the first part of an essay meant as an answer to one by Thomas Love Peacock, which appeared in 1820 in *Ollier's Literary Miscellany*, where also Shelley's *Defence* was to have appeared had the magazine been continued. Mrs. Shelley, when first giving the *Defence of Poetry* to the world in the *Essays* &c. (1840), characterized it in her Preface (page vii) as "the only entirely finished prose work Shelley left." The *Defence* was written shortly after *Epipsychidion*. Writing to Mr. Ollier on the 20th of January, 1821, Shelley says (*Shelley Memorials*, where the letter is given at pages 135–6, but dated 1820), "the moment I get rid of my ophthalmia, I mean to see about an answer to" *The Four Ages of Poetry*: he adds "It is very clever, but, I think, very false." Writing again on the 22nd of February, 1821, he says (*Shelley Memorials*, page 154), "Peacock's essay is at Florence at present,—I have sent for it and will transmit to you my paper as soon as it is written which will be in a very few days. Nevertheless, I should be sorry that you delayed your Magazine through any dependence on me.—I will not accept anything for this paper, as I had determined to write it, and promised it you, before, I heard of your liberal arrangements . . ." In a letter dated the 20th or 22nd of March, 1821, he says, "I send you the Defence of Poetry, Part I.—It is transcribed, I hope, legibly"; and he gives Mr. Ollier leave to omit, but not to "alter or add." In a postscript he requests that a copy of the Magazine containing the *Defence* may be sent to Peacock as from him. In a letter to Peacock dated the 21st of March, 1821 (*Fraser's Magazine*, March, 1860, page 315), he says "I dispatch by this post the first part of an essay, intended to consist of three parts, which I design for an antidote to your *Four Ages of Poetry*"; and Peacock says in a note that, as Shelley wrote it, "it contained many allusions to the article and its author, such as 'If I know the knight by the device of his shield, I have only to inscribe Cassandra, Antigone, or Alcestis on mine to blunt the point of his spear;' taking one instance of a favourite character from each of the three great Greek tragedians. All these allusions were struck out by Mr. John Hunt when he prepared the paper for publication in the *Liberal*. The demise of that periodical prevented the publication, and Mrs. Shelley subsequently printed it from Mr. Hunt's *rifacciamento*, as she received it. The paper as it now stands is a defence without an attack. Shelley intended this paper to be in three parts, but the other two were not written." I am not aware how the paper passed from Mr. Ollier to Mr. Hunt. In a letter to Mr. Ollier dated the 25th of September, 1821 (*Shelley Memorials*, page 159), Shelley says, "Pray give me notice against what time you want the second part of my *Defence of Poetry*—I give you this Defence, and you may do what you will with it." Mr. Garnett (*Relics*, page 48) mentions as existing among Shelley's MSS. a fair copy of this essay, prepared for the printer, but damaged by sea-water,—so much so, Mr. Garnett tells me, that only a word here and there can be deciphered. The publication in the *Relics* of some passages from the "original exordium" seems to indicate the existence of some of Shelley's notes, or parts of the draft. I have a complete MS. of it in the handwriting of Miss Clairmont; but, though it presents some variations from the printed text, it would seem to be copied, not from the original, but from the *rifacciamento*. In the MS. Note-book, however, containing the Notes on Sculpture, &c., is a fragment of the original *Defence*, including one of the cancelled references to *The Four Ages*. For the following text I have collated the editions of 1840 and 1852, and Miss Clairmont's transcript,—all three representing the same original, and have as a rule silently adopted the best reading in each case. The variations are usually of too slight and accidental a character to record. Peacock's Essay has a real interest independent of the help it gives in appreciating Shelley's mental attitude. It is therefore reprinted in the Appendix.—H. B. F.]

A DEFENCE OF POETRY.[1]

PART I.

ACCORDING to one mode of regarding those two classes of mental action, which are called reason and imagination, the former may be considered as mind contemplating the relations borne by one thought to another, however produced; and the latter, as mind acting upon those thoughts so as to colour them with its own light, and composing from them as from elements, other thoughts, each containing within itself the principle of its own integrity. The one is the τὸ ποιεῖν, or the principle of

[1] The following fragments are from the *Relics of Shelley*. Mr. Garnett, in first giving them to the public, pointed out (p. 89) that they "seem to have formed part of the original exordium of the *Defence of Poetry*, the composition of which was interrupted by an attack of ophthalmia."

"In one mode of considering those two classes of action of the human mind which are called reason and imagination, the former may be considered as mind employed upon the relations borne by one thought to another, however produced, and imagination as mind combining the elements of thought itself. It has been termed the power of association; and on an accurate anatomy of the functions of mind, it would be difficult to assign any other origin to the mass of what we perceive and know than this power. Association is, however, rather a law according

synthesis, and has for its object those forms which are common to universal nature and existence itself; the other is the τὸ λογίζειν, or principle of analysis, and its action regards the relations of things, simply as relations; considering thoughts, not in their integral unity, but as the algebraical representations which conduct to certain general results. Reason is the enumeration of quantities already known; imagination is the perception of the value of those quantities, both separately and as a whole. Reason respects the differences, and imagination the similitudes of things. Reason is to imagination as the instrument to the agent, as the body to the spirit, as the shadow to the substance.

Poetry, in a general sense, may be defined to be "the expression of the imagination:" and poetry is connate with the origin of man. Man is an instrument over which a series of external and internal impressions are driven, like the alternations of an ever-changing wind over an Æolian lyre, which move it by their motion to ever-changing melody. But there is a principle within the human being, and perhaps within all sentient beings,

to which this power is exerted than the power itself; in the same manner as gravitation is a passive expression of the reciprocal tendency of heavy bodies towards their respective centres. Were these bodies conscious of such a tendency, the name which they would assign to that consciousness would express the cause of gravitation; and it were a vain inquiry as to what might be the cause of that cause. Association bears the same relation to imagination as a mode to a source of action: when we look upon shapes in the fire or the clouds, and image to ourselves the resemblance of familiar objects, we do no more than seize the relation of certain points of visible objects, and fill up, blend together, . . .

"The imagination is a faculty not less imperial and essential to the happiness and dignity of the human being, than the reason.

"It is by no means indisputable that what is true, or rather that which the disciples of a certain mechanical and superficial philosophy call true, is more excellent than the beautiful."

which acts otherwise than in a lyre, and produces not melody alone, but harmony, by an internal adjustment of the sounds and motions thus excited to the impressions which excite them. It is as if the lyre could accommodate its chords to the motions of that which strikes them, in a determined proportion of sound; even as the musician can accommodate his voice to the sound of the lyre. A child at play by itself will express its delight by its voice and motions; and every inflexion of tone and every gesture will bear exact relation to a corresponding antitype in the pleasurable impressions which awakened it; it will be the reflected image of that impression; and as the lyre trembles and sounds after the wind has died away, so the child seeks, by prolonging in its voice and motions the duration of the effect, to prolong also a consciousness of the cause. In relation to the objects which delight a child, these expressions are what poetry is to higher objects. The savage (for the savage is to ages what the child is to years) expresses the emotions produced in him by surrounding objects in a similar manner; and language and gesture, together with plastic or pictorial imitation, become the image of the combined effect of those objects and his apprehension of them. Man in society, with all his passions and his pleasures, next becomes the object of the passions and pleasures of man; an additional class of emotions produces an augmented treasure of expression; and language, gesture, and the imitative arts, become at once the representation and the medium, the pencil and the picture, the chisel and the statue, the chord and the harmony. The social sympathies, or those laws from which as from its elements society results, begin to develope themselves from the moment that two human beings coexist; the future is contained within the present as the plant within the seed; and equality, diversity, unity, contrast, mutual dependence, become the principles alone capable of affording the motives according to which the will of a social being is determined to action, inasmuch as he is social; and constitute pleasure in sensation, virtue in sentiment, beauty in art, truth in reasoning, and love in the intercourse of kind. Hence men, even in the infancy of society, observe a certain order in their words and actions, distinct from that of the objects and the impressions represented by them, all expression being subject to the laws of that from which it proceeds. But let us dismiss those more general considerations which might involve an inquiry into the principles of society itself, and restrict our view to the manner in which the imagination is expressed upon its forms.

In the youth of the world, men dance and sing and imitate natural objects, observing in these actions, as in all others, a certain rhythm or order. And, although all men observe a similar, they observe not the same order, in the motions of the dance, in the melody of the song, in the combinations of language, in the series of their imitations of natural objects. For there is a certain order or rhythm belonging to each of these classes of mimetic representation, from which the hearer and the spectator receive an intenser and purer pleasure than from any other: the sense of an approximation to this order has been called taste by modern writers. Every man in the infancy of art, observes an order which approximates more or less closely to that from which this highest delight results: but the diversity is not sufficiently marked, as that its gradations should be sensible, except in those instances where the predominance of this faculty of approximation to the beautiful (for so we may be permitted to name the relation between this highest pleasure and its cause) is very great. Those in whom it exists to excess are poets, in the most universal sense of the word; and the pleasure resulting from the manner in which they express the influence of society or nature upon their own minds, communicates itself to others, and gathers a sort of reduplication from the community. Their language is vitally metaphorical; that is, it marks the before unapprehended relations of things, and perpetuates their apprehension, until words, which represent them, become, through time, signs for portions or classes of thought, instead of pictures of integral thoughts; and then, if no new poets should arise to create afresh the associations which have been thus disorganized, language will be dead to all the nobler purposes of human intercourse. These similitudes or relations are finely said by Lord Bacon to be "the same footsteps of nature impressed upon the various subjects of the world"[1]—and he considers the faculty which perceives them as the storehouse of axioms common to all knowledge. In the infancy of society every author is necessarily a poet, because language itself is poetry; and to be a poet is to apprehend the true and the beautiful, in a word, the good which exists in the relation subsisting, first between existence and perception, and secondly between perception and expression. Every original language near to its source is in itself the chaos of a cyclic poem: the copiousness of lexicography and the distinctions of grammar are the works of a later age, and are merely the catalogue and the forms of the creations of poetry.

[1] De Augment. Scient., cap. 1, lib. iii. [SHELLEY'S NOTE.]

But poets, or those who imagine and express this indestructible order, are not only the authors of language and of music, of the dance, and architecture, and statuary, and painting; they are the institutors of laws and the founders of civil society, and the inventors of the arts of life, and the teachers, who draw into a certain propinquity with the beautiful and the true, that partial apprehension of the agencies of the invisible world which is called religion. Hence all original religions are allegorical, or susceptible of allegory, and like Janus have a double face of false and true. Poets, according to the circumstances of the age and nation in which they appeared, were called, in the earlier epochs of the world, legislators or prophets: a poet essentially comprises and unites both these characters. For he not only beholds intensely the present as it is, and discovers those laws according to which present things ought to be ordered, but he beholds the future in the present, and his thoughts are the germs of the flower and the fruit of latest time. Not that I assert poets to be prophets in the gross sense of the word, or that they can foretell the form as surely as they foreknow the spirit of events: such is the pretence of superstition, which would make poetry an attribute of prophecy, rather than prophecy an attribute of poetry. A poet participates in the eternal, the infinite, and the one; as far as relates to his conceptions, time and place and number are not. The grammatical forms which express the moods of time, and the difference of persons, and the distinction of place, are convertible with respect to the highest poetry without injuring it as poetry; and the choruses of Æschylus, and the book of Job, and Dante's Paradise, would afford, more than any other writings, examples of this fact, if the limits of this essay did not forbid citation. The creations of music, sculpture, and painting, are illustrations still more decisive.

Language, colour, form, and religious and civil habits of action, are all the instruments and materials of poetry; they may be called poetry by that figure of speech which considers the effect as a synonyme of the cause. But poetry in a more restricted sense expresses those arrangements of language, and especially metrical language, which are created by that imperial faculty, whose throne is curtained within the invisible nature of man. And this springs from the nature itself of language, which is a more direct representation of the actions and passions of our internal being, and is susceptible of more various and delicate combinations, than colour, form, or motion, and is more plastic and obedient to the controul of that faculty of which it is the creation. For language is arbitrarily produced by the imagination, and has relation to thoughts alone; but all other materials, instruments, and conditions of art, have relations among each other, which limit and interpose between conception and expression. The former is as a mirror which reflects, the latter as a cloud which enfeebles, the light of which both are mediums of communication. Hence the fame of sculptors, painters, and musicians, although the intrinsic powers of the great masters of these arts may yield in no degree to that of those who have employed language as the hieroglyphic of their thoughts, has never equalled that of poets in the restricted sense of the term; as two performers of equal skill will produce unequal effects from a guitar and a harp. The fame of legislators and founders of religions, so long as their institutions last, alone seems to exceed that of poets in the restricted sense; but it can scarcely be a question, whether, if we deduct the celebrity which their flattery of the gross opinions of the vulgar usually conciliates, together with that which belonged to them in their higher character of poets, any excess will remain.

We have thus circumscribed the word poetry within the limits of that art which is the most familiar and the most perfect expression of the faculty itself. It is necessary, however, to make the circle still narrower, and to determine the distinction between measured and unmeasured language; for the popular division into prose and verse is inadmissible in accurate philosophy.

Sounds as well as thoughts have relation both between each other and towards that which they represent, and a perception of the order of those relations has always been found connected with a perception of the order of the relations of thought. Hence the language of poets has ever affected a sort of[1] uniform and harmonious recurrence of sound, without which it were not poetry, and which is scarcely less indispensable to the communication of its influence, than the words themselves without reference to that peculiar order. Hence the vanity of translation; it were as wise to cast a violet into a crucible that you might discover the formal principles of its colour and odour, as seek to transfuse from one language into another the creations of a poet. The plant must spring again from its seed, or it will bear no flower—and this is the burthen of the curse of Babel.

An observation of the regular mode of the recurrence of harmony in the language of poetical minds, together with its relation to music, produced metre, or a certain system of traditional forms of harmony and language. Yet it is by no means essential that a poet should accommodate his language to this traditional form, so that the harmony, which is its spirit, be observed. The practice is indeed convenient and popular, and to be preferred

[1] In the edition of 1852, *certain* for *sort of*.

especially in such composition as includes much action: but every great poet must inevitably innovate upon the example of his predecessors in the exact structure of his peculiar versification. The distinction between poets and prose writers is a vulgar error. The distinction between philosophers and poets has been anticipated. Plato was essentially a poet—the truth and splendour of his imagery, and the melody of his language, are the most intense that it is possible to conceive. He rejected the harmony[1] of the epic, dramatic, and lyrical forms, because he sought to kindle a harmony in thoughts divested of shape and action, and he forbore to invent any regular plan of rhythm which would include, under determinate forms, the varied pauses of his style. Cicero sought to imitate the cadence of his periods, but with little success. Lord Bacon was a poet.[2] His language has a sweet and majestic rhythm, which satisfies the sense, no less than the almost superhuman wisdom of his philosophy satisfies the intellect; it is a strain which distends, and then bursts the circumference of the reader's mind, and pours itself forth together with it into the universal element with which it has perpetual sympathy. All the authors of revolutions in opinion are not only necessarily poets as they are inventors, nor even as their words unveil the permanent analogy of things by images which participate in the life of truth; but as their periods are harmonious and rhythmical, and contain in themselves the elements of verse; being the echo of the eternal music. Nor are those supreme poets, who have employed traditional forms of rhythm on account of the form and action of their subjects, less capable of perceiving and teaching the truth of

[1] In the edition of 1852, *measure* for *harmony*.

[2] See the Filum Labyrinthi, and the Essay on Death particularly. [SHELLEY'S NOTE.]

things, than those who have omitted that form. Shakespeare, Dante, and Milton (to confine ourselves to modern writers) are philosophers of the very loftiest power.

A poem is the very image of life expressed in its eternal truth. There is this difference between a story and a poem, that a story is a catalogue of detached facts, which have no other connexion than time, place, circumstance, cause, and effect; the other is the creation of actions according to the unchangeable forms of human nature, as existing in the mind of the creator, which is itself the image of all other minds. The one is partial, and applies only to a definite period of time, and a certain combination of events which can never again recur; the other is universal, and contains within itself the germ of a relation to whatever motives or actions have place in the possible varieties of human nature. Time, which destroys the beauty and the use of the story of particular facts, stripped of the poetry which should invest them, augments that of poetry, and for ever developes new and wonderful applications of the eternal truth which it contains. Hence epitomes have been called the moths of just history; they eat out the poetry of it. A story of particular facts is as a mirror which obscures and distorts that which should be beautiful: poetry is a mirror which makes beautiful that which is distorted.

The parts of a composition may be poetical, without the composition as a whole being a poem. A single sentence may be considered as a whole, though it may be found in the midst of a series of unassimilated portions; a single word even may be a spark of inextinguishable thought. And thus all the great historians, Herodotus,

Plutarch, Livy, were poets; and although the plan of these writers, especially that of Livy, restrained them from developing this faculty in its highest degree, they made copious and ample amends for their subjection, by filling all the interstices of their subjects with living images.

Having determined what is poetry, and who are poets, let us proceed to estimate its effects upon society.

Poetry is ever accompanied with pleasure: all spirits on which it falls open themselves to receive the wisdom which is mingled with its delight. In the infancy of the world, neither poets themselves nor their auditors are fully aware of the excellency of poetry: for it acts in a divine and unapprehended manner, beyond and above consciousness; and it is reserved for future generations to contemplate and measure the mighty cause and effect in all the strength and splendour of their union. Even in modern times, no living poet ever arrived at the fulness of his fame; the jury which sits in judgment upon a poet, belonging as he does to all time, must be composed of his peers: it must be impannelled by Time from the selectest of the wise of many generations. A poet is a nightingale, who sits in darkness and sings to cheer its own solitude with sweet sounds; his auditors are as men entranced by the melody of an unseen musician, who feel that they are moved and softened, yet know not whence or why. The poems of Homer and his contemporaries were the delight of infant Greece; they were the elements of that social system which is the column upon which all succeeding civilization has reposed. Homer embodied the ideal perfection of his age in human character; nor can we doubt that those who read his verses were awakened to an ambition of becoming like to Achilles, Hector, and Ulysses: the truth and beauty of friendship, patriotism, and persevering devotion to an object, were unveiled to their depths in these immortal creations: the sentiments of the auditors must have been refined and enlarged by a sympathy with such great and lovely impersonations, until from admiring they imitated, and from imitation they identified themselves with the objects of their admiration. Nor let it be objected, that these characters are remote from moral perfection, and that they are by no means to be considered as edifying patterns for general imitation. Every epoch, under names more or less specious, has deified its peculiar errors; Revenge is the naked idol of the worship of a semibarbarous age; and Self-deceit is the veiled image of unknown evil, before which luxury and satiety lie prostrate. But a poet considers the vices of his contemporaries as the temporary dress in which his creations must be arrayed, and which cover without concealing the eternal proportions of their beauty. An epic or dramatic personage is understood to wear them around his soul, as he may the ancient armour or modern uniform around his body; whilst it is easy to conceive a dress more graceful than either. The beauty of the internal nature cannot be so far concealed by its accidental vesture, but that the spirit of its form shall communicate itself to the very disguise, and indicate the shape it hides from the manner in which it is worn. A majestic form and graceful motions will express themselves through the most barbarous and tasteless costume. Few poets of the highest class have chosen to exhibit the beauty of their conceptions in its naked truth and splendour; and it is doubtful whether the alloy of costume, habit, &c., be not necessary to temper this planetary music for mortal ears.

The whole objection, however, of the immorality of poetry rests upon a misconception of the manner in which poetry acts to produce the moral improvement of man. Ethical science arranges the elements which poetry has created, and propounds schemes and proposes examples of civil and domestic life: nor is it for want of admirable doctrines that men hate, and despise, and censure, and deceive, and subjugate one another. But poetry acts in another and diviner manner. It awakens and enlarges the mind itself by rendering it the receptacle of a thousand unapprehended combinations of thought. Poetry lifts the veil from the hidden beauty of the world, and makes familiar objects be as if they were not familiar; it reproduces all that it represents, and the impersonations clothed in its Elysian light stand thenceforward in the minds of those who have once contemplated them, as memorials of that gentle and exalted content which extends itself over all thoughts and actions with which it coexists. The great secret of morals is love; or a going out of our own nature, and an identification of ourselves with the beautiful which exists in thought, action, or person, not our own. A man, to be greatly good, must imagine intensely and comprehensively; he must put himself in the place of another and of many others; the pains and pleasures of his species must become his own. The great instrument of moral good is the imagination; and poetry administers to the effect by acting upon the cause. Poetry enlarges the circumference of the imagination by replenishing it with thoughts of ever new delight, which have the power of attracting and assimilating to their own nature all other thoughts, and which form new intervals and interstices whose void for ever craves fresh food. Poetry strengthens the faculty which is the organ of the moral nature of man, in the same manner as exercise strengthens a limb.[1] A poet therefore would do ill to embody his own conceptions of right and wrong, which are usually those of his place and time, in his poetical creations, which participate in neither. By this assumption of the inferior office of interpreting the effect, in which perhaps after all he might acquit himself but imperfectly, he would resign a glory in the participation of the cause. There was little danger that Homer, or any of the eternal poets, should have so far misunderstood themselves as to have abdicated this throne of their widest dominion. Those in whom the poetical faculty, though great, is less intense, as Euripides, Lucan, Tasso, Spenser, have frequently affected a moral aim, and the effect of their poetry is diminished in exact proportion to the degree in which they compel us to advert to this purpose.

Homer and the cyclic poets were followed at a certain interval by the dramatic and lyrical poets of Athens, who flourished contemporaneously with all that is most perfect

[1] Whether the slight laxity in the use of the word *organ* in this profound sentence is the result of haste in transcription we shall perhaps never know. It seems probable that Shelley perceived and meant to propound a great truth even now only admitted by investigators and thinkers in the fore-front of that battle wherein he was so notable a warrior. It cannot be rightly said that a *faculty* is the *organ of the moral nature*, except indeed in a figurative sense; and Shelley may have meant to describe imagination (the faculty strengthened by poetry) as the organ or, as he says higher up, instrument, of the moral nature. The words bear that sense as they stand; but that would be mere repetition; and the thought would really seem to point to the strengthening of an organ by the exercise of its function, *in the same manner as exercise strengthens a limb.* If *organ* was in fact, as I suppose, meant to be used in that sense, it must have been so used because the writer perceived the moral nature to be a function; and, although this is not proved, the tendency of physiological science is to find that organ in the great sympathetic nervous system. Had Shelley *known* of what organ the moral nature was a function, he would of course have turned the phrase differently.

in the kindred expressions of the poetical faculty; architecture, painting, music, the dance, sculpture, philosophy, and we may add, the forms of civil life. For although the scheme of Athenian society was deformed by many imperfections which the poetry existing in chivalry and Christianity has erased from the habits and institutions of modern Europe; yet never at any other period has so much energy, beauty and virtue, been developed; never was blind strength and stubborn form so disciplined and rendered subject to the will of man, or that will less repugnant to the dictates of the beautiful and the true, as during the century which preceded the death of Socrates. Of no other epoch in the history of our species have we records and fragments stamped so visibly with the image of the divinity in man. But it is poetry alone, in form, in action, and in language, which has rendered this epoch memorable above all others, and the storehouse of examples to everlasting time. For written poetry existed at that epoch simultaneously with the other arts, and it is an idle inquiry to demand which gave and which received the light, which all, as from a common focus, have scattered over the darkest periods of succeeding time. We know no more of cause and effect than a constant conjunction of events: poetry is ever found to co-exist with whatever other arts contribute to the happiness and perfection of man. I appeal to what has already been established to distinguish between the cause and the effect.

It was at the period here adverted to, that the drama had its birth; and however a succeeding writer may have equalled or surpassed those few great specimens of the Athenian drama which have been preserved to us, it is indisputable that the art itself never was understood or practised according to the true philosophy of it, as at Athens. For the Athenians employed language, action, music, painting, the dance, and religious institution, to produce a common effect in the representation of the highest idealisms of passion and of power; each division in the art was made perfect in its kind by artists of the most consummate skill, and was disciplined into a beautiful proportion and unity one towards the other. On the modern stage a few only of the elements capable of expressing the image of the poet's conception are employed at once. We have tragedy without music and dancing, and music and dancing without the highest impersonations of which they are the fit accompaniment, and both without religion and solemnity. Religious institution has indeed been usually banished from the stage. Our system of divesting the actor's face of a mask, on which the many expressions appropriated to his dramatic character might be moulded into one permanent and unchanging expression, is favourable only to a partial and inharmonious effect; it is fit for nothing but a monologue, where all the attention may be directed to some great master of ideal mimicry. The modern practice of blending comedy with tragedy, though liable to great abuse in point of practice, is undoubtedly an extension of the dramatic circle; but the comedy should be as in King Lear, universal, ideal, and sublime. It is perhaps the intervention of this principle which determines the balance in favour of King Lear against the Œdipus Tyrannus or the Agamemnon, or, if you will, the trilogies with which they are connected; unless the intense power of the choral poetry, especially that of the latter, should be considered as restoring the equilibrium. King Lear, if it can sustain this comparison, may be judged to be the most perfect specimen of the dramatic art existing in the world; in spite of the narrow conditions to which the poet was subjected by the ignorance of the philosophy of the drama which has prevailed in modern Europe. Calderon, in his religious Autos, has attempted to fulfil some of the high conditions of dramatic representation neglected by Shakespeare; such as the establishing a relation between the drama and religion, and the accommodating them to music and dancing; but he omits the observation of conditions still more important, and more is lost than gained by the substitution of the rigidly-defined and ever-repeated idealisms of a distorted superstition for the living impersonations of the truth of human passion.

But I digress.—The connexion of scenic exhibitions with the improvement or corruption of the manners of men, has been universally recognized: in other words, the presence or absence of poetry in its most perfect and universal form, has been found to be connected with good and evil in conduct or habit. The corruption which has been imputed to the drama as an effect, begins, when the poetry employed in its constitution ends: I appeal to the history of manners whether the periods of the growth[1] of the one and the decline of the other have not corresponded with an exactness equal to any example of moral cause and effect.

The drama at Athens, or wheresoever else it may have approached to its perfection, ever co-existed with the moral and intellectual greatness of the age. The tragedies of the Athenian poets are as mirrors in which the spectator

[1] In the transcript, *whether the quick growth* &c.

beholds himself, under a thin disguise of circumstance, stript of all but that ideal perfection and energy which every one feels to be the internal type of all that he loves, admires, and would become. The imagination is enlarged by a sympathy with pains and passions so mighty, that they distend in their conception the capacity of that by which they are conceived; the good affections are strengthened by pity, indignation, terror and sorrow; and an exalted calm is prolonged from the satiety of this high exercise of them into the tumult of familiar life: even crime is disarmed of half its horror and all its contagion by being represented as the fatal consequence of the unfathomable agencies of nature; error is thus divested of its wilfulness; men can no longer cherish it as the creation of their choice. In the drama of the highest order there is little food for censure or hatred; it teaches rather self-knowledge and self-respect. Neither the eye nor the mind can see itself, unless reflected upon that which it resembles. The drama, so long as it continues to express poetry, is a prismatic and many-sided mirror, which collects the brightest rays of human nature and divides and reproduces them from the simplicity of their elementary forms, and touches them with majesty and beauty, and multiplies all that it reflects, and endows it with the power of propagating its like wherever it may fall.

But in periods of the decay of social life, the drama sympathizes with that decay. Tragedy becomes a cold imitation of the forms of the great masterpieces of antiquity, divested of all harmonious accompaniment of the kindred arts; and often the very form misunderstood, or a weak attempt to teach certain doctrines, which the writer considers as moral truths, and which are usually no more than specious flatteries of some gross vice or weakness, with which the author, in common with his auditors, are infected. Hence what has been called the classical and domestic drama. Addison's "Cato" is a specimen of the one; and would it were not superfluous to cite examples of the other! To such purposes poetry cannot be made subservient. Poetry is a sword of lightning, ever unsheathed, which consumes the scabbard that would contain it. And hence we observe that all dramatic writings of this nature are unimaginative in a singular degree; they affect sentiment and passion, which, divested of imagination, are other names for caprice and appetite. The period in our own history of the grossest degradation of the drama is the reign of Charles II., when all forms in which poetry had been accustomed to be expressed became hymns to the triumph of kingly power over liberty and virtue. Milton stood alone illuminating an age unworthy of him. At such periods the calculating principle pervades all the forms of dramatic exhibition, and poetry ceases to be expressed upon them. Comedy loses its ideal universality: wit succeeds to humour; we laugh from self-complacency and triumph, instead of pleasure; malignity, sarcasm, and contempt, succeed to sympathetic merriment; we hardly laugh, but we smile. Obscenity, which is ever blasphemy against the divine beauty in life, becomes, from the very veil which it assumes, more active if less disgusting: it is a monster for which the corruption of society for ever brings forth new food, which it devours in secret.

The drama being that form under which a greater number of modes of expression of poetry are susceptible of being combined than any other, the connexion of poetry and social good is more observable in the drama than in whatever other form. And it is indisputable that the highest perfection of human society has ever corresponded with the highest dramatic excellence; and that the corruption or the extinction of the drama in a nation where it has once flourished, is a mark of a corruption of manners, and an extinction of the energies which sustain the soul of social life. But, as Machiavelli says of political institutions, that life may be preserved and renewed, if men should arise capable of bringing back the drama to its principles. And this is true with respect to poetry in its most extended sense: all language, institution and form, require not only to be produced but to be sustained: the office and character of a poet participates in the divine nature as regards providence, no less than as regards creation.

Civil war, the spoils of Asia, and the fatal predominance first of the Macedonian, and then of the Roman arms, were so many symbols of the extinction or suspension of the creative faculty in Greece. The bucolic writers, who found patronage under the lettered tyrants of Sicily and Egypt, were the latest representatives of its most glorious reign. Their poetry is intensely melodious; like the odour of the tuberose, it overcomes and sickens the spirit with excess of sweetness; whilst the poetry of the preceding age was as a meadow-gale of June, which mingles the fragrance of all the flowers of the field, and adds a quickening and harmonizing spirit of its own which endows the sense with a power of sustaining its extreme delight. The bucolic and erotic delicacy in written poetry is correlative with that softness in statuary, music, and the kindred arts, and even in manners and institutions, which distinguished the epoch to which I now refer. Nor is it the poetical faculty itself, or any misapplication of it, to which this want of harmony is to be imputed. An equal sensibility to the influence of the senses and the affections is to be found in the writings of Homer and Sophocles: the former, especially, has clothed sensual and pathetic images with irresistible attractions. Their superiority over these succeeding writers consists in the presence of those thoughts which belong to the inner faculties of our nature, not in the absence of those which are connected with the external: their incomparable perfection consists in an harmony of the union of all. It is not what the erotic poets have, but what they have not, in which their imperfection consists. It is not inasmuch as they were poets, but inasmuch as they were not poets, that they can be considered with any plausibility as connected with the corruption of their age. Had that corruption availed so as to extinguish in them the sensibility to pleasure, passion, and natural scenery, which is imputed to them as an imperfection, the last triumph of evil would have been achieved. For the end of social corruption is to destroy all sensibility to pleasure; and therefore it is corruption. It begins at the imagination and the intellect as at the core, and distributes itself thence as a paralysing venom, through the affections into the very appetites, until all become a torpid mass in which hardly sense survives. At the approach of such a period, poetry ever addresses itself to those faculties which are the last to be destroyed, and its voice is heard, like the footsteps of Astræa, departing from the world. Poetry ever communicates all the pleasure which men are capable of receiving:

it is ever still the light of life; the source of whatever of beautiful or generous or true can have place in an evil time. It will readily be confessed that those among the luxurious citizens of Syracuse and Alexandria who were delighted with the poems of Theocritus, were less cold, cruel, and sensual than the remnant of their tribe. But corruption must utterly have destroyed the fabric of human society before poetry can ever cease. The sacred links of that chain have never been entirely disjoined, which descending through the minds of many men, is attached to those great minds, whence as from a magnet the invisible effluence is sent forth; which at once connects, animates, and sustains the life of all.[1] It is the faculty which contains within itself the seeds at once of its own and of social renovation. And let us not circumscribe the effects of the bucolic and erotic poetry within the limits of the sensibility of those to whom it was addressed. They may have perceived the beauty of those immortal compositions, simply as fragments and isolated portions: those who are more finely organized, or born in an happier age, may recognize them as episodes to that great poem, which all poets, like the co-operating thoughts of one great mind, have built up since the beginning of the world.

The same revolution within a narrower sphere had place in ancient Rome; but the actions and forms of its social life never seem to have been perfectly saturated with the poetical element. The Romans appear to have considered the Greeks as the selectest treasuries of the selectest forms of manners and of nature, and to have abstained from creating in measured language, sculpture, music, or architecture, any thing which might bear a particular relation to their own condition, whilst it should

[1] *Cf.* Plato's *Ion.* (See p. 263 of this volume.)

bear a general one to the universal constitution of the world. But we judge from partial evidence, and we judge perhaps partially. Ennius, Varro, Pacuvius, and Accius, all great poets, have been lost. Lucretius is in the highest, and Virgil in a very high sense, a creator. The chosen delicacy of expressions of the latter, are as a mist of light which conceal from us the intense and exceeding truth of his conceptions of nature. Livy is instinct with poetry. Yet Horace, Catullus, Ovid, and generally the other great writers of the Virgilian age, saw man and nature in the mirror of Greece. The institutions also, and the religion of Rome, were less poetical than those of Greece, as the shadow is less vivid than the substance. Hence poetry in Rome, seemed to follow, rather than accompany, the perfection of political and domestic society. The true poetry of Rome lived in its institutions; for whatever of beautiful, of true and majestic, they contained, could have sprung only from the faculty which creates the order in which they consist. The life of Camillus, the death of Regulus; the expectation of the senators, in their godlike state, of the victorious Gauls; the refusal of the republic to make peace with Hannibal after the battle of Cannæ, were not the consequences of a refined calculation of the probable personal advantage to result from such a rhythm and order in the shows of life, to those who were at once the poets and the actors of these immortal dramas. The imagination beholding the beauty of this order, created it out of itself according to its own idea; the consequence was empire, and the reward everlasting fame. These things are not the less poetry, *quia carent vate sacro.* They are the episodes of that cyclic poem written by Time upon the memories of men. The Past, like an inspired rhapsodist, fills the theatre of everlasting generations with their harmony.

At length the ancient system of religion and manners had fulfilled the circle of its evolutions. And the world would have fallen into utter anarchy and darkness, but that there were found poets among the authors of the Christian and chivalric systems of manners and religion, who created forms of opinion and action never before conceived; which, copied into the imaginations of men, became as generals to the bewildered armies of their thoughts. It is foreign to the present purpose to touch upon the evil produced by these systems: except that we protest, on the ground of the principles already established, that no portion of it can be attributed to the poetry they contain.

It is probable that the poetry of Moses, Job, David, Solomon, and Isaiah, had produced a great effect upon the mind of Jesus and his disciples. The scattered fragments preserved to us by the biographers of this extraordinary person, are all instinct with the most vivid poetry. But his doctrines seem to have been quickly distorted. At a certain period after the prevalence of a system of opinions founded upon those promulgated by him, the three forms into which Plato had distributed the faculties of mind underwent a sort of apotheosis, and became the object of the worship of the civilized world. Here it is to be confessed that "Light" seems to "thicken,"

> And the crow makes wing to the rooky wood;
> Good things of day begin to droop and drowse;
> Whiles night's black agents to their preys do rouse.[1]

But mark how beautiful an order has sprung from the dust and blood of this fierce chaos! how the world, as

[1] This quotation from *Macbeth* (Act III, Sc. 2) is not given correctly in former editions; but it seems doubtful whether the errors were Shelley's own.

from a resurrection, balancing itself on the golden wings of knowledge and of hope, has reassumed its yet unwearied flight into the heaven of time. Listen to the music, unheard by outward ears, which is as a ceaseless and invisible wind, nourishing its everlasting course with strength and swiftness.

The poetry in the doctrines of Jesus Christ, and the mythology and institutions of the Celtic conquerors of the Roman empire, outlived the darkness and the convulsions connected with their growth and victory, and blended themselves in a new fabric of manners and opinion. It is an error to impute the ignorance of the dark ages to the Christian doctrines or the predominance of the Celtic nations. Whatever of evil their agencies may have contained sprang from the extinction of the poetical principle, connected with the progress of despotism and superstition. Men, from causes too intricate to be here discussed, had become insensible and selfish: their own will had become feeble, and yet they were its slaves, and thence the slaves of the will of others: lust, fear, avarice, cruelty, and fraud, characterized a race amongst whom no one was to be found capable of *creating* in form, language, or institution. The moral anomalies of such a state of society are not justly to be charged upon any class of events immediately connected with them, and those events are most entitled to our approbation which could dissolve it most expeditiously. It is unfortunate for those who cannot distinguish words from thoughts, that many of these anomalies have been incorporated into our popular religion.

It was not until the eleventh century that the effects

of the poetry of the Christian and chivalric systems began to manifest themselves. The principle of equality had been discovered and applied by Plato in his Republic, as the theoretical rule of the mode in which the materials of pleasure and of power produced by the common skill and labour of human beings ought to be distributed among them. The limitations of this rule were asserted by him to be determined only by the sensibility of each, or the utility to result to all. Plato, following the doctrines of Timæus and Pythagoras, taught also a moral and intellectual system of doctrine, comprehending at once the past, the present, and the future condition of man. Jesus Christ divulged the sacred and eternal truths contained in these views to mankind, and Christianity, in its abstract purity, became the exoteric expression of the esoteric doctrines of the poetry and wisdom of antiquity. The incorporation of the Celtic nations with the exhausted population of the south, impressed upon it the figure of the poetry existing in their mythology and institutions. The result was a sum of the action and reaction of all the causes included in it; for it may be assumed as a maxim that no nation or religion can supersede any other without incorporating into itself a portion of that which it supersedes. The abolition of personal and domestic slavery, and the emancipation of women from a great part of the degrading restraints of antiquity, were among the consequences of these events.

The abolition of personal slavery is the basis of the highest political hope that it can enter into the mind of man to conceive. The freedom of women produced the poetry of sexual love. Love became a religion, the idols of whose worship were ever present. It was as if the statues of Apollo and the Muses had been endowed with life and motion, and had walked forth among their worshippers; so that earth became peopled by the inhabitants of a diviner world. The familiar appearances and proceedings of life became wonderful and heavenly, and a paradise was created as out of the wrecks of Eden. And as this creation itself is poetry, so its creators were poets; and language was the instrument of their art: "Galeotto fù il libro, e chi lo scrisse." The Provençal Trouveurs, or inventors, preceded Petrarch, whose verses are as spells, which unseal the inmost inchanted fountains of the delight which is in the grief of love. It is impossible to feel them without becoming a portion of that beauty which we contemplate: it were superfluous to explain how the gentleness and elevation of mind connected with these sacred emotions can render men more amiable, more generous and wise, and lift them out of the dull vapours of the little world of self. Dante understood the secret things of love even more than Petrarch. His *Vita Nuova* is an inexhaustible fountain of purity of sentiment and language: it is the idealized history of that period, and those intervals of his life which were dedicated to love. His apotheosis of Beatrice in Paradise, and the gradations of his own love and her loveliness, by which as by steps he feigns himself to have ascended to the throne of the Supreme Cause, is the most glorious imagination of modern poetry. The acutest critics have justly reversed the judgment of the vulgar, and the order of the great acts of the Divina Commedia,[1] in the measure of the admiration which they accord to the Hell, Purgatory, and Paradise. The latter is a

[1] In the edition of 1852, *Divine Drama*.

perpetual hymn of everlasting love. Love, which found a worthy poet in Plato alone of all the ancients, has been celebrated by a chorus of the greatest writers of the renovated world; and the music has penetrated the caverns of society, and its echoes still drown the dissonance of arms and superstition. At successive intervals, Ariosto, Tasso, Shakespeare, Spenser, Calderon, Rousseau, and the great writers of our own age, have celebrated the dominion of love, planting as it were trophies in the human mind of that sublimest victory over sensuality and force. The true relation borne to each other by the sexes into which human kind is distributed, has become less misunderstood; and if the error which confounded diversity with inequality of the powers of the two sexes has been partially recognized in the opinions and institutions of modern Europe, we owe this great benefit to the worship of which chivalry was the law, and poets the prophets.

The poetry of Dante may be considered as the bridge thrown over the stream of time, which unites the modern and ancient world. The distorted notions of invisible things which Dante and his rival Milton have idealized, are merely the mask and the mantle in which these great poets walk through eternity enveloped and disguised. It is a difficult question to determine how far they were conscious of the distinction which must have subsisted in their minds between their own creeds and that of the people. Dante at least appears to wish to mark the full extent of it by placing Riphæus, whom Virgil calls *justissimus unus*, in Paradise, and observing a most heretical[1] caprice in his distribution of rewards and punishments. And Milton's poem contains within itself a

[1] In the first edition, *poetical*.

philosophical refutation of that system of which, by a strange and natural antithesis, it has been a chief popular support.[1] Nothing can exceed the energy and magnificence of the character of Satan as expressed in Paradise Lost. It is a mistake to suppose that he could ever have been intended for the popular personification of evil. Implacable hate, patient cunning, and a sleepless refinement of device to inflict the extremest anguish on an enemy, these things are evil; and, although venial in a slave, are not to be forgiven in a tyrant; although redeemed by much that ennobles his defeat in one subdued, are marked by all that dishonours his conquest in the victor. Milton's Devil as a moral being is as far superior to his God, as one who perseveres in some purpose which he has conceived to be excellent in spite of adversity and torture, is to one who in the cold security of undoubted triumph inflicts the most horrible

[1] It is extremely unlikely that Shelley ever saw William Blake's wonderful book, *The Marriage of Heaven and Hell*, which is even now not well enough known to make superfluous the transcription of the following remarkable parallel passage:

"Those who restrain desire, do so because theirs is weak enough to be restrained; and the restrainer or reason usurps its place & governs the unwilling.

"And being restrained it by degrees becomes passive till it is only the shadow of desire.

"The history of this is written in Paradise Lost. & the Governor or Reason is call'd Messiah.

"And the original Archangel or possessor of the command of the heavenly host is call'd the Devil or Satan and his children are call'd Sin & Death.

"But in the Book of Job Milton's Messiah is call'd Satan.

"For this history has been adopted by both parties.

"It indeed appear'd to Reason as if Desire was cast out, but the Devil's account is, that the Messiah fell, & formed a heaven of what he stole from the Abyss.

"This is shewn in the Gospel, where he prays to the Father to send the comforter or Desire that Reason may have Ideas to build on, the Jehovah of the Bible being no other than he who dwells in flaming fire.

"Know that after Christ's death, he became Jehovah.

"But in Milton; the Father is Destiny, the Son, a Ratio of the five senses, & the Holy-ghost, Vacuum.

"Note. The reason Milton wrote in fetters when he wrote of Angels and God, and at liberty when of Devils & Hell, is because he was a true Poet and of the Devil's party without knowing it."

revenge upon his enemy, not from any mistaken notion of inducing him to repent of a perseverance in enmity, but with the alleged design of exasperating him to deserve new torments. Milton has so far violated the popular creed (if this shall be judged to be a violation) as to have alleged no superiority of moral virtue to his god over his devil. And this bold neglect of a direct moral purpose is the most decisive proof of the supremacy of Milton's genius. He mingled as it were the elements of human nature as colours upon a single pallet, and arranged them in the composition of his great picture according to the laws of epic truth, that is, according to the laws of that principle by which a series of actions of the external universe and of intelligent and ethical beings is calculated to excite the sympathy of succeeding generations of mankind. The Divina Commedia and Paradise Lost have conferred upon modern mythology a systematic form; and when change and time shall have added one more superstition to the mass of those which have arisen and decayed upon the earth, commentators will be learnedly employed in elucidating the religion of ancestral Europe, only not utterly forgotten because it will have been stamped with the eternity of genius.

Homer was the first and Dante the second epic poet, that is, the second poet, the series of whose creations bore a defined and intelligible relation to the knowledge and sentiment and religion of the age in which he lived, and of the ages which followed it: developing itself in correspondence with their developement. For Lucretius had limed the wings of his swift spirit in the dregs of the sensible world; and Virgil, with a modesty that ill became his genius, had affected the fame of an imitator, even whilst he created anew all that he copied; and none among the flock of mock-birds, though their notes are sweet, Apollonius Rhodius, Quintus Calaber, Smyrnæus, Nonnus, Lucan, Statius, or Claudian, have sought even to fulfil a single condition of epic truth. Milton was the third epic poet. For if the title of epic in its highest sense be refused to the Æneid, still less can it be conceded to the Orlando Furioso, the Gerusalemme Liberata, the Lusiad, or the Fairy Queen.

Dante and Milton were both deeply penetrated with the ancient religion of the civilized world; and its spirit exists in their poetry probably in the same proportion as its forms survived in the unreformed worship of modern Europe. The one preceded and the other followed the Reformation at almost equal intervals. Dante was the first religious reformer, and Luther surpassed him rather in the rudeness and acrimony, than in the boldness of his censures, of papal usurpation. Dante was the first awakener of entranced Europe; he created a language, in itself music and persuasion, out of a chaos of inharmonious barbarisms. He was the congregator of those great spirits who presided over the resurrection of learning; the Lucifer of that starry flock which in the thirteenth century shone forth from republican Italy, as from a heaven, into the darkness of the benighted world. His very words are instinct with spirit; each is as a spark, a burning atom of inextinguishable thought; and many yet lie covered in the ashes of their birth, and pregnant with a lightning which has yet found no conductor. All high poetry is infinite; it is as the first acorn, which contained all oaks potentially. Veil after veil may be undrawn, and the inmost naked beauty of the meaning never exposed. A great poem is a fountain for ever overflowing with the waters of wisdom and delight; and after one person and one age has exhausted all its divine effluence which their peculiar relations enable them to share, another and yet another succeeds, and new relations are ever developed, the source of an unforeseen and an unconceived delight.

The age immediately succeeding to that of Dante, Petrarch, and Boccaccio, was characterized by a revival of painting, sculpture, and architecture. Chaucer caught the sacred inspiration, and the superstructure of English literature is based upon the materials of Italian invention.

But let us not be betrayed from a defence into a critical history of poetry and its influence on society. Be it enough to have pointed out the effects of poets, in the large and true sense of the word, upon their own and all succeeding times.

But poets have been challenged to resign the civic crown to reasoners and mechanists, on another plea. It is admitted that the exercise of the imagination is most delightful, but it is alleged that that of reason is more useful. Let us examine, as the grounds of this distinction, what is here meant by utility. Pleasure or good, in a general sense, is that which the consciousness of a sensitive and intelligent being seeks, and in which, when found, it acquiesces. There[1] are two kinds of

[1] The fragment of the original Defence referred to at page 98 corresponds with the passage beginning here and ending with the close of the next paragraph but one. The variations are so considerable that it is best to give the whole fragment just as it stands:

"In one sense Utility expresses the means for producing and fixing the most intense and durable and universal pleasure, and has relation to our inetellctual being; in another it expresses the means of banishing the importunity of the wants of our animal nature; and surrounding us

pleasure, one durable, universal and permanent; the other transitory and particular. Utility may either express the means of producing the former or the latter. In the former sense, whatever strengthens and purifies the affections, enlarges the imagination, and adds spirit to sense, is useful. But a narrower meaning may be assigned to the word utility, confining it to express that which banishes the importunity of the wants of our animal nature, the surrounding men with security of life, the dispersing the grosser delusions of superstition, and the conciliating such a degree of mutual forbearance among men as may consist with the motives of personal advantage.

Undoubtedly the promoters of utility, in this limited sense, have their appointed office in society. They follow the footsteps of poets, and copy the sketches of their creations into the book of common life. They make space, and give time. Their exertions are of the highest value, so long as they confine their administration of the

with security and tranquillity of life, destroying the grosser desires, superstition, &c., and conciliating such a degree of mutual forbearance between men as may spring from motives consistent with their own present and manifest advantage.—The author of The Four Ages of Poetry employs it solely in the latter sense.

"Undoubtedly the promoters of Utility, in this limited sense, have their due praise; they have their appointed office in society; they follow the footsteps of poets and copy their creations into the book of familiar life, and their exertions are of the highest value so long as they confine their administration of the concerns of the inferior powers of our nature within the limits of what is consistent with what is due to the superior ones. But whilst the sceptic destroys gross superstitions, let him not as some French writers have done, destroy the eternal truths written upon the minds and imaginations of men. Whilst the mechanist abridges, and the political economist combines labour, let them beware that the consequences of their speculations do not tend, as they have in modern England, to exasperate at once the extremes of luxury and want. But without an intermixture of the poetical element, such are the effects which must ever flow from the unmitigated exercise of the reason. The

concerns of the inferior powers of our nature within the limits due to the superior ones. But whilst the sceptic destroys gross superstitions, let him spare to deface, as some of the French writers have defaced, the eternal truths charactered upon the imaginations of men. Whilst the mechanist abridges, and the political economist combines labour, let them beware that their speculations, for want of correspondence with those first principles which belong to the imagination, do not tend, as they have in modern England, to exasperate at once the extremes of luxury and of want. They have exemplified the saying, "To him that hath, more shall be given; and from him that hath not, the little that he hath shall be taken away." The rich have become richer, and the poor have become poorer; and the vessel of the state is driven between the Scylla and Charybdis

rich become richer, and the poor become poorer; and tyranny and anarchy alternately furious.

"It is difficult to define pleasure in the highest sense, without combining a number of words which produce apparent paradoxes on account of the incommunicability of popular and philosophical
from an inexplicable want of harmony in the constitution of our mortal being. The pain of the inferior is frequently synonymous with the pleasure of the superior portions of our nature, and terror, anguish, sorrow, despair itself, are often the selectest expressions of our approximation to this good. On this depends our pleasure with tragic fiction. Our pleasure in tragic fiction depends on this principle; and tragedy produces pleasure by affording a shadow of the pleasure which exists in intense . This is the source also of the melancholy which is inseparable from the sweetest melody. The pleasure in sorrow is far intenser than that of pleasure itself, and it is sweeter to enter into the house of mourning than into the house of mirth. The pleasure of comedy is to that of tragedy as the pleasure of the senses to that of the imagination."

The phrase in the text, "so long as they confine their administration of the concerns of the inferior powers of our nature within the limits due to the superior ones," has always struck me as one of the passages tampered with. The form in which it occurs in the foregoing fragment is such as would tempt any redactor; but it is of course possible that it was Shelley himself who redacted the form at some slight sacrifice of sense.

of anarchy and despotism. Such are the effects which must ever flow from an unmitigated exercise of the calculating faculty.

It is difficult to define pleasure in its highest sense; the definition involving a number of apparent paradoxes. For, from an inexplicable defect of harmony in the constitution of human nature, the pain of the inferior is frequently connected with the pleasures of the superior portions of our being. Sorrow, terror, anguish, despair itself, are often the chosen expressions of an approximation to the highest good. Our sympathy in tragic fiction depends on this principle; tragedy delights by affording a shadow of that pleasure which exists in pain. This is the source also of the melancholy which is inseparable from the sweetest melody. The pleasure that is in sorrow is sweeter than the pleasure of pleasure itself. And hence the saying, "It is better to go to the house of mourning than to the house of mirth." Not that this highest species of pleasure is necessarily linked with pain. The delight of love and friendship, the ecstasy of the admiration of nature, the joy of the perception and still more of the creation of poetry, is often wholly unalloyed.

The production and assurance of pleasure in this highest sense is true utility. Those who produce and preserve this pleasure are poets or poetical philosophers.

The exertions of Locke, Hume, Gibbon, Voltaire, Rousseau,[1] and their disciples, in favour of oppressed and

[1] Although Rousseau has been thus classed, he was essentially a poet. The others, even Voltaire, were mere reasoners. [SHELLEY'S NOTE.]

deluded humanity, are entitled to the gratitude of mankind. Yet it is easy to calculate the degree of moral and intellectual improvement which the world would have exhibited, had they never lived. A little more nonsense would have been talked for a century or two; and perhaps a few more men, women, and children, burnt as heretics. We might not at this moment have been congratulating each other on the abolition of the Inquisition in Spain. But it exceeds all imagination to conceive what would have been the moral condition of the world if neither Dante, Petrarch, Boccaccio, Chaucer, Shakespeare, Calderon, Lord Bacon, nor Milton, had ever existed; if Raphael and Michael Angelo[1] had never been born; if the Hebrew poetry had never been translated; if a revival of the study of Greek literature had never taken place; if no monuments of ancient sculpture had been handed down to us; and if the poetry of the religion of the ancient world had been extinguished together with its belief. The human mind could never, except by the intervention of these excitements, have been awakened to the invention of the grosser sciences, and that application of analytical reasoning to the aberrations of society, which it is now attempted to exalt over the direct expression of the inventive and creative faculty itself.

We have more moral, political, and historical wisdom, than we know how to reduce into practice; we have more scientific and economical knowledge than can be

[1] This classification of Michael Angelo should prevent any misconception as to the precise bearing of the depreciatory remarks on some of that great man's productions,—such remarks for instance as those in the note on the Bacchus at p. 71 of the present volume, or those on the Last Judgment, in the letter of the 25th of February, 1819, published in *Fraser's Magazine* for March, 1860.

accommodated to the just distribution of the produce which it multiplies. The poetry, in these systems of thought, is concealed by the accumulation of facts and calculating processes. There is no want of knowledge respecting what is wisest and best in morals, government, and political economy, or at least what is wiser and better than what men now practise and endure. But we let "*I dare not* wait upon *I would*, like the poor cat in the adage."[1] We want the creative faculty to imagine that which we know; we want the generous impulse to act that which we imagine; we want the poetry of life: our calculations have outrun conception; we have eaten more than we can digest. The cultivation of those sciences which have enlarged the limits of the empire of man over the external world, has, for want of the poetical faculty, proportionally circumscribed those of the internal world; and man, having enslaved the elements, remains himself a slave. To what but a cultivation of the mechanical arts in a degree disproportioned to the presence of the creative faculty, which is the basis of all knowledge, is to be attributed the abuse of all invention for abridging and combining labour, to the exasperation of the inequality of mankind? From what other cause has it arisen that the discoveries which should have lightened, have added a weight to the curse imposed on Adam? Poetry, and the principle of Self of which money is the visible incarnation, are the God and Mammon of the world.

[1] This is a most curious instance of the persistency of ideas and expressions in Shelley's mind and work. He had already taken a fancy to this saying of Lady Macbeth's as early as 1810, or perhaps 1809, for it appears first at the head of Chapter IX of *Zastrozzi.* In 1812 it served in the Irish campaign, for we find it in the *Proposals for an Association.* (See Vol. I, p. 376.) And here we have it still doing duty in 1821, in what is usually considered to be Shelley's prose master-piece.

The functions of the poetical faculty are twofold; by one it creates new materials of knowledge, and power, and pleasure; by the other it engenders in the mind a desire to reproduce and arrange them according to a certain rhythm and order, which may be called the beautiful and the good. The cultivation of poetry is never more to be desired than at periods when, from an excess of the selfish and calculating principle, the accumulation of the materials of external life exceed the quantity of the power of assimilating them to the internal laws of human nature. The body has then become too unwieldy for that which animates it.

Poetry is indeed something divine. It is at once the centre and circumference of knowledge; it is that which comprehends all science, and that to which all science must be referred. It is at the same time the root and blossom of all other systems of thought; it is that from which all spring, and that which adorns all; and that which, if blighted, denies the fruit and the seed, and withholds from the barren world the nourishment and the succession of the scions of the tree of life. It is the perfect and consummate surface and bloom of all things; it is as the odour and the colour of the rose to the texture of the elements which compose it, as the form and splendour of unfaded beauty to the secrets of anatomy and corruption. What were virtue, love, patriotism, friendship,—what were the scenery of this beautiful universe which we inhabit; what were our consolations on this side of the grave—and what were our aspirations beyond it, if poetry did not ascend to bring light and fire from those eternal regions where the owl-winged faculty of calculation dare not ever soar? Poetry is not like reasoning, a power to be exerted according to the determination of the will. A man cannot say, "I will compose poetry." The greatest poet even cannot say it; for the mind in creation is as a fading coal, which some invisible influence, like an inconstant wind, awakens to transitory brightness; this power arises from within, like the colour of a flower which fades and changes as it is developed, and the conscious portions of our nature are unprophetic either of its approach or its departure. Could this influence be durable in its original purity and force, it is impossible to predict the greatness of the results; but when composition begins, inspiration is already on the decline, and the most glorious poetry that has ever been communicated to the world is probably a feeble shadow of the original conceptions of the poet. I appeal to the greatest poets of the present day, whether it is not an error to assert that the finest passages of poetry are produced by labour and study. The toil and the delay recommended by critics, can be justly interpreted to mean no more than a careful observation of the inspired moments, and an artificial connexion of the spaces between their suggestions, by the intertexture of conventional expressions; a necessity only imposed by the limitedness of the poetical faculty itself: for Milton conceived the Paradise Lost as a whole before he executed it in portions. We have his own authority also for the muse having "dictated" to him the "unpremeditated song." And let this be an answer to those who would allege the fifty-six various readings of the first line of the Orlando Furioso. Compositions so produced are to poetry what mosaic is to painting. The instinct and intuition of the poetical faculty is still more observable in the plastic and pictorial arts: a great statue or picture grows under the power of the artist as a child in the mother's womb; and the very mind which directs the hands in formation, is incapable of accounting to itself for the origin, the gradations, or the media of the process.

Poetry is the record of the best and happiest moments of the happiest and best minds. We are aware of evanescent visitations of thought and feeling, sometimes associated with place or person, sometimes regarding our own mind alone, and always arising unforeseen and departing unbidden, but elevating and delightful beyond all expression: so that even in the desire and the regret they leave, there cannot but be pleasure, participating as it does in the nature of its object. It is as it were the interpenetration of a diviner nature through our own; but its footsteps are like those of a wind over the sea, which the morning[1] calm erases, and whose traces remain only, as on the wrinkled sand which paves it. These and corresponding conditions of being are experienced principally by those of the most delicate sensibility and the most enlarged imagination; and the state of mind produced by them is at war with every base desire. The enthusiasm of virtue, love, patriotism, and friendship, is essentially linked with such emotions; and whilst they last, self appears as what it is, an atom to a universe. Poets are not only subject to these experiences as spirits of the most refined organization, but they can colour all that they combine with the evanescent hues of this æthereal world; a word, a trait in the representation of a scene or a passion, will touch the inchanted chord, and re-animate, in those who have ever experienced these emotions, the sleeping, the cold, the buried image of the

[1] In the edition of 1852, *coming* for *morning*.

past. Poetry thus makes immortal all that is best and most beautiful in the world; it arrests the vanishing apparitions which haunt the interlunations of life, and veiling them, or in language or in form, sends them forth among mankind, bearing sweet news of kindred joy to those with whom their sisters abide—abide, because there is no portal of expression from the caverns of the spirit which they inhabit into the universe of things. Poetry redeems from decay the visitations of the divinity in man.

Poetry turns all things to loveliness; it exalts the beauty of that which is most beautiful, and it adds beauty to that which is most deformed; it marries exultation and horror, grief and pleasure, eternity and change; it subdues to union, under its light yoke, all irreconcilable things. It transmutes all that it touches, and every form moving within the radiance of its presence is changed by wondrous sympathy to an incarnation of the spirit which it breathes: its secret alchemy turns to potable gold the poisonous waters which flow from death through life; it strips the veil of familiarity from the world, and lays bare the naked and sleeping beauty, which is the spirit of its forms.

All things exist as they are perceived; at least in relation to the percipient.

> The mind is its own place, and in itself
> Can make a Heav'n of Hell, a Hell of Heav'n.[1]

But poetry defeats the curse which binds us to be sub-

[1] The quotation from *Paradise Lost* (Book I, 254-5) is printed as if it were prose in former editions, —*of itself* being substituted for *in itself*. *Cf.* Byron's *Manfred*, Act III, Sc. 4:

> The mind which is immortal makes itself
> Requital for its good or evil thoughts—
> Is its own origin of ill and end—
> And its own place and time—its innate sense,
> When stripp'd of this mortality, derives
> No colour from the fleeting things without;
> But is absorb'd in sufferance or in joy,
> Born from the knowledge of its own desert.

jected to the accident of surrounding impressions. And whether it spreads its own figured curtain, or withdraws life's dark veil from before the scene of things, it equally creates for us a being within our being. It makes us the inhabitant of a world to which the familiar world is a chaos. It reproduces the common universe of which we are portions and percipients, and it purges from our inward sight the film of familiarity which obscures from us the wonder of our being. It compels us to feel that which we perceive, and to imagine that which we know. It creates anew the universe, after it has been annihilated in our minds by the recurrence of impressions blunted by reiteration. It justifies the bold and true word of Tasso: *Non merita nome di creatore, se non Iddio ed il Poeta.*[1]

A poet, as he is the author to others of the highest wisdom, pleasure, virtue and glory, so he ought personally to be the happiest, the best, the wisest, and the most illustrious of men. As to his glory, let time be challenged to declare whether the fame of any other institutor of human life be comparable to that of a poet. That he is the wisest, the happiest, and the best, inasmuch as he is a poet, is equally incontrovertible: the greatest poets have been men of the most spotless virtue, of the most consummate prudence, and, if we would look into the interior of their lives, the most fortunate of men: and the exceptions, as they regard those who possessed the poetic faculty in a high yet inferior degree, will be found on consideration to confirm[2] rather than destroy the rule.

[1] Shelley quotes the same saying of Tasso in his letter of the 16th of August, 1818, to Peacock, who, in printing the letter in *Fraser's Magazine* for March, 1860, gave the words quoted as *Non c'è in mondo chi merita nome di creatore, che Dio ed il Poeta.*

[2] So in the first edition, but *confine* in that of 1852 and in the transcript.

Let us for a moment stoop to the arbitration of popular breath, and usurping and uniting in our own persons the incompatible characters of accuser, witness, judge and executioner, let us decide without trial, testimony, or form, that certain motives of those who are "there sitting where we dare not soar," are reprehensible. Let us assume that Homer was a drunkard, that Virgil was a flatterer, that Horace was a coward, that Tasso was a madman, that Lord Bacon was a peculator, that Raphael was a libertine, that Spenser was a poet laureate. It is inconsistent with this division of our subject to cite living poets, but posterity has done ample justice to the great names now referred to. Their errors have been weighed and found to have been dust in the balance; if their sins "were as scarlet, they are now white as snow:" they have been washed in the blood of the mediator and redeemer, time. Observe in what a ludicrous chaos the imputations of real or fictitious crime have been confused in the contemporary calumnies against poetry and poets; consider how little is as it appears—or appears as it is; look to your own motives, and judge not, lest ye be judged.

Poetry, as has been said, differs in this respect from logic, that it is not subject to the controul of the active powers of the mind, and that its birth and recurrence have no necessary connexion with the consciousness or will. It is presumptuous to determine that these are the necessary conditions of all mental causation, when mental effects are experienced insusceptible of being referred to them. The frequent recurrence of the poetical power, it is obvious to suppose, may produce in the mind an habit of order and harmony correlative with its own nature and with its effects upon other minds. But in the intervals of inspiration, and they may be frequent without being durable, a poet becomes a man, and is abandoned to the sudden reflux of the influences under which others habitually live. But as he is more delicately organized than other men, and sensible to pain and pleasure, both his own and that of others, in a degree unknown to them, he will avoid the one and pursue the other with an ardour proportioned to this difference. And he renders himself obnoxious to calumny, when he neglects to observe the circumstances under which these objects of universal pursuit and flight have disguised themselves in one another's garments.

But there is nothing necessarily evil in this error, and thus cruelty, envy, revenge, avarice, and the passions purely evil, have never formed any portion of the popular imputations on the lives of poets.

I have thought it most favourable to the cause of truth to set down these remarks according to the order in which they were suggested to my mind, by a consideration of the subject itself, instead of observing the formality of a polemical reply; but if the view which they contain be just, they will be found to involve a refutation of the arguers against poetry, so far at least as regards the first division of the subject. I can readily conjecture what should have moved the gall of some learned and intelligent writers who quarrel with certain versifiers; I, like them, confess myself unwilling to be stunned by the Theseids of the hoarse Codri of the day. Bavius and Mævius undoubtedly are, as they ever were, insufferable persons. But it belongs to a philosophical critic to distinguish rather than confound.

The first part of these remarks has related to poetry in its elements and principles; and it has been shewn, as well as the narrow limits assigned them would permit, that what is called poetry in a restricted sense, has a common source with all other forms of order and of beauty, according to which the materials of human life are susceptible of being arranged, and which is poetry in an universal sense.

The second part will have for its object an application of these principles to the present state of the cultivation of poetry, and a defence of the attempt to idealize the modern forms of manners and opinions, and compel them into a subordination to the imaginative and creative faculty. For the literature of England, an energetic developement of which has ever preceded or accompanied a great and free developement of the national will, has arisen as it were from a new birth. In spite of the low-thoughted envy which would undervalue contemporary merit, our own will be a memorable age in intellectual achievements, and we live among such philosophers and poets as surpass beyond comparison any who have appeared since the last national struggle for civil and religious liberty. The most unfailing herald, companion, and follower of the awakening of a great people to work a beneficial change in opinion or institution, is poetry. At such periods there is an accumulation of the power of communicating and receiving intense and impassioned conceptions respecting man and nature. The persons in whom this power resides, may often, as far as regards many portions of their nature, have little apparent correspondence with that spirit of good of which they are the ministers. But even whilst they deny and abjure they are yet compelled to serve, the power which is seated on the throne of their own soul. It is impossible to read the compositions of the most celebrated writers of the present day without being startled with the electric life which burns within their words. They measure the circumference and sound the depths of human nature with a comprehensive and all-penetrating spirit, and they are themselves perhaps the most sincerely astonished at its manifestations; for it is less their spirit than the spirit of the age. Poets are the hierophants of an unapprehended inspiration; the mirrors of the gigantic shadows which futurity casts upon the present; the words which express what they understand not; the trumpets which sing to battle and feel not what they inspire; the influence which is moved not, but moves. Poets are the unacknowledged legislators of the world.

THREE FRAGMENTS ON BEAUTY.[1]

I.

Why is the reflection in that canal more beautiful than the objects it reflects? The colours are more vivid, and yet blended with more harmony; the openings from within into the soft and tender colours of the distant wood, and the intersection of the mountain lines, surpass and misrepresent truth.

II.

The mountains sweep to the plain like waves that meet in a chasm—the olive woods are as green as a sea and are waving in the wind—the shadows of the clouds are spotting the bosoms of the hills—a heron comes sailing over me—a butterfly flits near—at intervals the pines give forth their sweet and prolonged response to the wind—the myrtle bushes are in bud, and the soil beneath me is carpeted with odoriferous flowers.

[1] These three fragments from the *Relics of Shelley*, assigned by Mr. Garnett to the year 1821, may fitly follow the *Defence of Poetry*.

III.

It is sweet to feel the beauties of nature in every pulsation, in every nerve—but it is far sweeter to be able to express this feeling to one who loves you. To feel all that is divine in the green-robed earth and the starry sky is a penetrating yet vivid pleasure which, when it is over, presses like the memory of misfortune; but if you can express those feelings—if, secure of sympathy (for without sympathy it is worse than the taste of those apples whose core is as bitter ashes), if thus secure you can pour forth into another's most attentive ear the feelings by which you are entranced, there is an exultation of spirit in the utterance—a glory of happiness which far transcends all human transports, and seems to invest the soul as the saints are with light, with a halo untainted, holy, and undying.

TRANSLATIONS.

[When Mrs. Shelley's two volumes of *Essays, Letters from Abroad, Translations, and Fragments* were published, the translations were not placed in a group apart; and, were the present edition merely a reprint of those two volumes, there would have been no occasion to disturb the order adopted in them. They, however, consisted almost wholly of posthumous prose writings, and bear the same relation to Shelley's whole works in prose as the volume of *Posthumous Poems* (1824) bears to his whole poetical works. In arranging the whole mass of prose work issued during and after his life-time, it seemed desirable to separate the translations. In the following pages are brought together those remarks in Mrs. Shelley's Preface which refer to the translations.—H. B. F.]

MRS. SHELLEY'S REMARKS ON THE TRANSLATIONS.

In allusion to the *Discourse on the Manners of the Ancients relative to the subject of Love,*[1] and the *Preface to the Banquet of Plato,* Mrs. Shelley says:—

"The fragments that follow form an introduction to *The Banquet* or *Symposium* of Plato—and that noble piece of writing follows; which for the first time introduces the Athenian to the English reader in a style worthy of him. No prose author in the history of mankind has exerted so much influence over the world as Plato. From him the fathers and commentators of early Christianity derived many of their most abstruse notions and spiritual ideas. His name is familiar to our lips, and he is regarded even by the unlearned as the possessor of the highest imaginative faculty ever displayed by man—the creator of much of the purity of sentiment which in another guise was adopted by the founders of

[1] Printed in the *Essays* &c. under the title of *Essay on the Literature, Arts, and Manners of the Athenians—a Fragment.*

chivalry—the man who endowed Socrates with a large portion of that reputation for wisdom and virtue, which surrounds him evermore with an imperishable halo of glory.

"With all this, how little is really known of Plato! The translation we have is so harsh and un-English in its style, as universally to repel. There are excellent abstracts of some of his dialogues in a periodical publication called the *Monthly Repository*;[1] and the mere English reader must feel deeply obliged to the learned translator. But these abstracts are defective from their very form of abridgment; and, though I am averse to speak disparagingly of pages from which I have derived so much pleasure and knowledge, they want the radiance and delicacy of language with which the ideas are invested in the original, and are dry and stiff compared with the soaring poetry, the grace, subtlety, and infinite variety of Plato. They want, also, the dramatic vivacity and the touch of nature, that vivifies the pages of the Athenian. These are all found here. Shelley commands language splendid and melodious as Plato, and renders faithfully the elegance and the gaiety which make the *Symposium* as amusing as it is sublime. The whole mechanism of the drama, for such in some sort it is,—the enthusiasm of Apollodorus, the sententiousness of Eryximachus, the wit of Aristophanes, the rapt and golden eloquence of Agathon, the subtle dialectics and grandeur of aim of Socrates, the drunken outbreak of Alcibiades,—are given with grace and animation. The picture presented reminds us of that talent which, in a less

[1] It is perhaps not generally known that these abstracts are the work of the late John Stuart Mill. See his Autobiography, p. 198.

degree, we may suppose to have dignified the orgies of the last generation of free-spirited wits,—Burke, Fox, Sheridan, and Curran. It has something of license, —too much, indeed, and perforce omitted; but of coarseness, that worst sin against our nature, it has nothing.

"Shelley's own definition of Love follows; and reveals the secrets of the most impassioned, and yet the purest and softest heart that ever yearned for sympathy, and was ready to give its own, in lavish measure, in return. 'The Coliseum' is a continuation to a great degree of the same subject. Shelley had something of the idea of a story in this. The stranger was a Greek,—nurtured from infancy exclusively in the literature of his progenitors,—and brought up as a child of Pericles might have been; and to heighten the resemblance, Shelley conceived[1] the idea of a woman, whom he named Diótima, who was his instructress and guide.

* * * * * *

"I do not know why Shelley selected the 'Ion' of Plato to translate. Probably because he thought it characteristic; that it unfolded peculiar ideas, and those Platonic, with regard to poetry; and gave insight into portions of Athenian manners, pursuits, and views, which would have been otherwise lost to us. We find manifestation here of the exceeding partiality felt by the Greeks, for every exhibition of eloquence. It testifies that love of interchanging and enlarging ideas by conversation, which in modern society, through our domestic

[1] So in the edition of 1852; but, in the original edition we read, *and the greater the resemblance, since Shelley conceived* &c. It is to be assumed that the change is Mrs. Shelley's own.

system of life, is too often narrowed to petty objects, and which, from their fashion of conversing in streets and under porticos, and in public places, became a passion far more intense than with us. Among those who ministered exclusively to this taste, were the rhapsodists; and among rhapsodists, Ion himself tells us, he was the most eminent of his day; that he was a man of enthusiastic and poetic temperament, and abundantly gifted with the power of arranging his thoughts in glowing and fascinating language, his success proves. But he was singularly deficient in reason. When Socrates presses on him the question of, whether he as a rhapsodist is as well versed in nautical, hippodromic, and other arts, as sailors, charioteers, and various artisans? he gives up the point with the most foolish inanity. One would fancy that practice in his pursuit would have caused him to reply, that though he was neither mariner nor horseman, nor practically skilled in any other of the pursuits in question, yet that he had consulted men versed in them; and enriching his mind with the knowledge afforded by adepts in all arts, he was better qualified by study and by his gift of language and enthusiasm to explain these, as they form a portion of Homer's poetry, than any individual whose knowledge was limited to one subject only. But Ion had no such scientific view of his profession. He gives up point after point, till, as Socrates observes, he most absurdly strives at victory, under the form of an expert leader of armies. In this, as in all the other of Plato's writings, we are perpetually referred, with regard to the enthusiastic and ideal portion of our intellect, to something above and beyond our sphere, the inspiration of the God—the influence exercised over the human mind,—either through the direct agency of the deities, or our own half-blind memory of divine knowledge acquired by the soul in its antenatal state. Shelley left Ion imperfect—I thought it better that it should appear as a whole—but at the same time have marked with brackets the passages that have been added; the rest appears exactly as Shelley left it.[1]

"Respect for the name of Plato as well as that of Shelley, and reliance on the curiosity that the English reader must feel with regard to the sealed book of the Ancient Wonder, caused me to include in this volume the fragment of *Menexenus*, and passages from *The Republic*. In the first we have another admirable specimen of Socratic irony. In the latter the opinions and views of Plato enounced in *The Republic*, which appeared remarkable to Shelley, are preserved, with the addition, in some instances, of his own brief observations on them."

[1] See note on this subject at p. 250.

THE BANQUET.

TRANSLATED FROM THE GREEK OF PLATO.

[This happy task seems to have been undertaken in the early part of Shelley's residence in Italy. In a letter to Mr. and Mrs. Gisborne, dated "Bagni di Lucca, July 10th, 1818," he says, "I am employed just now, having little better to do, in translating into my faint and inefficient periods, the divine eloquence of Plato's Symposium; only as an exercise, or, perhaps, to give Mary some idea of the manners and feelings of the Athenians—so different on many subjects from that of any other community that ever existed. Writing to Godwin on the 25th of the same month, he says he has been constantly occupied in literature, but has written little except some translations of Plato, done "in despair of producing anything original." He specifies the *Symposium* as what he has been at work upon; and on the same date he writes to Peacock (*Fraser's Magazine*, March, 1860, page 302), "I have lately found myself totally incapable of original composition. I employed my mornings, therefore, in translating the *Symposium*, which I accomplished in ten days. Mary is now transcribing it, and I am writing a prefatory essay." In 1821 this work was missing; and Shelley wrote to Medwin (Trelawny's *Records of Shelley*, &c., 1878, Vol. II, page 42), "I think you must have put up by mistake a MS. translation of the Symposium of Plato; if so, pray contrive to send it to me." On the 4th of July, 1822, he wrote to Mrs. Shelley from Pisa that he had "found the translation of the Symposium," presumably at Pisa.—H. B. F.]

PREFACE.

[BY SHELLEY.]

THE dialogue entitled "The Banquet," was selected by the translator as the most beautiful and perfect among all the works of Plato.[1] He despairs of having communicated to the English language any portion of the surpassing graces of the composition, or having done more than present an imperfect shadow of the language and the sentiment of this astonishing production.

Plato is eminently the greatest among the Greek philosophers, and from, or, rather, perhaps through him, from his master Socrates, have proceeded those emanations of moral and metaphysical knowledge, on which a long series and an incalculable variety of popular superstitions

[1] The Republic, though replete with considerable errors of speculation, is, indeed, the greatest repository of important truths of all the works of Plato. This, perhaps, is because it is the longest. He first, and perhaps last, maintained that a state ought to be governed, not by the wealthiest, or the most ambitious, or the most cunning, but by the wisest; the method of selecting such rulers, and the laws by which such a selection is made, must correspond with and arise out of the moral freedom and refinement of the people. [SHELLEY'S NOTE.]

have sheltered their absurdities from the slow contempt of mankind. Plato exhibits the rare union of close and subtle logic, with the Pythian enthusiasm of poetry, melted by the splendour and harmony of his periods into one irresistible stream of musical impressions, which hurry the persuasions onward, as in a breathless career. His language is that of an immortal spirit, rather than a man. Lord Bacon is, perhaps, the only writer, who, in these particulars, can be compared with him: his imitator, Cicero, sinks in the comparison into an ape mocking the gestures of a man. His views into the nature of mind, and existence are often obscure, only because they are profound; and though his theories respecting the government of the world, and the elementary laws of moral action, are not always correct, yet there is scarcely any of his treatises, which do not, however stained by puerile sophisms, contain the most remarkable intuitions into all that can be the subject of the human mind. His excellence consists especially in intuition, and it is this faculty which raises him far above Aristotle, whose genius though vivid and various, is obscure in comparison with that of Plato.

The dialogue entitled the "Banquet," is called 'Ερωτικός, or a Discussion upon Love, and is supposed to have taken place at the house of Agathon, at one of a series of festivals given by that poet, on the occasion of his gaining the prize of tragedy at the Dionysiaca. The account of the debate on this occasion is supposed to have been given by Apollodorus, a pupil of Socrates, many years after it had taken place, to a companion who was curious to hear it. This Apollodorus appears, both from the style in which he is represented in this piece, as well as from a passage in the Phædon, to have been a person of an impassioned and enthusiastic disposition; to borrow an image from the Italian painters, he seems to have been the St. John of the Socratic group. The drama (for so the lively distinction of character and the various and well-wrought circumstances of the story almost entitle it to be called) begins by Socrates persuading Aristodemus to sup at Agathon's, uninvited. The whole of this introduction affords the most lively conception of refined Athenian manners.

[UNFINISHED.]

NOTE ON THE BANQUET.[1]

The wonderful description of Love in Plato, Sympos. p. 214—particularly 214, l. 8—*l. ultima, et passim* 218.

I should say in answer, that Ἔρως neither loved nor was loved, but is the cause of Love in others—a subtlety to beat Plato. *Agathon,* a poem.

[1] This note is from the *Relics of Shelley,* and is assigned by Mr. Garnett to the year 1817. I do not know to what edition of Plato Shelley's figures apply. The reference is likely to be to the descriptions given by Agathon and Diotima. (See pp. 195 to 199 and 209 to 212 of this volume). Mr. Garnett's impression of the last three words in this note is that Shelley thought the Agathon of this Dialogue a good subject for a poem.

THE BANQUET.

THE PERSONS OF THE DIALOGUE.

Apollodorus.
A Friend of Apollodorus.
Glauco.
Aristodemus.
Socrates.
Agathon.
Phædrus.
Pausanias.
Eryximachus.
Aristophanes.
Diotima.
Alcibiades.

THE BANQUET.

TRANSLATED FROM PLATO.

APOLLODORUS.

I THINK that the subject of your inquiries is still fresh in my memory; for yesterday, as I chanced to be returning home from Phaleros, one of my acquaintance, seeing me before him, called out to me from a distance, jokingly, "Apollodorus, you Phalerian, will you not wait a minute?"—I waited for him, and as soon as he overtook me, "I have just been looking for you, Apollodorus," he said, "for I wished to hear what those discussions were on Love, which took place at the party, when Agathon, Socrates, Alcibiades, and some others, met at supper. Some one who heard it from Phœnix, the son of Philip, told me that you could give a full account, but he could relate nothing distinctly himself. Relate to me, then, I intreat you, all the circumstances. I know you are a faithful reporter of the discussions of your friends; but, first tell me, were you present at the party or not?"

"Your informant," I replied, "seems to have given you no very clear idea of what you wish to hear, if he thinks that these discussions took place so lately as that I could have been of the party."

"Indeed, I thought so," replied he.

"For how," said I, "O Glauco! could I have been present? Do you not know that Agathon has been absent from the city many years? But, since I began to converse with Socrates, and to observe each day all his words and actions, three years are scarcely past. Before this time I wandered about wherever it might chance, thinking that I did something, but being, in truth, a most miserable wretch, not less than you are now, who believe that you ought to do anything rather than practise the love of wisdom."

"Do not cavil," interrupted Glauco, "but tell me, when did this party take place?"

"Whilst we were yet children," I replied, "when Agathon first gained the prize of tragedy, and the day after that on which he and the chorus made sacrifices in celebration of their success."

"A long time ago, it seems. But who told you all the circumstances of the discussion? Did you hear them from Socrates himself?"

"No, by Jupiter! but the same person from whom Phœnix had his information, one Aristodemus, a Cydathenean,—a little man who always went about without sandals. He was present at this feast, being, I believe, more than any of his contemporaries, a lover and admirer of Socrates. I have questioned Socrates concerning some of the circumstances of his narration, who confirms all that I have heard from Aristodemus."

"Why, then," said Glauco, "why not relate them, as we walk, to me? The road to the city is every way convenient, both for those who listen and those who speak."

Thus as we walked I gave him some account of those discussions concerning Love; since, as I said before, I remember them with sufficient accuracy. If I am required to relate them also to you, that shall willingly be done; for, whensoever either I myself talk of philosophy, or listen to others talking of it, in addition to the improvement which I conceive there arises from such conversation, I am delighted beyond measure; but whenever I hear your discussions about monied men and great proprietors, I am weighed down with grief, and pity you, who, doing nothing, believe that you are doing something. Perhaps you think that I am a miserable wretch; and, indeed, I believe that you think truly. I do not think, but well know, that you are miserable.

COMPANION.

You are always the same, Apollodorus—always saying some ill of yourself and others. Indeed, you seem to me to think every one miserable except Socrates, beginning with yourself. I do not know what could have entitled you to the surname of the "Madman," for I am sure you are consistent enough, for ever inveighing with bitterness against yourself and all others, except Socrates.

APOLLODORUS.

My dear friend, it is manifest that I am out of my wits from this alone—that I have such opinions as you describe concerning myself and you.

COMPANION.

It is not worth while, Apollodorus, to dispute now about these things; but do what I intreat you, and relate to us what were these discussions.

APOLLODORUS.

They were such as I will proceed to tell you. But let me attempt to relate them in the order which Aristodemus observed in relating them to me. He said that he met Socrates washed, and, contrary to his usual custom, sandalled, and having inquired whither he went so gaily dressed, Socrates replied, "I am going to sup at Agathon's; yesterday I avoided it, disliking the crowd, which would attend at the prize sacrifices then celebrated; to-day I promised to be there, and I made myself so gay, because one ought to be beautiful to approach one who is beautiful. But you, Aristodemus, what think you of coming uninvited to supper?"

"I will do," he replied, "as you command."

"Follow, then, that we may, by changing its application, disarm that proverb which says, *To the feasts of the good, the good come uninvited.* Homer, indeed, seems not only to destroy, but to outrage the proverb; for, describing Agamemnon as excellent in battle, and Menelaus but a faint-hearted warrior, he represents Menelaus as coming uninvited to the feast of one better and braver than himself."

Aristodemus hearing this, said, "I also am in some danger, Socrates, not as you say, but according to Homer, of approaching like an unworthy inferior, the banquet of one more wise and excellent than myself. Will you not, then, make some excuse for me? for, I shall not confess that I came uninvited, but shall say that I was invited by you."

"As we walk together," said Socrates, "we will consider together what excuse to make—but let us go."

Thus discoursing, they proceeded. But, as they walked, Socrates, engaged in some deep contemplation, slackened his pace, and, observing Aristodemus waiting for him, he desired him to go on before. When Aristodemus arrived at Agathon's house he found the door open, and it occurred somewhat comically, that a slave met him at the vestibule, and conducted him where he found the guests already reclined. As soon as Agathon saw him, "You arrive just in time to sup with us, Aristodemus," he said; "if you have any other purpose in your visit, defer it to a better opportunity. I was looking for you yesterday, to invite you to be of our party; I could not find you anywhere. But how is it that you do not bring Socrates with you?"

But he turning round, and not seeing Socrates behind him, said to Agathon, "I just came hither in his company, being invited by him to sup with you."

"You did well," replied Agathon, "to come; but where is Socrates?"

"He just now came hither behind me; I myself wonder where he can be."

"Go and look, boy," said Agathon, "and bring Socrates in; meanwhile, you, Aristodemus, recline there near Eryximachus." And he bade a slave wash his feet that he might recline. Another slave, meanwhile, brought word that Socrates had retired into a neighbouring vestibule, where he stood, and, in spite of his message, refused to come in.

"What absurdity you talk," cried Agathon, "call him, and do not leave him till he comes."

"Leave him alone, by all means," said Aristodemus, "it is customary with him sometimes to retire in this way and stand wherever it may chance. He will come presently, I do not doubt; do not disturb him."

"Well, be it as you will," said Agathon; "as it is, you boys, bring supper for the rest; put before us what you will, for I resolved that there should be no master of the feast. Consider me, and these, my friends, as guests, whom you have invited to supper, and serve them so that we may commend you."

After this they began supper, but Socrates did not come in. Agathon ordered him to be called, but Aristodemus perpetually forbade it. At last he came in, much about the middle of supper, not having delayed so long as was his custom. Agathon (who happened to be reclining at the end of the table, and alone,) said, as he entered, "Come hither, Socrates, and sit down by me; so that by the mere touch of one so wise as you are, I may enjoy the fruit of your meditations in the vestibule ; for, I well know, you would not have departed till you had discovered and secured it."

Socrates having sate down as he was desired, replied, " It would be well, Agathon, if wisdom were of such a nature, as that when we touched each other, it would overflow of its own accord, from him who possesses much to him who possesses little ; like the water in two chalices, which will flow through a flock of wool from the fuller into the emptier, until both are equal. If wisdom had this property, I should esteem myself most fortunate in reclining near to you. I should thus soon be filled, I think, with the most beautiful and various wisdom. Mine, indeed, is something obscure, and doubtful, and dreamlike. But yours is radiant, and has been crowned with amplest reward ; for, though you are yet so young, it shone forth from you, and became so manifest yesterday, that more than thirty thousand Greeks can bear testimony to its excellence and loveliness."

" You are laughing at me, Socrates," said Agathon, " but you and I will decide this controversy about wisdom by and by, taking Bacchus for our judge. At present turn to your supper."

After Socrates and the rest had finished supper, and had reclined back on their couches, and the libations had been poured forth, and they had sung hymns to the god, and all other rites which are customary had been performed, they turned to drinking.

Then Pausanias made this kind of proposal. "Come, my friends," said he, "in what manner will it be pleasantest for us to drink? I must confess to you that, in reality, I am not very well from the wine we drank last night, and I have need of some intermission. I suspect that most of you are in the same condition, for you were here yesterday. Now, consider how we shall drink most easily and comfortably."

"'Tis a good proposal, Pausanias," said Aristophanes, "to contrive, in some way or other, to place moderation in our cups. I was one of those who were drenched last night."

Eryximachus, the son of Acumenius, hearing this, said: "I am of your opinion; I only wish to know one thing—whether Agathon is in the humour for hard drinking?"

"Not at all," replied Agathon; "I confess that I am not able to drink much this evening."

"It is an excellent thing for us," replied Eryximachus, "I mean myself, Aristodemus, Phædrus, and these others, if you who are such invincible drinkers, now refuse to drink. I ought to except Socrates, for he is capable of drinking everything, or nothing; and whatever we shall determine will equally suit him. Since, then, no one present has any desire to drink much wine, I shall perhaps give less offence, if I declare the nature of drunkenness. The science of medicine teaches us that drunkenness is very pernicious: nor would I choose to drink immoderately myself, or counsel another to do so, especially if he had been drunk the night before."

"Yes," said Phædrus, the Myrinusian, interrupting him, "I have been accustomed to confide in you, especially in your directions concerning medicine; and I would now willingly do so, if the rest will do the same." All then agreed that they would drink at this present banquet not for drunkenness, but for pleasure.

"Since, then," said Eryximachus, "it is decided that no one shall be compelled to drink more than he pleases, I think that we may as well send away the flute-player to play to herself; or, if she likes, to the women within. Let us devote the present occasion to conversation between ourselves, and if you wish, I will propose to you what shall be the subject of our discussion."

All present desired and entreated that he would explain.

"The exordium of my speech," said Eryximachus, "will be in the style of the Menalippe of Euripides, for the story which I am about to tell belongs not to me, but to Phædrus. Phædrus has often indignantly complained to me, saying—'Is it not strange, Eryximachus, that there are innumerable hymns and pæans composed for the other gods, but that not one of the many poets who spring up in the world has ever composed a verse in honour of Love, who is such and so great a god? Nor any one of those accomplished sophists, who, like the famous Prodicus, have celebrated the praise of Hercules and others, have ever celebrated that of Love; but what is more astonishing, I have lately met with the book of some philosopher, in which salt is extolled on account of its utility, and many other things of the same nature are in like manner celebrated with elaborate praise. That so much serious thought is expended on such trifles, and that no man has dared to this day to frame a hymn in honour of Love, who being so great a deity, is thus neglected, may well be sufficient to excite my indignation.'

"There seemed to me some justice in these complaints of Phædrus; I propose, therefore, at the same time for the sake of giving pleasure to Phædrus, and that we may on the present occasion do something well and befitting us, that this God should receive from those who are now present the honour which is most due to him. If you agree to my proposal, an excellent discussion might arise on the subject. Every one ought, according to my plan, to praise Love with as much eloquence as he can. Let Phædrus begin first, both because he reclines the first in order, and because he is the father of the discussion."

"No one will vote against you, Eryximachus," said Socrates, "for how can I oppose your proposal, who am ready to confess that I know nothing on any subject but love? Or how can Agathon, or Pausanias, or even Aristophanes, whose life is one perpetual ministration to Venus and Bacchus? Or how can any other whom I see here? Though we who sit last are scarcely on an equality with you; for if those who speak before us shall have exhausted the subject with their eloquence and reasonings, our discourses will be superfluous. But in the name of Good Fortune, let Phædrus begin and praise Love."

The whole party agreed to what Socrates said, and intreated Phædrus to begin.

What each then said on this subject, Aristodemus did not intirely recollect, nor do I recollect all that he related to me; but only the speeches of those who said what was most worthy of remembrance. First, then, Phædrus began thus:—

"Love is a mighty deity, and the object of admiration, both to Gods and men, for many and for various claims; but especially on account of his origin. For that he is to be honoured as one of the most ancient of the gods, this may serve as a testimony, that Love has no parents, nor is there any poet or other person who has ever affirmed that there are such. Hesiod says, that first 'Chaos was produced; then the broad-bosomed Earth, to be a secure foundation for all things; then Love.' He says, that after Chaos these two were produced, the Earth and Love. Parmenides, speaking of generation, says:—'But he created Love before any of the gods.' Acusileus agrees with Hesiod. Love, therefore, is universally acknowledged to be among the oldest of things. And in addition to this, Love is the author of our greatest advantages; for I cannot imagine a greater happiness and advantage to one who is in the flower of youth than an amiable lover, or to a lover, than an amiable object of his love. For neither birth, nor wealth, nor honours, can awaken in the minds of men the principles which should guide those who from their youth aspire to an honourable and excellent life, as Love awakens them. I speak of the fear of shame, which deters them from that which is disgraceful; and the love of glory, which incites to honourable deeds. For it is not possible that a state or private person should accomplish, without these incitements, anything beautiful or great. I assert, then, that should one who loves be discovered in any dishonourable action, or tamely enduring insult through cowardice, he would feel more anguish and shame if observed by the object of his passion, than if he were observed by his father, or his companions, or any other person. In like manner among warmly attached friends, a man is especially grieved to be discovered by his friend in any dishonourable act. If then, by any contrivance, a state or army could be composed of friends bound by strong attachment, it is beyond calculation how excellently they would administer their affairs, refraining from any thing base, contending with each other for the acquirement of fame, and exhibiting such valour in battle as that, though few in numbers, they might subdue all mankind. For should one friend desert the ranks or cast away his arms in the presence of the other, he would suffer far acuter shame from that one person's regard, than from the regard of all other men. A thousand times would he prefer to die, rather than desert the object of his attachment, and not succour him in danger.

"There is none so worthless whom Love cannot impel, as it were by a divine inspiration, towards virtue, even so that he may through this inspiration become equal to one who might naturally be more excellent; and, in truth, as Homer says: The God breathes vigour into certain heroes—so Love breathes into those who love, the spirit which is produced from himself. Not only men, but even women who love, are those alone who willingly expose themselves to die for others. Alcestis, the daughter of Pelias, affords to the Greeks a remarkable example of this opinion; she alone being willing to die for her husband, and so surpassing his parents in the affection with which love inspired her towards him, as to make them appear, in the comparison with her, strangers to their own child, and related to him merely in name; and so lovely and admirable did this action appear, not only to men, but even to the Gods, that, although they conceded the prerogative of bringing back the spirit from death to few among the many who then performed excellent and honourable deeds, yet, delighted with this action, they redeemed her soul from the infernal regions: so highly do the Gods honour zeal and devotion in love. They sent back indeed Orpheus, the son of Œagrus, from Hell, with his purpose unfulfilled, and, showing him only the spectre of her for whom he came, refused to render up herself. For Orpheus seemed to them, not as Alcestis, to have dared die for the sake of her whom he loved, and thus to secure to himself a perpetual intercourse with her in the regions to which she had preceded him, but like a cowardly musician, to have contrived to descend alive into Hell; and, indeed, they appointed as a punishment for his cowardice, that he should be put to death by women.

"Far otherwise did they reward Achilles, the son of Thetis, whom they sent to inhabit the islands of the blessed. For Achilles, though informed by his mother that his own death would ensue upon his killing Hector, but that if he refrained from it he might return home and die in old age, yet preferred revenging and honouring his beloved Patroclus; not to die for him merely, but to disdain and reject that life which he had ceased to share. Therefore the Greeks honoured Achilles beyond all other men, because he thus preferred his friend to all things else.

* * * * * *

"On this account have the Gods rewarded Achilles more amply than Alcestis; permitting his spirit to inhabit the islands of the blessed. Hence do I assert that Love is the most ancient and venerable of deities, and most powerful to endow mortals with the possession of happiness and virtue, both whilst they live and after they die."

Thus Aristodemus reported the discourse of Phædrus; and after Phædrus, he said that some others spoke, whose discourses he did not well remember. When they had ceased, Pausanias began thus:—

"Simply to praise Love, O Phædrus, seems to me too bounded a scope for our discourse. If Love were one, it would be well. But since Love is not one, I will endeavour to distinguish which is the Love whom it becomes us to praise, and having thus discriminated one from the other, will attempt to render him who is the subject of our discourse the honour due to his divinity. We all know that Venus is never without Love; and if Venus were one, Love would be one; but since there are two Venuses, of necessity also must there be two Loves. For assuredly are there two Venuses; one, the eldest, the daughter of Uranus, born without a mother, whom we call the Uranian; the other younger, the daughter of Jupiter and Dione, whom we call the Pandemian;—of necessity must there also be two Loves, the Uranian and Pandemian companions of these goddesses. It is becoming to praise all the Gods, but the attributes which fall to the lot of each may be distinguished and selected. For any particular action whatever, in itself is neither good nor evil; what we are now doing—drinking, singing, talking, none of these things are good in themselves, but the mode in which they are done stamps them with its own nature; and that which is done well, is good, and that which is done ill, is evil. Thus, not all love, nor every mode of love is beautiful, or worthy of commendation, but that alone which excites us to love worthily. The Love, therefore, which attends upon Venus Pandemos is, in truth, common to the vulgar, and presides over transient and fortuitous connexions, and is worshipped by the least excellent of mankind. The votaries of this deity seek the body rather than the soul, and the ignorant rather than the wise, disdaining all that is honourable and lovely, and considering how they shall best satisfy their sensual necessities. This Love is derived from the younger goddess, who partakes in her nature both of male and female. But the attendant on the other, the Uranian, whose nature is entirely masculine, is the Love who inspires us with affection, and exempts us from all wantonness and libertinism. Those who are inspired by this divinity seek the affections of those who are endowed by nature with greater excellence and vigour both of body and mind. And it is easy to distinguish those who especially exist under the influence of this power, by their choosing in early youth as the objects of their love those in whom the intellectual faculties have begun to develope. For those who begin to love in this manner, seem to me to be preparing to pass their whole life together in a community of good and evil, and not ever lightly deceiving those who love them, to be faithless to their vows. There ought to be a law that none should love the very young; so much serious affection as this deity enkindles should not be doubtfully bestowed; for the body and mind of those so young are yet unformed, and it is difficult to foretell what will be their future tendencies and power. The good voluntarily impose this law upon themselves, and those vulgar lovers ought to be compelled to the same observance, as we deter them with all the power of the laws from the love of free matrons. For these are the persons whose shameful actions embolden those who observe their importunity and intemperance to assert, that it is dishonourable to serve and gratify the objects of our love. But no one who does this gracefully and according to law, can justly be liable to the imputation of blame.

* * * * * *

"Not only friendship, but philosophy and the practice of the gymnastic exercises, are represented as dishonourable by the tyrannical governments under which the barbarians live. For I imagine it would little conduce to the benefit of the governors, that the governed should be disciplined to lofty thoughts and to the unity and communion of steadfast friendship, of which admirable effects the tyrants of our own country have also learned that Love is the author. For the love of Harmodius and Aristogeiton, strengthened into a firm friendship, dissolved the tyranny. Wherever, therefore, it is declared dishonourable in any case to serve and benefit friends, that law is a mark of the depravity of the legislator, the avarice and tyranny of the rulers, and the cowardice of those who are ruled. Wherever it is simply declared to be honourable without distinction of cases, such a declaration denotes dulness and want of subtlety of mind in the authors of the regulation. Here the degrees of praise or blame to be attributed by law are far better regulated; but it is yet difficult to determine the cases to which they should refer.

"It is evident, however, for one in whom passion is enkindled, it is more honourable to love openly than secretly; and most honourable to love the most excellent and virtuous, even if they should be less beautiful than others. It is honourable for the lover to exhort and sustain the object of his love in virtuous conduct. It is considered honourable to attain the love of those whom we seek, and the contrary shameful; and to facilitate this attainment, opinion has given to the lover the permission of acquiring favour by the most extraordinary devices, which if a person should practise for any purpose besides this, he would incur the severest reproof of philosophy. For if any one desirous of accumulating money, or ambitious of procuring power, or seeking any other advantage, should, like a lover seeking to acquire the favour of his beloved, employ prayers and intreaties in his necessity, and swear such oaths as lovers swear, and sleep before the threshold, and offer to subject himself to such slavery as no slave even would endure; he would be frustrated of the attainment of what he sought, both by his enemies and friends, these reviling him for his flattery, those sharply admonishing him, and taking to themselves the shame of his servility. But there is a certain grace in a lover who does all these things, so that he alone may do them without dishonour. It is commonly said that the Gods accord pardon to the lover alone if he should break his oath, and that there is no oath by Venus. Thus, as our law declares, both Gods and men have given to lovers all possible indulgence.

* * * * * *

"The affair, however, I imagine, stands thus:—As I

have before said, love cannot be considered in itself as either honourable or dishonourable: if it is honourably pursued, it is honourable; if dishonourably, dishonourable: it is dishonourable basely to serve and gratify a worthless person; it is honourable honourably to serve a person of virtue. That Pandemic lover who loves rather the body than the soul is worthless, nor can be constant and consistent, since he has placed his affections on that which has no stability. For as soon as the flower of the form, which was the sole object of his desire, has faded, then he departs and is seen no more; bound by no faith nor shame of his many promises and persuasions. But he who is the lover of virtuous manners is constant during life, since he has placed himself in harmony and desire with that which is consistent with itself.

"These two classes of persons we ought to distinguish with careful examination, so that we may serve and converse with the one and avoid the other; determining, by that inquiry, by what a man is attracted, and for what the object of his love is dear to him. On the same account it is considered as dishonourable to be inspired with love at once, lest time should be wanting to know and approve the character of the object. It is considered dishonourable to be captivated by the allurements of wealth and power, or terrified through injuries to yield up the affections, or not to despise in the comparison with an unconstrained choice all political influence and personal advantage. For no circumstance is there in wealth or power so invariable and consistent, as that no generous friendship can ever spring up from amongst them. We have an opinion with respect to lovers which declares that it shall not be considered servile or disgraceful, though the lover should submit himself to any species of slavery for the sake of his beloved. The same opinion holds with respect to those who undergo any degradation for the sake of virtue. And also it is esteemed among us, that if any one chooses to serve and obey another for the purpose of becoming more wise or more virtuous through the intercourse that might thence arise, such willing slavery is not the slavery of a dishonest flatterer. Through this we should consider in the same light a servitude undertaken for the sake of love as one undertaken for the acquirement of wisdom or any other excellence, if indeed the devotion of a lover to his beloved is to be considered a beautiful thing. For when the lover and the beloved have once arrived at the same point, the province of each being distinguished; * * * the one able to assist in the cultivation of the mind and in the acquirement of every other excellence; the other yet requiring education, and seeking the possession of wisdom; then alone, by the union of these conditions, and in no other case, is it honourable for the beloved to yield up the affections to the lover. In this servitude alone there is no disgrace in being deceived and defeated of the object for which it was undertaken, whereas every other is disgraceful, whether we are deceived or no.

* * * * * *

"On the same principle, if any one seeks the friendship of another, believing him to be virtuous, for the sake of becoming better through such intercourse and affection, and is deceived, his friend turning out to be worthless, and far from the possession of virtue; yet it is honourable to have been so deceived. For such a one seems to have submitted to a kind of servitude, because he would endure any thing for the sake of becoming more virtuous and wise; a disposition of mind eminently beautiful.

"This is that Love who attends on the Uranian deity, and is Uranian; the author of innumerable benefits both to the state and to individuals, and by the necessity of whose influence those who love are disciplined into the zeal of virtue. All other loves are the attendants on Venus Pandemos. So much, although unpremeditated, is what I have to deliver on the subject of Love, O Phædrus."

Pausanias having ceased (for so the learned teach me to denote the changes of the discourse), Aristodemus said that it came to the turn of Aristophanes to speak; but it happened that, from repletion or some other cause, he had an hiccough which prevented him; so he turned to Eryximachus, the physician, who was reclining close beside him, and said—

"Eryximachus, it is but fair that you should cure my hiccough, or speak instead of me until it is over."

"I will do both," said Eryximachus; "I will speak in your turn, and you, when your hiccough has ceased, shall speak in mine. Meanwhile, if you hold your breath some time, it will subside. If not, gargle your throat with water; and if it still continue, take something to stimulate your nostrils, and sneeze; do this once or twice, and even though it should be very violent it will cease."

"Whilst you speak," said Aristophanes, "I will follow your directions."

Eryximachus then began:—

"Since Pausanias, beginning his discourse excellently, placed no fit completion and developement to it, I think it necessary to attempt to fill up what he has left unfinished. He has reasoned well in defining love as of a double nature. The science of medicine, to which I have addicted myself, seems to teach me that the love which impels towards those who are beautiful, does not subsist only in the souls of men, but in the bodies also of those of all other living beings which are produced upon earth, and, in a word, in all things which are. So wonderful and mighty is this divinity, and so widely is his influence extended over all divine and human things! For the honour of my profession, I will begin by adducing a proof from medicine. The nature of the body contains within itself this double love. For that which is healthy and that which is diseased in a body differ and are unlike: that which is unlike, loves and desires that which is unlike. Love, therefore, is different in a sane and in a diseased body. Pausanias has asserted rightly that it is honourable to gratify those things in the body which are good and healthy, and in this consists the skill of the physician; whilst those which are bad and diseased, ought to be treated with no indulgence. The science of medicine, in a word, is a knowledge of the love affairs of the body, as they bear relation to repletion and evacuation; and he is the most skilful physician who can trace those operations of the good and evil love, can make the one change places with the other, and attract love into those parts from which he is absent, or expel him from those which he ought not to occupy. He ought to make those things which are most inimical, friendly, and excite them to mutual love. But those things are most inimical which are most opposite to each other; cold to heat, bitterness to sweetness, dryness to moisture. Our progenitor, Æsculapius, as the poets inform us, (and indeed I believe them,) through the skill which he possessed to inspire love and concord in these contending principles, established the science of medicine.

"The gymnastic arts and agriculture, no less than medicine, are exercised under the dominion of this God. Music, as any one may perceive, who yields a very slight attention to the subject, originates from the same source; which Heraclitus probably meant, though he could not express his meaning very clearly in words, when he says, 'One though apparently differing, yet so agrees with itself, as the harmony of a lyre and a bow.' It is great absurdity to say that a harmony differs, and can exist between things whilst they are dissimilar; but probably he meant that from sounds which first differed, like the grave and the acute, and which afterwards agreed, harmony was produced according to musical art. For no harmony can arise from the grave and the acute whilst yet they differ. But harmony is symphony: symphony is, as it were, concord. But it is impossible that concord should subsist between things that differ, so long as they differ. Between things which are discordant and dissimilar there is then no harmony. A rhythm is produced from that which is quick, and that which is slow, first being distinguished and opposed to each other, and then made accordant; so does medicine, no less than music, establish a concord between the objects of its art, producing love and agreement between adverse things.

"Music is then the knowledge of that which relates to love in harmony and system. In the very system of harmony and rhythm, it is easy to distinguish love. The double love is not distinguishable in music itself; but it is required to apply it to the service of mankind by system and harmony, which is called poetry, or the composition of melody; or by the correct use of songs and measures already composed, which is called discipline; then one can be distinguished from the other, by the aid of an extremely skilful artist. And the better love ought to be honoured and preserved for the sake of those who are virtuous, and that the nature of the vicious may be changed through the inspiration of its spirit. This is that beautiful Uranian love, the attendant on the Uranian muse: the Pandemian is the attendant of Polyhymnia; to whose influence we should only so far subject ourselves, as to derive pleasure from it without indulging to excess; in the same manner as, according to our art, we are instructed to seek the pleasures of the table, only so far as we can enjoy them without the consequences of disease. In music, therefore, and in medicine, and in all other things, human and divine, this double love ought to be traced and discriminated; for it is in all things.

"Even the constitution of the seasons of the year is penetrated with these contending principles. For so often as heat and cold, dryness and moisture, of which I spoke before, are influenced by the more benignant love, and are harmoniously and temperately intermingled with the seasons, they bring maturity and health to men, and to all the other animals and plants. But when the evil and injurious love assumes the dominion of the seasons of the year, destruction is spread widely abroad. Then pestilence is accustomed to arise, and many other blights and diseases fall upon animals and plants: and hoar frosts, and hails, mildew on the corn, are produced from that excessive and disorderly love, with which each season of the year is impelled towards the other; the motions of which and the knowledge of the stars, is called astronomy. All sacrifices, and all those things in which divination is concerned, (for these things are the links by which is maintained an intercourse and communion between the Gods and men,) are nothing else than the science of preservation and right government of Love. For impiety is accustomed to spring up, so soon as any one ceases to serve the more honourable Love, and worship him by the sacrifice of good actions; but submits himself to the influences of the other, in relation to his duties towards his parents, and the Gods, and the living, and the dead. It is the object of divination to distinguish and remedy the effects of these opposite loves; and divination is therefore the author of the friendship of Gods and men, because it affords the knowledge of what in matters of love is lawful or unlawful to men.

"Thus every species of love possesses collectively a various and vast, or rather universal power. But love which incites to the acquirement of its objects according to virtue and wisdom, possesses the most exclusive dominion, and prepares for his worshippers the highest happiness through the mutual intercourse of social kindness which it promotes among them, and through the benevolence which he attracts to them from the Gods, our superiors.

"Probably in thus praising Love, I have unwillingly omitted many things; but it is your business, O Aristophanes, to fill up all that I have left incomplete; or, if you have imagined any other mode of honouring the divinity; for I observe your hiccough is over."

"Yes," said Aristophanes, "but not before I applied the sneezing. I wonder why the harmonious construction of our body should require such noisy operations as sneezing; for it ceased the moment I sneezed."

"Do you not observe what you do, my good Aristophanes?" said Eryximachus; "you are going to speak, and you predispose us to laughter, and compel me to watch for the first ridiculous idea which you may start in your discourse, when you might have spoken in peace."

"Let me unsay what I have said, then," replied Aristophanes, laughing. "Do not watch me, I intreat you; though I am not afraid of saying what is laughable, (since that would be all gain, and quite in the accustomed spirit of my muse,) but lest I should say what is ridiculous."

"Do you think to throw your dart, and escape with impunity, Aristophanes? Attend, and what you say be careful you maintain; then, perhaps, if it pleases me, I may dismiss you without question."

"Indeed, Eryximachus," proceeded Aristophanes, "I have designed that my discourse should be very different from yours and that of Pausanias. It seems to me that mankind are by no means penetrated with a conception of the power of Love, or they would have built sumptuous temples and altars, and have established magnificent rites of sacrifice in his honour; he deserves worship and homage more than all the other Gods, and he has yet received none. For Love is of all the Gods the most friendly to mortals; and the physician of those wounds, whose cure would be the greatest happiness which could be conferred upon the human race. I will endeavour to unfold to you his true power, and you can relate what I declare to others.

"You ought first to know the nature of man, and the adventures he has gone through; for his nature was anciently far different from that which it is at present. First, then, human beings were formerly not divided into two sexes, male and female; there was also a third, common to both the others, the name of which remains, though the sex itself has disappeared. The androgynous sex, both in appearance and in name, was common both to male and female; its name alone remains, which labours under a reproach.

"At the period to which I refer, the form of every human being was round, the back and the sides being circularly joined, and each had four arms and as many legs; two faces fixed upon a round neck, exactly like each other; one head between the two faces; four ears, and every thing else as from such proportions it is easy to conjecture. Man walked upright as now, in whatever direction he pleased; but when he wished to go fast he made use of all his eight limbs, and proceeded in a rapid motion by rolling circularly round,—like tumblers, who, with their legs in the air, tumble round and round. We account for the production of three sexes by supposing that, at the beginning, the male was produced from the sun, the female from the earth; and that sex which participated in both sexes, from the moon, by reason of the androgynous nature of the moon. They were round, and their mode of proceeding was round, from the similarity which must needs subsist between them and their parent.

"They were strong also, and had aspiring thoughts. They it was who levied war against the Gods; and what Homer writes concerning Ephialtes[1] and Otus, that they sought to ascend heaven and dethrone the Gods, in reality relates to this primitive people. Jupiter and the other Gods debated what was to be done in this emergency. For neither could they prevail on themselves to destroy them, as they had the giants, with thunder, so that the race should be abolished; for in that case they would be deprived of the honours of the sacrifices which they were in the custom of receiving from them; nor could they permit a continuance of their insolence and impiety. Jupiter, with some difficulty having desired silence, at length spoke. 'I think,' said he, 'I have contrived a method by which we may, by rendering the human race more feeble, quell the insolence which they exercise, without proceeding to their utter destruction. I will cut each of them in half; and so they will at once be weaker and more useful on account of their numbers. They shall walk upright on two legs. If they show any more insolence, and will not keep quiet, I will cut them up in half again, so they shall go about hopping on one leg.'

"So saying, he cut human beings in half, as people cut eggs before they salt them, or as I have seen eggs cut with hairs. He ordered Apollo to take each one as he cut him, and turn his face and half his neck towards the

[1] In previous editions, *Ephialtus*.

operation, so that by contemplating it he might become more cautious and humble; and then, to cure him, Apollo turned the face round, and drawing the skin upon what we now call the belly, like a contracted pouch, and leaving one opening, that which is called the navel, tied it in the middle. He then smoothed many other wrinkles, and moulded the breast with much such an instrument as the leather-cutters use to smooth the skins upon the block. He left only a few wrinkles in the belly, near the navel, to serve as a record of its former adventure. Immediately after this division, as each desired to possess the other half of himself, these divided people threw their arms around and embraced each other, seeking to grow together; and from this resolution to do nothing without the other half, they died of hunger and weakness: when one half died and the other was left alive, that which was thus left sought the other and folded it to its bosom; whether that half were an entire woman (for we now call it a woman) or a man; and thus they perished. But Jupiter, pitying them, thought of another contrivance. * * * In this manner is generation now produced, by the union of male and female; so that from the embrace of a man and woman the race is propagated.

"From this period, mutual love has naturally existed between human beings; that reconciler and bond of union of their original nature, which seeks to make two, one, and to heal the divided nature of man. Every one of us is thus the half of what may be properly termed a man, and like a pselta cut in two, is the imperfect portion of an entire whole, perpetually necessitated to seek the half belonging to him.

* * * * * *

"Such as I have described is ever an affectionate lover and a faithful friend, delighting in that which is in conformity with his own nature. Whenever, therefore, any such as I have described are impetuously struck, through the sentiment of their former union, with love and desire and the want of community, they are unwilling to be divided even for a moment. These are they who devote their whole lives to each other, with a vain and inexpressible longing to obtain from each other something they know not what; for it is not merely the sensual delights of their intercourse for the sake of which they dedicate themselves to each other with such serious affection; but the soul of each manifestly thirsts for, from the other, something which there are no words to describe, and divines that which it seeks, and traces obscurely the footsteps of its obscure desire. If Vulcan should say to persons thus affected, 'My good people, what is it that you want with one another?' And if while they were hesitating what to answer, he should proceed to ask, 'Do you not desire the closest union and singleness to exist between you, so that you may never be divided night or day? If so, I will melt you together, and make you grow into one, so that both in life and death ye may be undivided. Consider, is this what you desire? Will it content you if you become that which I propose?' We all know that no one would refuse such an offer, but would at once feel that this was what he had ever sought; and intimately to mix and melt and to be melted together with his beloved, so that one should be made out of two.

"The cause of this desire is, that according to our original nature, we were once entire. The desire and the pursuit of integrity and union is that which we all love. First, as I said, we were entire, but now we have been dwindled through our own weakness, as the Arcadians by the Lacedemonians. There is reason to fear, if we are guilty of any additional impiety towards the Gods, that we may be cut in two again, and may go about like those figures painted on the columns, divided through the middle of our nostrils, as thin as lispæ. On which account every man ought to be exhorted to pay due reverence to the Gods, that we may escape so severe a punishment, and obtain those things which Love, our general and commander, incites us to desire; against whom let none rebel by exciting the hatred of the Gods. For if we continue on good terms with them, we may discover and possess those lost and concealed objects of our love; a good-fortune which now befalls so few.

* * * * * *

"I assert, then, that the happiness of all, both men and women, consists singly in the fulfilment of their love, and in that possession of its objects by which we are in some degree restored to our ancient nature. If this be the completion of felicity, that must necessarily approach nearest to it, in which we obtain the possession and society of those whose natures most intimately accord with our own. And if we would celebrate any God as the author of this benefit, we should justly celebrate Love with hymns of joy; who, in our present condition, brings good assistance in our necessity, and affords great hopes, if we persevere in piety towards the Gods, that he will restore us to our original state, and confer on us the complete happiness alone suited to our nature.

"Such, Eryximachus, is my discourse on the subject of Love; different indeed from yours, which I nevertheless intreat you not to turn into ridicule, that we may not interrupt what each has separately to deliver on the subject."

"I will refrain at present," said Eryximachus, "for your discourse delighted me. And if I did not know that Socrates and Agathon were profoundly versed in the science of love affairs, I should fear that they had nothing new to say, after so many and such various imaginations. As it is, I confide in the fertility of their geniuses."

"Your part of the contest, at least, was strenuously fought, Eryximachus," said Socrates, "but if you had been in the situation in which I am, or rather shall be, after the discourse of Agathon, like me, you would then have reason to fear, and be reduced to your wits' end."

"Socrates," said Agathon, "wishes to confuse me with the inchantments of his wit, sufficiently confused already with the expectation I see in the assembly in favour of my discourse."

"I must have lost my memory, Agathon," replied Socrates, "if I imagined that you could be disturbed by a few private persons, after having witnessed your firmness and courage in ascending the rostrum with the actors, and in calmly reciting your compositions in the presence of so great an assembly as that which decreed you the prize of tragedy."

"What then, Socrates," retorted Agathon, "do you

think me so full of the theatre as to be ignorant that the judgment of a few wise is more awful than that of a multitude of others, to one who rightly balances the value of their suffrages?"

"I should judge ill indeed, Agathon," answered Socrates, "in thinking you capable of any rude and unrefined conception, for I well know that if you meet with any whom you consider wise, you esteem such alone of more value than all others. But we are far from being entitled to this distinction, for we were also of that assembly, and to be numbered among the rest But should you meet with any who are really wise, you would be careful to say nothing in their presence which you thought they would not approve—is it not so?"

"Certainly," replied Agathon.

"You would not then exercise the same caution in the presence of the multitude in which they were included?"

"My dear Agathon," said Phædrus, interrupting him, "if you answer all the questions of Socrates, they will never have an end; he will urge them without conscience so long as he can get any person, especially one who is so beautiful, to dispute with him. I own it delights me to hear Socrates discuss; but at present, I must see that Love is not defrauded of the praise, which it is my province to exact from each of you. Pay the God his due, and then reason between yourselves if you will."

"Your admonition is just, Phædrus," replied Agathon,

" nor need any reasoning I hold with Socrates impede me: we shall find many future opportunities for discussion. I will begin my discourse then; first having defined what ought to be the subject of it. All who have already spoken seem to me not so much to have praised Love, as to have felicitated mankind on the many advantages of which that deity is the cause; what he is, the author of these great benefits, none have yet declared. There is one mode alone of celebration which would comprehend the whole topic, namely, first to declare what are those benefits, and then what he is who is the author of those benefits, which are the subject of our discourse. Love ought first to be praised, and then his gifts declared. I assert, then, that although all the Gods are immortally happy, Love, if I dare trust my voice to express so awful a truth, is the happiest, and most excellent, and the most beautiful. That he is the most beautiful is evident; first, O Phædrus, from this circumstance, that he is the youngest of the Gods; and, secondly, from his fleetness, and from his repugnance to all that is old; for he escapes with the swiftness of wings from old age; a thing in itself sufficiently swift, since it overtakes us sooner than there is need; and which Love, who delights in the intercourse of the young, hates, and in no manner can be induced to enter into community with. The ancient proverb, which says that like is attracted by like, applies to the attributes of Love. I concede many things to you, O Phædrus, but this I do not concede, that Love is more ancient than Saturn and Jupiter. I assert that he is not only the youngest of the Gods, but invested with everlasting youth. Those ancient deeds among the Gods recorded by Hesiod and Parmenides, if their relations are to be considered as true, were produced not by Love, but by Necessity. For if Love had been then in Heaven, those violent and sanguinary crimes never would have taken place; but there would ever have subsisted that affection and peace, in which the Gods now live, under the influence of Love.

"He is young, therefore, and being young is tender and soft. There were need of some poet like Homer to celebrate the delicacy and tenderness of Love. For Homer says, that the goddess Calamity is delicate, and that her feet are tender. 'Her feet are soft,' he says, 'for she treads not upon the ground, but makes her path upon the heads of men.' He gives as an evidence of her tenderness, that she walks not upon that which is hard, but that which is soft. The same evidence is sufficient to make manifest the tenderness of Love. For Love walks not upon the earth, nor over the heads of men, which are not indeed very soft; but he dwells within, and treads on the softest of existing things, having established his habitation within the souls and inmost nature of Gods and men; not indeed in all souls—for wherever he chances to find a hard and rugged disposition, there he will not inhabit, but only where it is most soft and tender. Of needs must he be the most delicate of all things, who touches lightly with his feet only the softest parts of those things which are the softest of all.

"He is then the youngest and the most delicate of all divinities; and in addition to this, he is, as it were, the most moist and liquid. For if he were otherwise, he could not, as he does, fold himself around every thing, and secretly flow out and into every soul. His loveliness, that which Love possesses far beyond all other things, is a manifestation of the liquid and flowing symmetry of his form; for between deformity and Love there is eternal contrast and repugnance. His life is spent among flowers, and this accounts for the immortal fairness of his skin; for the winged Love rests not in his flight on any form, or within any soul the flower of whose loveliness is faded, but there remains most willingly where is the odour and the radiance of blossoms, yet unwithered. Concerning the beauty of the God, let this be sufficient, though many things must remain unsaid. Let us next consider the virtue and power of Love.

"What is most admirable in Love is, that he neither inflicts nor endures injury in his relations either with Gods or men. Nor if he suffers any thing does he suffer it through violence, nor doing any thing does he act it with violence, for Love is never even touched with violence. Every one willingly administers every thing to Love; and that which every one voluntarily concedes to another, the laws, which are the kings of the republic, decree that it is just for him to possess. In addition to justice, Love participates in the highest temperance; for if temperance is defined to be the being superior to and holding under dominion pleasures and desires; then Love, than whom no pleasure is more powerful, and who is thus more powerful than all persuasions and delights, must be excellently temperate. In power and valour Mars cannot contend with Love: the love of Venus possesses Mars; the possessor is always superior to the possessed, and he who subdues the most powerful must of necessity be the most powerful of all.

"The justice and temperance and valour of the God

have been thus declared;—there remains to exhibit his wisdom. And first, that, like Eryximachus, I may honour my own profession, the God is a wise poet; so wise that he can even make a poet one who was not before: for every one, even if before he were ever so undisciplined, becomes a poet as soon as he is touched by Love;—a sufficient proof that Love is a great poet, and well skilled in that science according to the discipline of music. For what any one possesses not, or knows not, that can he neither give nor teach another. And who will deny that the divine poetry, by which all living things are produced upon the earth, is[1] harmonized by the wisdom of Love? Is it not evident that Love was the author of all the arts of life with which we are acquainted, and that he whose teacher has been Love, becomes eminent and illustrious, whilst he who knows not Love, remains forever unregarded and obscure? Apollo invented medicine, and divination, and archery, under the guidance of desire and Love; so that Apollo was the disciple of Love. Through him the Muses discovered the arts of literature, and Vulcan that of moulding brass, and Minerva the loom, and Jupiter the mystery of the dominion which he now exercises over gods and men. So were the Gods taught and disciplined by the love of that which is beautiful; for there is no love towards deformity.

"At the origin of things, as I have before said, many fearful deeds are reported to have been done among the Gods, on account of the dominion of Necessity. But so soon as this deity sprang forth from the desire which forever tends in the universe towards that which is lovely, then all blessings descended upon all living things, human

[1] The word *not* occurs before *harmonized* in previous editions.

and divine. Love seems to me, O Phædrus, a divinity the most beautiful and the best of all, and the author to all others of the excellencies with which his own nature is endowed. Nor can I restrain the poetic enthusiasm which takes possession of my discourse, and bids me declare that Love is the divinity who creates peace among men, and calm upon the sea, the windless silence of storms, repose and sleep in sadness. Love divests us of all alienation from each other, and fills our vacant hearts with overflowing sympathy; he gathers us together in such social meetings as we now delight to celebrate, our guardian and our guide in dances, and sacrifices, and feasts. Yes, Love, who showers benignity upon the world, and before whose presence all harsh passions flee and perish; the author of all soft affections; the destroyer of all ungentle thoughts; merciful, mild; the object of the admiration of the wise, and the delight of gods; possessed by the fortunate, and desired by the unhappy, therefore unhappy because they possess him not; the father of grace, and delicacy, and gentleness, and delight, and persuasion, and desire; the cherisher of all that is good, the abolisher of all evil; our most excellent pilot, defence, saviour and guardian in labour and in fear, in desire and in reason; the ornament and governor of all things human and divine; the best, the loveliest; in whose footsteps every one ought to follow, celebrating him excellently in song, and bearing each his part in that divinest harmony which Love sings to all things which live and are, soothing the troubled minds of Gods and men. This, O Phædrus, is what I have to offer in praise of the divinity; partly composed, indeed, of thoughtless and playful fancies, and partly of such serious ones, as I could well command."

No sooner had Agathon ceased, than a loud murmur of applause arose from all present; so becomingly had the fair youth spoken, both in praise of the God, and in extenuation of himself.

Then Socrates, addressing Eryximachus, said—

"Was not my fear reasonable, son of Acumenus? Did I not divine what has, in fact, happened,—that Agathon's discourse would be so wonderfully beautiful, as to preoccupy all interest in what I should say?"

"You, indeed, divined well so far, O Socrates," said Eryximachus, "that Agathon would speak eloquently, but not that, therefore, you would be reduced to any difficulty."

"How, my good friend, can I or any one else be otherwise than reduced to difficulty, who speak after a discourse so various and so eloquent, and which otherwise had been sufficiently wonderful, if, at the conclusion, the splendour of the sentences, and the choice selection of the expressions, had not struck all the hearers with astonishment; so that I, who well know that I can never say anything nearly so beautiful as this, would, if there had been any escape, have run away for shame. The story of Gorgias came into my mind, and I was afraid lest in reality I should suffer what Homer describes; and lest Agathon, scanning my discourse with the head of the eloquent Gorgias, should turn me to stone for speechlessness. I immediately perceived how ridiculously I had engaged myself with you to assume a part in rendering praise to love, and had boasted that I was well skilled in amatory matters, being so ignorant of the manner in which it is becoming to render him honour, as I now perceive myself to be. I, in my simplicity, imagined that the truth ought to be spoken concerning each of the topics of our praise, and that it would be sufficient, choosing those which are the most honourable to the God, to place them in as luminous an arrangement as we could. I had therefore, great hopes that I should speak satisfactorily, being well aware that I was acquainted with the true foundations of the praise which we have engaged to render. But since, as it appears, our purpose has been, not to render Love his due honour, but to accumulate the most beautiful and the greatest attributes of his divinity, whether they in truth belong to it or not, and that the proposed question is not how Love ought to be praised, but how we should praise him most eloquently, my attempt must of necessity fail. It is on this account, I imagine, that in your discourses you have attributed everything to Love, and have described him to be the author of such and so great effects as, to those who are ignorant of his true nature, may exhibit him as the most beautiful and the best of all things. Not, indeed, to those who know the truth. Such praise has a splendid and imposing effect, but as I am unacquainted with the art of rendering it, my mind, which could not foresee what would be required of me, absolves me from that which my tongue promised. Farewell then, for such praise I can never render.

"But if you desire, I will speak what I feel to be true; and that I may not expose myself to ridicule, I intreat you to consider that I speak without entering into competition with those who have preceded me. Consider, then, Phædrus, whether you will exact from me such a discourse, containing the mere truth with respect to Love, and composed of such unpremeditated expressions as may chance to offer themselves to my mind."

Phædrus and the rest bade him speak in the manner which he judged most befitting.

"Permit me, then, O Phædrus, to ask Agathon a few questions, so that, confirmed by his agreement with me, I may proceed."

"Willingly," replied Phædrus, "ask."

Then Socrates thus began :—

"I applaud, dear Agathon, the beginning of your discourse, where you say, we ought first to define and declare what Love is, and then his works. This rule I particularly approve. But, come, since you have given us a discourse of such beauty and majesty concerning Love, you are able, I doubt not, to explain this question, whether Love is the love of something or nothing? I do not ask you of what parents Love is; for the inquiry, of whether Love is the love of any father or mother, would be sufficiently ridiculous. But if I were asking you to describe that which a father is, I should ask, not whether a father was the love of any one, but whether a father was the father of any one or not; you would undoubtedly reply, that a father was the father of a son or daughter; would you not?"

"Assuredly."

"You would define a mother in the same manner?"

"Without doubt?"

"Yet bear with me, and answer a few more questions, for I would learn from you that which I wish to know. If I should inquire, in addition, is not a brother, through the very nature of his relation, the brother of some one?"

"Certainly."

"Of a brother or sister, is he not?"

"Without question."

"Try to explain to me then the nature of Love; Love is the love of something or nothing?"

"Of something, certainly."

"Observe and remember this concession. Tell me yet farther, whether Love desires that of which it is the Love or not?"

"It desires it, assuredly."

"Whether possessing that which it desires and loves, or not possessing it, does it desire and love?"

"Not possessing it, I should imagine."

"Observe now, whether it does not appear, that, of

necessity, desire desires that which it wants and does not possess, and no longer desires that which it no longer wants: this appears to me, Agathon, of necessity to be; how does it appear to you?"

"It appears so to me also."

"Would any one who was already illustrious, desire to be illustrious; would any one already strong, desire to be strong? From what has already been conceded, it follows that he would not. If any one already strong, should desire to be strong; or any one already swift, should desire to be swift; or any one already healthy, should desire to be healthy, it must be concluded that they still desired the advantages of which they already seemed possessed. To destroy the foundation of this error, observe, Agathon, that each of these persons must possess the several advantages in question, at the moment present to our thoughts, whether he will or no. And, now, is it possible that those advantages should be at that time the objects of his desire? For, if any one should say, being in health, 'I desire to be in health'; being rich, 'I desire to be rich, and thus still desire those thing which I already possess'; we might say to him, 'You, my friend, possess health, and strength, and riches; you do not desire to possess now, but to continue to possess them in future; for, whether you will or no, they now belong to you. Consider then, whether, when you say that you desire things present to you, and in your own possession, you say anything else than that you desire the advantages to be for the future also in your possession.' What else could he reply?"

"Nothing, indeed."

"Is not Love, then, the love of that which is not within its reach, and which cannot hold in security, for the future, those things of which it obtains a present and transitory possession?"

"Evidently."

"Love, therefore, and every thing else that desires anything, desires that which is absent and beyond his reach, that which it has not, that which is not itself, that which it wants; such are the things of which there are desire and love."

"Assuredly."

"Come," said Socrates, "let us review your concessions. Is Love anything else than the love first of something; and, secondly, of those things of which it has need?"

"Nothing."

"Now, remember of those things you said in your discourse, that Love was the love—if you wish I will remind you. I think you said something of this kind, that all the affairs of the gods were admirably disposed through the love of the things which are beautiful; for there was no love of things deformed; did you not say so?"

"I confess that I did."

"You said what was most likely to be true, my friend; and if the matter be so, the love of beauty must be one thing, and the love of deformity another."

"Certainly."

"It is conceded then, that Love loves that which he wants but possesses not?"

"Yes, certainly."

"But Love wants and does not possess beauty?"

"Indeed it must necessarily follow."

"What, then! call you that beautiful which has need of beauty and possesses not?"

"Assuredly no."

"Do you still assert, then, that Love is beautiful, if all that we have said be true?"

"Indeed, Socrates," said Agathon, "I am in danger of being convicted of ignorance, with respect to all that I then spoke."

"You spoke most eloquently, my dear Agathon; but bear with my questions yet a moment. You admit that things which are good are also beautiful?"

"No doubt."

"If Love, then, be in want of beautiful things, and things which are good are beautiful, he must be in want of things which are good?"

"I cannot refute your arguments, Socrates."

"You cannot refute truth, my dear Agathon: to refute Socrates is nothing difficult. But I will dismiss these questionings. At present let me endeavour, to the best of my power, to repeat to you, on the basis of the points which have been agreed upon between me and Agathon, a discourse concerning love, which I formerly heard from the prophetess Diotima, who was profoundly skilled in this and many other doctrines, and who, ten years before the pestilence, procured to the Athenians, through their sacrifices, a delay of the disease; for it was she who taught me the science of things relating to Love.

"As you well remarked, Agathon, we ought to declare who and what is Love, and then his works. It is easiest to relate them in the same order, as the foreign prophetess observed when, questioning me, she related them. For I said to her much the same things that Agathon has just said to me—that Love was a great deity, and that he was beautiful; and she refuted me with the same reasons as I have employed to refute Agathon, compelling me to infer that he was neither beautiful nor good, as I said.—'What, then,' I objected, 'O Diotima, is love ugly and evil?'—'Good words, I intreat you,' said Diotima; 'do you think that every thing which is not beautiful, must of necessity be ugly.'—'Certainly.'—'And every thing that is not wise, ignorant? Do you not perceive that there is something between ignorance and wisdom?'—'What is that?'—'To have a right opinion or conjecture. Observe, that this kind of opinion, for which no reason can be rendered, cannot be called knowledge; for how can that be called knowledge, which is without evidence or reason? Nor ignorance, on the other hand; for how can that be called ignorance which arrives at the persuasion of that which it really is? A right opinion is something between understanding and ignorance.'—I confessed that what she alleged was true.—'Do not then say,' she continued, 'that what is not beautiful is of necessity deformed, nor what is not good is of necessity evil; nor, since you have confessed that Love is neither beautiful nor good, infer, therefore, that he is deformed or evil, but rather something intermediate.'

"'But,' I said, 'love is confessed by all to be a great God.'—'Do you mean, when you say all, all those who know, or those who know not, what they say?'—'All, collectively.'—'And how can that be, Socrates?' said she laughing; 'how can he be acknowledged to be a great God, by those who assert that he is not even a God at all?'—'And who are they?' I said.—'You for one, and I for another.'—'How can you say that, Diotima?'—'Easily,' she replied, 'and with truth; for tell me, do you not own that all the Gods are beautiful and happy? or will you presume to maintain that any God is otherwise.'—'By Jupiter, not I!'—'Do you not call those alone happy who possess all things that are beautiful and good?'—'Certainly.'—'You have confessed that Love, through his desire for things beautiful and good, possesses not those materials of happiness.'—'Indeed, such was my concession.'—'But how can we conceive a God to be without the possession of what is beautiful and good?'—'In no manner, I confess.'—'Observe, then, that you do not consider Love to be a God.'—'What, then,' I said, 'is Love a mortal?'—'By no means.'—'But what, then?'—'Like those things which I have before instanced, he is neither mortal nor immortal, but something intermediate.'—'What is that, O Diotima?'—'A great dæmon, Socrates; and every thing dæmoniacal holds an intermediate place between what is divine and what is mortal.'

"'What is his power and nature?' I inquired.—'He interprets and makes a communication between divine and human things, conveying the prayers and sacrifices of men to the Gods, and communicating the commands and directions concerning the mode of worship most pleasing to them, from Gods to men. He fills up that intermediate space between these two classes of beings, so as to bind together, by his own power, the whole universe of things. Through him subsist all divination, and the science of sacred things as it relates to sacrifices, and expiations, and disenchantments, and prophecy, and magic. The divine nature cannot immediately communicate with what is human, but all that intercourse and converse which is conceded by the Gods to men, both whilst they sleep and when they wake, subsists through the intervention of Love; and he who is wise in the science of this intercourse is supremely happy, and participates in the dæmoniacal nature; whilst he who is wise in any other science or art, remains a mere ordinary slave. These dæmons are, indeed, many and various, and one of them is Love.'

"'Who are the parents of Love?' I inquired.—'The history of what you ask,' replied Diotima, 'is somewhat long; nevertheless I will explain it to you. On the birth of Venus the Gods celebrated a great feast, and among them came Plenty, the son of Metis. After supper, Poverty, observing the profusion, came to beg, and stood beside the door. Plenty being drunk with nectar, for wine was not yet invented, went out into Jupiter's garden, and fell into a deep sleep. Poverty wishing to have a child by Plenty, on account of her low estate, lay down by him, and from his embraces conceived Love. Love is, therefore, the follower and servant of Venus, because he was conceived at her birth, and because by nature he is a lover of all that is beautiful, and Venus was beautiful. And since Love is the child of Poverty and Plenty, his nature and fortune participate in that of his parents. He is for ever poor, and so far from being delicate and beautiful, as mankind imagine, he is squalid and withered; he flies low along the ground, and is homeless and unsandalled; he sleeps without covering before the doors, and in the unsheltered streets; possessing thus far his mother's nature, that he is ever the companion of want. But, inasmuch as he participates in that of his father, he is for ever scheming to obtain things which are good and beautiful; he is fearless, vehement, and strong; a dreadful hunter, for ever weaving some new contrivance; exceedingly cautious and prudent, and full of resources; he is also, during his whole existence, a philosopher, a powerful inchanter, a wizard, and a subtle sophist. And, as his nature is neither mortal nor immortal, on the same day when he is fortunate and successful, he will at one time flourish, and then die away, and then, according to his father's nature, again revive. All that he acquires perpetually flows away from him, so that Love is never either rich or poor, and holding for ever an intermediate state between ignorance and wisdom. The case stands thus;—no God philosophizes or desires to become wise, for he his wise; nor, if there exist any other being who is wise, does he philosophize. Nor do the ignorant philosophize, for they desire not to become wise; for this is the evil of ignorance, that he who has neither intelligence, nor virtue, nor delicacy of sentiment, imagines that he possesses all those things sufficiently. He seeks not, therefore, that possession, of whose want he is not aware.'—'Who, then, O Diotima,' I inquired, 'are philosophers, if they are neither the ignorant nor the wise?'—'It is evident, even to a child, that they are those intermediate persons, among whom is Love. For Wisdom is one of the most beautiful of all things; Love is that which thirsts for the beautiful, so that Love is of necessity a philosopher, philosophy being an intermediate state between ignorance and wisdom. His parentage accounts for his condition, being the child of a wise and well provided father, and of a mother both ignorant and poor.

"'Such is the dæmoniacal nature, my dear Socrates; nor do I wonder at your error concerning Love, for you thought, as I conjecture from what you say, that Love was not the lover but the beloved, and thence, well concluded that he must be supremely beautiful; for that which is the object of Love must indeed be fair, and delicate, and perfect, and most happy; but Love inherits, as I have declared, a totally opposite nature.'—'Your words have persuasion in them, O stranger,' I said; 'be it as you say. But this Love, what advantages does he afford to men?'—'I will proceed to explain it to you, Socrates. Love being such and so produced as I have described, is, indeed, as you say, the love of things which are beautiful. But if any one should ask us, saying; O Socrates and Diotima, why is Love the love of beautiful things? Or, in plainer words, what does the lover of that which is beautiful, love in the object of his love, and seek from it ?'—'He seeks,' I said, interrupting her, 'the property and possession of it.'—'But that,' she replied, 'might still be met with another question, What has he, who possesses that which is beautiful ?'—'Indeed, I cannot immediately reply.'—'But, if changing the beautiful for good, any one should inquire,—I ask, O Socrates, what is that which he who loves that which is good, loves in the object of his love ?'—'To be in his possession,' I replied. —'And what has he, who has the possession of good ?' —'This question is of easier solution, he is happy.'— 'Those who are happy, then, are happy through the possession ; and it is useless to inquire what he desires, who desires to be happy ; the question seems to have a complete reply. But do you think that this wish and this love are common to all men, and that all desire, that that which is good should be for ever present to them ?'— 'Certainly, common to all.'—'Why do we not say then, Socrates, that every one loves ? if, indeed, all love perpetually the same thing ? But we say that some love, and some do not.'—'Indeed I wonder why it is so.'— 'Wonder not,' said Diotima, 'for we select a particular species of love, and apply to it distinctively the appellation of that which is universal.'——

"'Give me an example of such a select application.'— 'Poetry ; which is a general name signifying every cause whereby anything proceeds from that which is not, into that which is ; so that the exercise of every inventive art is poetry, and all such artists poets. Yet they are not called poets, but distinguished by other names ; and one portion or species of poetry, that which has relation to music and rhythm, is divided from all others, and known by the name belonging to all. For this is alone properly called poetry, and those who exercise the art of this species of poetry, poets. So, with respect to Love. Love is indeed universally all that earnest desire for the possession of happiness and that which is good; the greatest and the subtlest love, and which inhabits the heart of every living being; but those who seek this object through the acquirement of wealth, or the exercise of the gymnastic arts, or philosophy, are not said to love, nor are called lovers; one species alone is called love, and those alone are said to be lovers, and to love, who seek the attainment of the universal desire through one species of love, which is peculiarly distinguished by the name belonging to the whole. It is asserted by some, that they love, who are seeking the lost half of their divided being. But I assert, that Love is neither the love of the half nor of the whole, unless, my friend, it meets with that which is good; since men willingly cut off their own hands and feet, if they think that they are the cause of evil to them. Nor do they cherish and embrace that which may belong to themselves, merely because it is their own; unless, indeed, any one should choose to say, that that which is good is attached to his own nature and is his own, whilst that which is evil is foreign and accidental; but love nothing but that which is good. Does it not appear so to you?'—'Assuredly.'—'Can we then simply affirm that men love that which is good?'—'Without doubt.'—'What, then, must we not add, that, in addition to loving that which is good, they love that it should be present to themselves?'—'Indeed that must be added.'—'And not merely that it should be present, but that it should ever be present?'—'This also must be added.'

"'Love, then, is collectively the desire in men that

good should be for ever present to them.'—'Most true.'—'Since this is the general definition of Love, can you explain in what mode of attaining its object, and in what species of actions, does Love peculiarly consist?'—'If I knew what you ask, O Diotima, I should not have so much wondered at your wisdom, nor have sought you out for the purpose of deriving improvement from your instructions.'—'I will tell you,' she replied: 'Love is the desire of generation in the beautiful, both with relation to the body and the soul.'—'I must be a diviner to comprehend what you say, for, being such as I am, I confess that I do not understand it.'—'But I will explain it more clearly. The bodies and the souls of all human beings are alike pregnant with their future progeny, and when we arrive at a certain age, our nature impels us to bring forth and propagate. This nature is unable to produce in that which is deformed, but it can produce in that which is beautiful. The intercourse of the male and female in generation, a divine work, through pregnancy and production, is, as it were, something immortal in mortality. These things cannot take place in that which is incongruous; for that which is deformed is incongruous, but that which is beautiful is congruous with what is immortal and divine. Beauty is, therefore, the fate, and the Juno Lucina to generation. Wherefore, whenever that which is pregnant with the generative principle, approaches that which is beautiful, it becomes transported with delight, and is poured forth in overflowing pleasure, and propagates. But when it approaches that which is deformed it is contracted by sadness, and being repelled and checked, it does not produce, but retains unwillingly that with which it is pregnant. Wherefore, to one pregnant, and, as it were, already bursting with the load of his desire, the impulse towards that which is beautiful is intense, on account of the great pain of retaining that which he has conceived. Love, then, O Socrates, is not as you imagine the love of the beautiful.'—'What, then?'—'Of generation and production in the beautiful.'—'Why then of generation?'—'Generation is something eternal and immortal in mortality. It necessarily, from what has been confessed, follows, that we must desire immortality together with what is good, since Love is the desire that good be for ever present to us. Of necessity Love must also be the desire of immortality.'

"Diotima taught me all this doctrine in the discourse we had together concerning Love; and, in addition, she inquired, 'What do you think, Socrates, is the cause of this love and desire? Do you not perceive how all animals, both those of the earth and of the air, are affected when they desire the propagation of their species, affected even to weakness and disease by the impulse of their love; first, longing to be mixed with each other, and then seeking nourishment for their offspring, so that the feeblest are ready to contend with the strongest in obedience to this law, and to die for the sake of their young, or to waste away with hunger, and do or suffer anything so that they may not want nourishment. It might be said that human beings do these things through reason, but can you explain why other animals are thus affected through love?'—I confessed that I did not know.—'Do you imagine yourself,' said she, 'to be skilful in the science of Love, if you are ignorant of these things?'—'As I said before, O Diotima, I come to you, well knowing how much I am in need of a teacher. But explain to me, I intreat you, the cause of these things and of the other things relating to Love.'—'If,' said Diotima, 'you believe that Love is of the same nature as we have mutually agreed upon, wonder not that such are its effects. For the mortal nature seeks, so far as it is able, to become deathless and eternal. But it can only accomplish this desire by generation, which for ever leaves another new in place of the old. For, although each human being be severally said to live, and be the same from youth to old age, yet, that which is called the same, never contains within itself the same things, but always is becoming new by the loss and change of that which it possessed before; both the hair, and the flesh, and the bones, and the intire body.

"'And not only does this change take place in the body, but also with respect to the soul. Manners, morals, opinions, desires, pleasures, sorrows, fears; none of these ever remain unchanged in the same persons; but some die away, and others are produced. And, what is yet more strange is, that not only does some knowledge spring up, and another decay, and that we are never the same with respect to our knowledge, but that each several object of our thoughts suffers the same revolution. That which is called meditation, or the exercise of memory, is the science of the escape or departure of memory; for forgetfulness is the going out of knowledge; and meditation, calling up a new memory in the place of that which has departed, preserves knowledge; so that, though for ever displaced and restored, it seems to be the same. In this manner every thing mortal is preserved: not that it is constant and eternal, like that which is divine; but that in the place of what has grown old and is departed, it leaves another new like that which it was itself. By this contrivance, O Socrates, does what is mortal, the body and all other things, partake of immortality; that which is immortal, is immortal in another manner. Wonder not, then, if every thing by nature cherishes that which was produced from itself, for this earnest Love is a tendency towards eternity.'

"Having heard this discourse, I was astonished, and asked, 'Can these things be true, O wisest Diotima?' And she, like an accomplished sophist, said, 'Know well, O Socrates, that if you only regard that love of glory which inspires men, you will wonder at your own unskilfulness in not having discovered all that I now declare. Observe with how vehement a desire they are affected to become illustrious and to prolong their glory into immortal time, to attain which object, far more ardently than for the sake of their children, all men are ready to engage in many dangers, and expend their fortunes, and submit to any labours and incur any death. Do you believe that Alcestis would have died in the place of Admetus, or Achilles for the revenge of Patroclus, or Codrus for the kingdom of his posterity, if they had not believed that the immortal memory of their actions, which we now cherish, would have remained after their death? Far otherwise; all such deeds are done for the sake of ever-living virtue, and this immortal glory which they have obtained; and inasmuch as any one is of an excellent nature, so much the more is he impelled to attain this reward. For they love what is immortal.

"'Those whose bodies alone are pregnant with this principle of immortality are attracted by women, seeking through the production of children what they imagine to be happiness and immortality and an enduring remembrance; but they whose souls are far more pregnant than their bodies, conceive and produce that which is more suitable to the soul. What is suitable to the soul? Intelligence, and every other power and excellence of the mind; of which all poets, and all other artists who are creative and inventive, are the authors. The greatest and most admirable wisdom is that which regulates the government of families and states, and which is called moderation and justice. Whosoever, therefore, from his youth feels his soul pregnant with the conception of these excellences, is divine; and when due time arrives, desires to bring forth; and wandering about, he seeks the beautiful in which he may propagate what he has conceived; for there is no generation in that which is deformed; he embraces those bodies which are beautiful rather than those which are deformed, in obedience to the principle which is within him, which is ever seeking to perpetuate itself. And if he meets, in conjunction with loveliness of form, a beautiful, generous and gentle soul, he embraces both at once, and immediately undertakes to educate this object of his love, and is inspired with an overflowing persuasion to declare what is virtue, and what he ought to be who would attain to its possession, and what are the duties which it exacts. For, by the intercourse with, and as it were, the very touch of that which is beautiful, he brings forth and produces what he had formerly conceived; and nourishes and educates that which is thus produced together with the object of his love, whose image, whether absent or present, is never divided from his mind. So that those who are thus united are linked by a nobler community and a firmer love, as being the common parents of a lovelier and more endearing progeny than the parents of other children. And every one who considers what posterity Homer and Hesiod, and the other great poets, have left behind them, the sources of their own immortal memory and renown, or what children of his soul Lycurgus has appointed to be the guardians, not only of Lacedæmon, but of all Greece; or what an illustrious progeny of laws Solon has produced, and how many admirable achievements, both among the Greeks and Barbarians, men have left as the pledges of that love which subsisted between them and the beautiful, would choose rather to be the parent of such children than those in a human shape. For divine honours have often been rendered to them on account of such children, but on account of those in human shape, never.

"'Your own meditation, O Socrates, might perhaps have initiated you in all these things which I have already taught you on the subject of Love. But those perfect and sublime ends to which these are only the means, I know not that you would have been competent to discover. I will declare them, therefore, and will render them as intelligible as possible: do you meanwhile strain all your attention to trace the obscure depth of the subject. He who aspires to love rightly, ought from his earliest youth to seek an intercourse with beautiful forms, and first to make a single form the object of his love, and therein to generate intellectual excellences. He ought, then, to consider that beauty in whatever form it resides is the brother of that beauty which subsists in another form; and if he ought to pursue that which is beautiful in form it would be absurd to imagine that beauty is not one and the same thing in all forms, and would therefore remit much of his ardent preference towards one, through his perception of the multitude of claims upon his love. In addition, he would consider the beauty which is in souls more excellent than that which is in form. So that one endowed with an admirable soul, even though the flower of the form were withered, would suffice him as the object of his love and care, and the companion with whom he might seek and produce such conclusions as tend to the improvement of youth; so that it might be led to observe the beauty and the conformity which there is in the observation of its duties and the laws, and to esteem little the mere beauty of the outward form. He would then conduct his pupil to science, so that he might look upon the loveliness of wisdom; and that contemplating thus the universal beauty, no longer would he unworthily and meanly enslave himself to the attractions of one form in love, nor one subject of discipline or science, but would turn towards the wide ocean of intellectual beauty, and from the sight of the lovely and majestic forms which it contains, would abundantly bring forth his conceptions in philosophy; until, strengthened and confirmed, he should at length steadily contemplate one science, which is the science of this universal beauty.

"'Attempt, I intreat you, to mark what I say with as keen an observation as you can. He who has been disciplined to this point in Love, by contemplating beautiful objects gradually, and in their order, now arriving at the end of all that concerns Love, on a sudden beholds a beauty wonderful in its nature. This is it, O Socrates, for the sake of which all the former labours were endured. It is eternal, unproduced, indestructible; neither subject to increase nor decay: not, like other things, partly beautiful and partly deformed; not at one time beautiful and at another time not; not beautiful in relation to one thing and deformed in relation to another; not here beautiful and there deformed; not beautiful in the estimation of one person and deformed in that of another; nor can this supreme beauty be figured to the imagination like a beautiful face, or beautiful hands, or any portion of the body, nor like any discourse, nor any science. Nor does it subsist in any other that lives or is, either in earth, or in heaven, or in any other place; but it is eternally uniform and consistent, and monoeidic with itself. All other things are beautiful through a participation of it, with this condition, that although they are subject to production and decay, it never becomes more or less, or endures any change. When any one, ascending from a correct system of Love, begins to contemplate this supreme beauty, he already touches the consummation of his labour. For such as discipline themselves upon this system, or are conducted by another beginning to ascend through these transitory objects which are beautiful, towards that which is beauty itself, proceeding as on steps from the love of one form to that of two, and from that of two, to that of all forms which are beautiful; and from beautiful forms to beautiful habits and institutions, and from institutions to beautiful doctrines; until, from the meditation of many doctrines, they arrive at that which is nothing else than the doctrine of the supreme beauty itself, in the knowledge and contemplation of which at length they repose.

"'Such a life as this, my dear Socrates,' exclaimed the stranger Prophetess, 'spent in the contemplation of the beautiful, is the life for men to live; which if you chance ever to experience, you will esteem far beyond gold and rich garments, and even those lovely persons whom you and many others now gaze on with astonishment, and are prepared neither to eat nor drink so that you may behold and live for ever with these objects of your love! What then shall we imagine to be the aspect of the supreme beauty itself, simple, pure, uncontaminated with the intermixture of human flesh and colours, and all other idle and unreal shapes attendant on mortality; the divine, the original, the supreme, the monoeidic beautiful itself? What must be the life of him who dwells with and gazes on that which it becomes us all to seek? Think you not that to him alone is accorded the prerogative of bringing forth, not images and shadows of virtue, for he is in contact not with a shadow but with reality; with virtue itself, in the production and nourishment of which he becomes dear to the Gods, and if such a privilege is conceded to any human being, himself immortal.'

"Such, O Phædrus, and my other friends, was what Diotima said. And being persuaded by her words, I have since occupied myself in attempting to persuade others, that it is not easy to find a better assistant than Love in seeking to communicate immortality to our human natures. Wherefore I exhort every one to honour Love; I hold him in honour, and chiefly exercise myself in amatory matters, and exhort others to do so; and now and ever do I praise the power and excellence of Love, in the best manner that I can. Let this discourse, if it pleases you, Phædrus, be considered as an encomium of Love; or call it by what other name you will."

The whole assembly praised his discourse, and Aristophanes was on the point of making some remarks on the allusion made by Socrates to him in a part of his discourse, when suddenly they heard a loud knocking at the door of the vestibule, and a clamour as of revellers, attended by a flute-player.

"Go boys," said Agathon, "and see who is there: if they are any of our friends, call them in; if not, say that we have already done drinking."

A minute afterwards, they heard the voice of Alcibiades in the vestibule excessively drunk and roaring out:—"Where is Agathon? Lead me to Agathon!"

The flute-player, and some of his companions then led him in, and placed him against the door-post, crowned with a thick crown of ivy and violets, and having a quantity of fillets on his head.

"My friends," he cried out, "hail! I am excessively drunk already, but I'll drink with you, if you will. If not, we will go away after having crowned Agathon, for which purpose I came. I assure you that I could not come yesterday, but I am now here with these fillets round my temples, that from my own head I may crown his who, with your leave, is the most beautiful and wisest of men. Are you laughing at me because I am drunk? Ay, I know what I say is true, whether you laugh or not. But tell me at once, whether I shall come in, or no. Will you drink with me?"

Agathon and the whole party desired him to come in, and recline among them; so he came in, led by his companions. He then unbound his fillets that he might crown Agathon, and though Socrates was just before his eyes, he did not see him, but sat down by Agathon, between Socrates and him, for Socrates moved out of the way to make room for him. When he sat down, he embraced Agathon and crowned him; and Agathon desired the slaves to untie his sandals, that he might make a third, and recline on the same couch.

"By all means," said Alcibiades, "but what third companion have we here?" And at the same time turning round and seeing Socrates, he leaped up and cried out:— "O Hercules! what have we here? You, Socrates, lying in ambush for me wherever I go! and meeting me just as you always do, when I least expected to see you! And, now, what are you come here for? Why have you chosen to recline exactly in this place, and not near Aristophanes, or any one else who is, or wishes to be ridiculous, but have contrived to take your place beside the most delightful person of the whole party?"

"Agathon," said Socrates, "see if you cannot defend me. I declare my friendship for this man is a bad business: from the moment that I first began to know him I have never been permitted to converse with, or so much as to look upon any one else. If I do, he is so jealous and suspicious that he does the most extravagant things, and hardly refrains from beating me. I intreat you to prevent him from doing anything of that kind at present. Procure a reconciliation: or, if he perseveres in attempting any violence, I intreat you to defend me."

"Indeed," said Alcibiades, "I will not be reconciled to

you; I shall find another opportunity to punish you for this. But now," said he, addressing Agathon, "lend me some of those fillets, that I may crown the wonderful head of this fellow, lest I incur the blame, that having crowned you, I neglected to crown him who conquers all men with his discourses, not yesterday alone as you did, but ever."

Saying this he took the fillets, and having bound the head of Socrates, and again having reclined, said: "Come, my friends, you seem to be sober enough. You must not flinch, but drink, for that was your agreement with me before I came in. I choose as president, until you have drunk enough—myself. Come, Agathon, if you have got a great goblet, fetch it out. But no matter, that wine-cooler will do; bring it, boy!" And observing that it held more than eight cups, he first drank it off, and then ordered it to be filled for Socrates, and said:—"Observe, my friends, I cannot invent any scheme against Socrates, for he will drink as much as any one desires him, and not be in the least drunk."

Socrates, after the boy had filled up, drank it off; and Eryximachus said:—"Shall we then have no conversation or singing over our cups, but drink down stupidly, just as if we were thirsty?"

And Alcibiades said: "Ah, Eryximachus, I did not see you before; hail, you excellent son of a wise and excellent father!"

"Hail to you also," replied Eryximachus, "but what shall we do?"

"Whatever you command, for we ought to submit to your directions; a physician is worth a hundred common men. Command us as you please."

"Listen then," said Eryximachus, "before you came in, each of us had agreed to deliver as eloquent a discourse as he could in praise of Love, beginning at the right hand; all the rest of us have fulfilled our engagement; you have not spoken, and yet have drunk with us: you ought to bear your part in the discussion; and having done so, command what you please to Socrates, who shall have the privilege of doing so to his right-hand neighbour, and so on to the others."

"Indeed, there appears some justice in your proposal, Eryximachus, though it is rather unfair to induce a drunken man to set his discourse in competition with that of those who are sober. And, besides, did Socrates really persuade you that what he just said about me was true, or do you not know that matters are in fact exactly the reverse of his representation? For I seriously believe that, should I praise in his presence, be he god or man, any other beside himself, he would not keep his hands off me. But I assure you, Socrates, I will praise no one beside yourself in your presence."

"Do so, then," said Eryximachus, "praise Socrates if you please."

"What," said Alcibiades, "shall I attack him, and punish him before you all?"

"What have you got into your head now," said

Socrates, "are you going to expose me to ridicule, and to misrepresent me? Or what are you going to do?"

"I will only speak the truth; will you permit me on this condition?"

"I not only permit, but exhort you to say all the truth you know," replied Socrates.

"I obey you willingly," said Alcibiades, "and if I advance anything untrue, do you, if you please, interrupt me, and convict me of misrepresentation, for I would never willingly speak falsely. And bear with me if I do not relate things in their order, but just as I remember them, for it is not easy for a man in my present condition to enumerate systematically all your singularities.

"I will begin the praise of Socrates by comparing him to a certain statue. Perhaps he will think that this statue is introduced for the sake of ridicule, but I assure you that it is necessary for the illustration of truth. I assert, then, that Socrates is exactly like those Silenuses that sit in the sculptors' shops, and which are carved holding flutes or pipes, but which, when divided in two, are found to contain withinside the images of the gods. I assert that Socrates is like the satyr Marsyas. That your form and appearance are like these satyrs, I think that even you will not venture to deny; and how like you are to them in all other things, now hear. Are you not scornful and petulant? If you deny this, I will bring witnesses. Are you not a piper, and far more wonderful a one than he? For Marsyas, and whoever now pipes the music that he taught, for that music which is of heaven, and[1] described as being taught by Marsyas, inchants men through the power of the mouth. For if any musician, be he skilful or not, awakens this music, it alone enables him to retain the minds of men, and from the divinity of its nature makes evident those who are in want of the gods and initiation. You differ only from Marsyas in this circumstance, that you effect without instruments, by mere words, all that he can do. For when we hear Pericles, or any other accomplished orator, deliver a discourse, no one, as it were, cares any thing about it. But when any one hears you, or even your words related by another, though ever so rude and unskilful a speaker, be that person a woman, man or child, we are struck and retained, as it were, by the discourse clinging to our mind.

"If I was not afraid that I am a great deal too drunk, I would confirm to you by an oath the strange effects which I assure you I have suffered from his words, and suffer still; for when I hear him speak, my heart leaps up far more than the hearts of those who celebrate the Corybantic mysteries; my tears are poured out as he talks, a thing I have seen happen to many others beside myself. I have heard Pericles and other excellent orators, and have been pleased with their discourses, but I suffered nothing of this kind; nor was my soul ever on those occasions disturbed and filled with self-reproach, as if it were slavishly laid prostrate. But this Marsyas here has often affected me in the way I describe, until the life which I lead seemed hardly worth living. Do not deny it, Socrates, for I well know that if even now I chose to listen to you, I could not resist, but should again suffer

[1] There can hardly be a doubt that *is* should be in the place of *and*. The sense of the original would then be rendered: now the sentence has no construction, and does not render the sense.

the same effects. For, my friends, he forces me to confess that while I myself am still in want of many things, I neglect my own necessities, and attend to those of the Athenians. I stop my ears, therefore, as from the Syrens, and flee away as fast as possible, that I may not sit down beside him and grow old in listening to his talk. For this man has reduced me to feel the sentiment of shame, which I imagine no one would readily believe was in me; he alone inspires me with remorse and awe. For I feel in his presence my incapacity of refuting what he says, or of refusing to do that which he directs; but when I depart from him, the glory which the multitude confers overwhelms me. I escape, therefore, and hide myself from him, and when I see him I am overwhelmed with humiliation, because I have neglected to do what I have confessed to him ought to be done; and often and often have I wished that he were no longer to be seen among men. But if that were to happen, I well know that I should suffer far greater pain; so that where I can turn, or what I can do with this man, I know not. All this have I and many others suffered from the pipings of this satyr.

"And observe, how like he is to what I said, and what a wonderful power he possesses. Know that there is not one of you who is aware of the real nature of Socrates; but since I have begun, I will make him plain to you. You observe how passionately Socrates affects the intimacy of those who are beautiful, and how ignorant he professes himself to be; appearances in themselves excessively Silenic. This, my friends, is the external form with which, like one of the sculptured Sileni, he has clothed himself; for if you open him, you will find within admirable temperance and wisdom. For he cares not for mere beauty, but despises more than any one can imagine all external possessions, whether it be beauty or wealth, or glory, or any other thing for which the multitude felicitates the possessor. He esteems these things and us who honour them, as nothing, and lives among men, making all the objects of their admiration the playthings of his irony. But I know not if any one of you have ever seen the divine images which are within, when he has been opened and is serious. I have seen them, and they are so supremely beautiful, so golden, so divine, and wonderful, that every thing which Socrates commands surely ought to be obeyed, even like the voice of a God.

* * * * * *

"At one time we were fellow-soldiers, and had our mess together in the camp before Potidæa. Socrates there overcame not only me, but every one beside, in endurance of toils: when, as often happens in a campaign, we were reduced to few provisions, there were none who could sustain hunger like Socrates; and when we had plenty, he alone seemed to enjoy our military fare. He never drank much willingly, but when he was compelled he conquered all even in that to which he was least accustomed; and what is most astonishing, no person ever saw Socrates drunk either then or at any other time. In the depth of winter (and the winters there are excessively rigid), he sustained calmly incredible hardships: and amongst other things, whilst the frost was intolerably severe, and no one went out of their tents, or if they went out, wrapt themselves up carefully, and put fleeces under their feet, and bound their legs with hairy skins, Socrates went out only with the same cloke on that he usually wore, and walked barefoot upon the ice; more easily, indeed, than those who had sandalled themselves so delicately: so that the soldiers thought that he did it to mock their want of fortitude. It would indeed be worth while to commemorate all that this brave man did and endured in that expedition. In one instance he was seen early in the morning, standing in one place wrapt in meditation; and as he seemed not to be able to unravel the subject of his thoughts, he still continued to stand as inquiring and discussing within himself, and when noon came, the soldiers observed him, and said to one another—'Socrates has been standing there thinking, ever since the morning.' At last some Ionians came to the spot, and having supped, as it was summer, bringing their blankets, they lay down to sleep in the cool; they observed that Socrates continued to stand there the whole night until morning, and that, when the sun rose, he saluted it with a prayer and departed.

"I ought not to omit what Socrates is in battle. For in that battle after which the generals decreed to me the prize of courage, Socrates alone of all men was the saviour of my life, standing by me when I had fallen and was wounded, and preserving both myself and my arms from the hands of the enemy. On that occasion I intreated the generals to decree the prize, as it was most due, to him. And this, O Socrates, you cannot deny, that while the generals, wishing to conciliate a person of my rank, desired to give me the prize, you were far more earnestly desirous than the generals that this glory should be attributed not to yourself, but me.

"But to see Socrates when our army was defeated and scattered in flight at Delius, was a spectacle worthy to behold. On that occasion I was among the cavalry, and he on foot, heavily armed. After the total rout of our troops, he and Laches retreated together; I came up by chance, and seeing them, bade them be of good cheer, for that I would not leave them. As I was on horseback, and therefore less occupied by a regard of my own situation, I could better observe than at Potidæa the beautiful spectacle exhibited by Socrates on this emergency. How superior was he to Laches in presence of mind and courage! Your representation of him on the stage, O Aristophanes, was not wholly unlike his real self on this occasion, for he walked and darted his regards around with a majestic composure, looking tranquilly both on his friends and enemies; so that it was evident to every one, even from afar, that whoever should venture to attack him would encounter a desperate resistance. He and his companion thus departed in safety; for those who are scattered in flight are pursued and killed, whilst men hesitate to touch those who exhibit such a countenance as that of Socrates even in defeat.

"Many other and most wonderful qualities might well be praised in Socrates; but such as these might singly be attributed to others. But that which is unparalleled in Socrates, is, that he is unlike and above comparison with all other men, whether those who have lived in ancient times, or those who exist now. For it may be conjectured, that Brasidas and many others are such as was Achilles. Pericles deserves comparison with Nestor and Antenor; and other excellent persons of various times may, with probability, be drawn into comparison with each other. But to such a singular man as this, both himself and his discourses are so uncommon, no one, should he seek, would find a parallel among the present or the past generations of mankind; unless they should say that he resembled those with whom I lately compared him, for, assuredly, he and his discourses are like nothing but the Sileni and the Satyrs. At first I forgot to make you observe how like his discourses are to those Satyrs when they are opened, for, if any one will listen to the talk of Socrates, it will appear to him at first extremely ridiculous; the phrases and expressions which he employs, fold around his exterior the skin, as it were, of a rude and wanton Satyr. He is always talking about great market-asses, and brass-founders, and leather-cutters, and skin-dressers; and this is his perpetual custom, so that any dull and unobservant person might easily laugh at his discourse. But if any one should see it opened, as it were, and get within the sense of his words, he would then find that they alone of all that enters into the mind of man to utter, had a profound and persuasive meaning, and that they were most divine; and that they presented to the mind innumerable images of every excellence, and that they tended towards objects of the highest moment, or rather towards all that he who seeks the possession of what is supremely beautiful and good need regard as essential to the accomplishment of his ambition.

"These are the things, my friends, for which I praise Socrates."

* * * * * *

Alcibiades having said this, the whole party burst into a laugh at his frankness, and Socrates said, "You seem to be sober enough, Alcibiades, else you would not have made such a circuit of words, only to hide the main design for which you made this long speech, and which, as it were carelessly, you just throw in at the last; now, as if you had not said all this for the mere purpose of dividing me and Agathon? You think that I ought to be your friend, and to care for no one else. I have found you out; it is evident enough for what design you invented all this Satyrical and Silenic drama. But, my dear Agathon, do not let his device succeed. I intreat you to permit no one to throw discord between us."

"No doubt," said Agathon, "he sate down between us only that he might divide us; but this shall not assist his scheme, for I will come and sit near you."

"Do so," said Socrates, "come, there is room for you by me."

"Oh, Jupiter!" exclaimed Alcibiades, "what I endure from that man! He thinks to subdue every way; but, at least, I pray you, let Agathon remain between us."

"Impossible," said Socrates, "you have just praised me; I ought to praise him sitting at my right hand. If Agathon is placed beside you, will he not praise me before I praise him? Now, my dear friend, allow the young man to receive what praise I can give him. I have a great desire to pronounce his encomium."

"Quick, quick, Alcibiades," said Agathon, "I cannot stay here, I must change my place, or Socrates will not praise me."

Agathon then arose to take his place near Socrates.

He had no sooner reclined than there came in a number of revellers—for some one who had gone out had left the door open—and took their places on the vacant couches, and everything became full of confusion ; and no order being observed, every one was obliged to drink a great quantity of wine. Eryximachus, and Phædrus, and some others, said Aristodemus, went home to bed ; that, for his part, he went to sleep on his couch, and slept long and soundly—the nights were then long—until the cock crew in the morning. When he awoke he found that some were still fast asleep, and others had gone home, and that Aristophanes, Agathon, and Socrates had alone stood it out, and were still drinking out of a great goblet which they passed round and round. Socrates was disputing between them. The beginning of their discussion Aristodemus said that he did not recollect, because he was asleep ; but it was terminated by Socrates forcing them to confess, that the same person is able to compose both tragedy and comedy, and that the foundations of the tragic and comic arts were essentially the same. They, rather convicted than convinced, went to sleep. Aristophanes first awoke, and then, it being broad daylight, Agathon. Socrates, having put them to sleep, went away, Aristodemus following him, and coming to the Lyceum he washed himself, as he would have done anywhere else, and after having spent the day there in his accustomed manner, went home in the evening.

A DISCOURSE ON THE MANNERS OF THE ANCIENTS

RELATIVE TO THE SUBJECT OF LOVE.

[In Shelley's letter to Godwin referred to at page 156 of the present volume, he says of the Symposium, "I have occupied myself in translating this, and it has excited me to attempt an Essay upon the cause of some differences in sentiment between the Ancients and Moderns, with respect to the subject of the dialogue." Mrs. Shelley affixed to this Fragment the title *Essay on the Literature, the Arts, and the Manners of the Athenians*, recording, however, in a note that Shelley named it as it is headed in the present edition, and that it "was intended to be a commentary" on the Symposium, but "breaks off at the moment when the main subject is about to be discussed." Referring to this and the Preface to the Banquet, Mrs. Shelley makes the observations already cited at page 42 as to "small portions of these and other Essays" having been "published by Captain Medwin in a newspaper." Under the title of *The Age of Pericles: With Critical Notices of the Sculpture in the Florence Gallery*, Medwin published in *The Shelley Papers* an excerpt from this Fragment (beginning at the beginning and going down to *extravagant fiction*, page 241), and the seven Notes on Sculpture indicated in the present volume (see pages 47 *et seq.*). The portion of this Fragment appeared first with the Niobe Note in *The Athenæum* for the 15th of September, 1832; and in the issue of the 29th of the same month will be found the Reflection on Love, which also is an excerpt from this Discourse. I have collated these excerpts of Medwin's with the authoritative version of Mrs. Shelley here given, and have not failed to note any variations of the slightest consequence.—H. B. F.]

A DISCOURSE ON THE MANNERS OF THE ANCIENTS

RELATIVE TO THE SUBJECT OF LOVE.

A FRAGMENT.

The period which intervened between the birth of Pericles and the death of Aristotle, is undoubtedly, whether considered in itself, or with reference to the effects which it has produced upon the subsequent destinies of civilized man, the most memorable in the history of the world. What was the combination of moral and political circumstances which produced so unparalleled a progress during that period in literature and the arts;—why that progress, so rapid and so sustained, so soon received a check, and became retrograde,—are problems left to the wonder and conjecture of posterity. The wrecks and fragments of those subtle and profound minds, like the ruins of a fine statue, obscurely suggest to us the grandeur and perfection of the whole. Their very language—a type of the understandings[1] of which it was the creation

[1] Medwin makes this word singular.

and the image—in variety, in simplicity, in flexibility, and in copiousness, excels every other language of the western world. Their sculptures are such as we,[1] in our presumption, assume to be the models of ideal truth and beauty, and to which no artist of modern times can produce forms in any degree comparable. Their paintings, according to Pliny and[2] Pausanias, were full of delicacy and harmony; and some even[3] were powerfully pathetic, so as to awaken, like tender music or tragic poetry, the most overwhelming emotions. We are accustomed to conceive the painters of the sixteenth century, as those who have brought their[4] art to the highest perfection, probably because none of the ancient paintings[5] have been preserved. For[6] all the inventive arts maintain, as it were, a sympathetic connexion between each other, being no more than various expressions of one internal power, modified by different circumstances, either of an individual, or of society; and[7] the paintings of that period would probably bear the same relation as is confessedly borne by the sculptures to all succeeding[8] ones. Of their music we know little; but the effects which it is said to have produced, whether they be attributed to the skill of the composer, or the sensibility of his audience, are far more powerful than any which we experience from the music of our own times; and if, indeed, the melody of their compositions were more tender and delicate, and inspiring, than the melodies of some modern European nations, their superiority in this art must have been something wonderful, and wholly beyond conception.

[1] Medwin omits *we*, and reads *perception* for *presumption*.

[2] Medwin omits *Pliny and*.

[3] The word *even* is omitted by Medwin.

[4] Medwin reads *this* for *their*.

[5] In Medwin's version, *pictures*.

[6] Medwin omits *For*.

[7] Medwin omits *and*, and makes this a fresh paragraph.

[8] In Medwin's version, *successive*.

Their poetry seems to maintain a very high, though not so disproportionate a rank, in the comparison. Perhaps Shakespeare, from the variety and comprehension of his genius, is to be considered, on the whole,[1] as the greatest individual mind, of which we have specimens remaining. Perhaps Dante created imaginations of greater loveliness and energy[2] than any that are to be found in the ancient literature of Greece. Perhaps nothing has been discovered in the fragments of the Greek lyric poets equivalent to the sublime and chivalric sensibility of Petrarch.—But, as a poet, Homer must be acknowledged to excel Shakespeare in the truth, the harmony, the sustained grandeur, the satisfying completeness of his images, their exact fitness to the illustration, and to that to which they belong. Nor could Dante, deficient in conduct, plan, nature, variety, and temperance, have been brought into comparison with these men,[3] but for those fortunate isles, laden with golden fruit, which alone could tempt any one to embark in the misty ocean of his dark and extravagant fiction.[4]

But, omitting the comparison of individual minds, which can afford no general inference, how superior was the spirit and system of their poetry to that of any other period! So that, had any other genius equal in other respects to the greatest that ever enlightened the world arisen in that age, he would have been superior to all, from this circumstance alone—that his conceptions would have assumed a more harmonious and perfect form. For it is worthy of observation, that whatever the poets of that age produced is as harmonious and perfect as pos-

[1] Medwin omits *on the whole*.

[2] Medwin reads *beauty* for *energy*.

[3] In Medwin's version the words *with these men* do not appear.

[4] At this point closes the excerpt issued by Medwin under the title of *The Age of Pericles*.

sible. If a drama, for instance, were the composition of a person of inferior talent, it was still homogeneous and free from inequalities; it was a whole, consistent with itself. The compositions of great minds bore throughout the sustained stamp of their greatness. In the poetry of succeeding ages the expectations are often exalted on Icarean wings, and fall, too much disappointed to give a memory and a name to the oblivious pool in which they fell.

In physical knowledge Aristotle and Theophrastus had already—no doubt assisted by the labours of those of their predecessors whom they criticize—made advances worthy of the maturity of science. The astonishing invention of geometry, that series of discoveries which have enabled man to command the elements and foresee future events, before the subjects of his ignorant wonder, and which have opened as it were the doors of the mysteries of nature, had already been brought to great perfection. Metaphysics, the science of man's intimate nature, and logic, or the grammar and elementary principles of that science, received from the latter philosophers of the Periclean age a firm basis. All our more exact philosophy is built upon the labours of these great men, and many of the words which we employ in metaphysical distinctions were invented by them to give accuracy and system to their reasonings. The science of morals, or the voluntary conduct of men in relation to themselves or others, dates from this epoch. How inexpressibly bolder and more pure were the doctrines of those great men, in comparison with the timid maxims which prevail in the writings of the most esteemed modern moralists! They were such as Phocion, and Epaminondas, and Timoleon, who formed themselves on their influence, were to the wretched heroes of our own age.

Their political and religious institutions are more difficult to bring into comparison with those of other times. A summary idea may be formed of the worth of any political and religious system, by observing the comparative degree of happiness and of intellect produced under its influence. And whilst many institutions and opinions, which in ancient Greece were obstacles to the improvement of the human race, have been abolished among modern nations, how many pernicious superstitions and new contrivances of misrule, and unheard-of complications of public mischief, have not been invented among them by the ever-watchful spirit of avarice and tyranny!

The modern nations of the civilized world owe the progress which they have made—as well in those physical sciences in which they have already excelled their masters, as in the moral and intellectual inquiries in which, with all the advantage of the experience of the latter, it can scarcely be said that they have yet equalled them,—to what is called the revival of learning; that is, the study of the writers of the age which preceded and immediately followed the government of Pericles, or of subsequent writers, who were, so to speak, the rivers flowing from those immortal fountains. And though there seems to be a principle in the modern world, which, should circumstances analogous to those which modelled the intellectual resources of the age to which we refer, into so harmonious a proportion, again arise, would arrest and perpetuate them, and consign their results to a more equal, extensive, and lasting improvement of the condition of man—though justice and the true meaning of human society are, if not more accurately, more generally understood; though perhaps men know more and therefore are more, as a mass, yet this principle has never been called into action, and requires indeed a universal and an almost appalling change in the system of existing things. The study of modern history is the study of kings, financiers, statesmen, and priests. The history of ancient Greece is the study of legislators, philosophers, and poets; it is the history of men, compared with the history of titles. What the Greeks were, was a reality, not a promise. And what we are and hope to be, is derived, as it were, from the influence and inspiration of these glorious generations.

Whatever tends to afford a further illustration of the manners and opinions of those to whom we owe so much, and who were perhaps, on the whole, the most perfect specimens of humanity of whom we have authentic record, were infinitely valuable. Let us see their errors, their weaknesses, their daily actions, their familiar conversation, and catch the tone of their society. When we discover how far the most admirable community ever framed, was removed from that perfection to which human society is impelled by some active power within each bosom, to aspire, how great ought to be our hopes, how resolute our struggles! For the Greeks of the Periclean age were widely different from us. It is to be lamented that no modern writer has hitherto dared to show them precisely as they were. Barthélemi cannot be denied the praise of industry and system; but he never forgets that he is a Christian and a Frenchman. Wieland, in his delightful novels, makes indeed a very tolerable Pagan, but cherishes too many political prejudices, and refrains from diminishing the interest of his romances by painting sentiments in which no European of modern times can possibly sympathize. There is no book which shows the Greeks precisely as they were; they seem all written for children, with the caution that no practice or sentiment, highly inconsistent with our present manners, should be mentioned, lest those manners should receive outrage and violation. But there are many to whom the Greek language is inaccessible, who ought not to be excluded by this prudery from possessing an exact and comprehensive conception of the history of man; for there is no knowledge concerning what man has been and may be, from partaking of which a person can depart, without becoming in some degree more philosophical, tolerant, and just.

One of the chief distinctions between the manners of ancient Greece and modern Europe, consisted in the regulations and the sentiments respecting sexual intercourse. Whether this difference arises from some imperfect influence of the doctrines of Jesus Christ, who alleges the absolute and unconditional equality of all human beings, or from the institutions of chivalry, or from a certain fundamental difference of physical nature existing in the Celts, or from a combination of all or any of these causes, acting on each other, is a question worthy of voluminous investigation. The fact is, that the modern Europeans have in this circumstance, and in the abolition of slavery, made an improvement the most decisive in the regulation of human society; and all the virtue and the wisdom of the Periclean age arose under other institutions, in spite of the diminution which personal slavery and the inferiority of women, recognized by law and opinion, must have produced in the delicacy, the strength, the comprehensiveness, and the accuracy of their conceptions, in moral, political, and metaphysical science, and perhaps in every other art and science.

The women, thus degraded, became such as it was expected they would become. They possessed, except with extraordinary exceptions, the habits and the qualities of slaves. They were probably not extremely beautiful; at least there was no such disproportion in the attractions of the external form between the female and male sex among the Greeks, as exists among the modern Europeans. They were certainly devoid of that moral and intellectual loveliness with which the acquisition of knowledge and the cultivation of sentiment animates, as with another life of overpowering grace, the lineaments and the gestures of every form which they inhabit. Their eyes could not have been deep and intricate from the workings of the mind, and could have entangled no heart in soul-inwoven labyrinths.

Let it not be imagined that because the Greeks were deprived of its legitimate object, they were incapable of sentimental love; and that this passion is the mere child of chivalry and the literature of modern times. This object[1] or its archetype for ever exists in the mind, which selects among those who resemble it that which most resembles it; and instinctively fills up the interstices of the imperfect image, in the same manner as the imagination moulds and completes the shapes in clouds, or in the fire, into the resemblances[2] of whatever form, animal,

[1] The Reflection on Love mentioned in the note at p. 238 as an excerpt given by Medwin from this Discourse opens at this point, but thus: "The mind selects among those who most resemble it, that which is most its archetype."

[2] Medwin reads *a resemblance*.

building, &c., happens to be present to it. Man is in his wildest state a social being[1]; a certain degree of civilization and refinement ever produces the want of sympathies still more intimate and complete; and the gratification of the senses is no longer all that is sought in sexual connexion.[2] It soon becomes a very small part of that profound and complicated sentiment which we call love, which is rather the universal thirst for a communion not only of the senses, but of our whole nature, intellectual, imaginative and sensitive, and which, when individualized becomes an imperious necessity, only to be satisfied by the complete or partial, actual[3] or supposed fulfilment of its claims. This want grows more powerful in proportion to the developement which our nature receives from civilization, for man never ceases to be a social being.[4] The sexual impulse, which is only one, and often a small part of those claims, serves, from its obvious and external nature, as a kind of type or expression of the rest, a common basis, an acknowledged and visible link. Still it is a claim which even derives a strength not its own from the accessory circumstances which surround it, and one which our nature thirsts to satisfy. To estimate this, observe the degree of intensity and durability of the love of the male towards the female in animals and savages; and acknowledge all the duration and intensity observable in the love of civilized beings beyond that of savages to be produced from other causes. In the

[1] Medwin reads *animal* for *being*; and the expression seems much too good for him to have invented,—indeed more characteristic and profound than the expression of the text.

[2] Here Medwin has doubtless toned Shelley down; for he reads instead of *all that is sought in sexual connexion* simply *all that is desired*, a phrase which does not explain itself.

[3] The word *actual* is omitted by Medwin.

[4] The Reflection on Love as given by Medwin ends here.

susceptibility of the external senses there is probably no important difference.

Among the ancient Greeks the male sex, one half of the human race, received the highest cultivation and refinement; whilst the other, so far as intellect is concerned, were educated as slaves, and were raised but few degrees in all that related to moral or intellectual excellence above the condition of savages. The gradations in the society of man present us with slow improvement in this respect. The Roman women held a higher consideration in society, and were esteemed almost as the equal partners with their husbands in the regulation of domestic economy and the education of their children. The practices and customs of modern Europe are essentially different from and incomparably less pernicious than either, however remote from what an enlightened mind cannot fail to desire as the future destiny of human beings.

ION, OR OF THE ILIAD;

TRANSLATED FROM THE GREEK OF PLATO.

[The translation of *Ion*, like that of *The Banquet*, was first given by Mrs. Shelley in the *Essays* &c. (1840); but, unlike the text of *The Banquet*, the text of *Ion* is not free from complications. Mrs. Shelley's remarks on this subject shew that she had to make good certain gaps in the translation as found among Shelley's papers; but her intention to indicate by means of brackets the portions not by Shelley was frustrated by what seems to be a printer's omission. Only two brackets appear in the printed texts of this dialogue; and these are both commencing brackets: the corresponding bracket, to shew where the interpolation ends, being in each case absent. Now I have in my possession a very careful transcript of this translation of Shelley's in the handwriting of the late Miss Claire Clairmont. Up to the point at which Mrs. Shelley's first bracket appears, or, strictly, up to the middle of the sentence preceding it, and within a few words of that point, the transcript and the printed text present no further variation than two transcribers of Shelley's rough MS. would be certain to produce by reason of alternative readings standing in the original. One word or phrase is often in Shelley's drafts placed above another without the rejected reading being struck through; and it is well known how large an option exists in making ready fair copies for the press from many of the poet's unfinished MSS. At the point where Mrs. Shelley indicates the beginning of the first gap, and for several pages, the transcript diverges so completely from the printed text, as to be clearly a different translation: then for half a dozen short speeches there is the same measure of correspondence as in the first portion; and then comes a gap in the version of the transcript and a note by Miss Clairmont that there is a gap. This gap is represented by four pages of printed text without any indication that it was supplied by Mrs. Shelley. This again is followed by a dozen short speeches extending to Mrs. Shelley's second mark of the beginning of a supplied passage—a dozen speeches shewing, when compared with the transcript, a high average of variation, as if taken from very rough and difficult notes, but unquestionably the work of the same hand. Mrs. Shelley's second hiatus would seem to be one of three pages and a half; for, from the bracket indicating where it begins, to the end of the dialogue, where I presume it to close, the printed text and the transcript differ wholly. These facts seem to indicate very clearly that Miss Clairmont's transcript, which is old-looking enough to have been written during Shelley's life-time, was made when the rough MS. was less confused and imperfect than when Mrs. Shelley performed her labour of love; and I have no doubt that the transcript is wholly from Shelley's notes. If, as I also feel sure, Mrs. Shelley's text of that part where there is a gap in the transcript was *not* meant to be included within one of the missing brackets, it results that we have the whole dialogue from Shelley's hand, and that the imperfections found in 1839 were the result of the same fortuitous circumstances which left the text of Shelley's other works a matter of gradual growth. To avoid risk of loss on either hand I have carefully collated the two sources of the following revised text, and noted all variations of consequence. Not knowing positively how far the passages added by Mrs. Shelley extend, I have inserted as foot-notes the whole of the two long passages which vary *in toto* from the transcript by Miss Clairmont. Throughout this, there are reference figures in the text evidently referring to notes on this dialogue; but whether Shelley wrote such notes, or only meant to write them, I know not. Miss Clairmont has left a space for the six verses quoted from the twenty-third book of the Iliad,—a space only just large enough for the original; and hence it may perhaps be fairly concluded that the extracts from Pope's translation, given in this and other cases in the printed editions, were inserted by Mrs. Shelley.—H. B. F.]

ION, OR OF THE ILIAD;

TRANSLATED FROM PLATO.

PERSONS OF THE DIALOGUE,

SOCRATES *and* ION.

SOCRATES.

HAIL to thee O Ion! from whence returnest thou amongst us now?—from thine own native Ephesus[1]?

ION.

No, Socrates; I come from Epidaurus and the feasts in honour of Æsculapius.[2]

SOCRATES.

Had the Epidaurians[3] instituted a contest of rhapsody in honour of the God?

[1] The transcript starts with an inauspicious but not unnatural clerical error, happily obvious, *spheres* for *Ephesus*. To avoid repetition, it is to be understood that all phrases printed in italics in foot-notes to this dialogue, without remark, are variations found in Miss Clairmont's transcript.

[2] *Epidaurus of the Æsculapians.*

[3] *Æsculapians.*

ION.

And not in rhapsodies alone; there were contests in every species of music.

SOCRATES.

And in which did you contend? And what was the success of your efforts?

ION.

I bore away the first prize at[1] the games O Socrates.

SOCRATES.

Well done! You have now only to consider how you shall win the Panathenæa.

ION.

That may also happen, God willing.

SOCRATES.

Your profession O Ion has often appeared to me an enviable one; for together with the nicest care of your person[2] and the most studied elegance of dress, it imposes upon you the necessity of a familiar acquaintance with many and excellent poets, and especially with Homer, the most admirable of them all. Nor is it merely because you can repeat the verses of this great poet, that I envy you, but because you fathom his inmost thoughts[3]; for he is no rhapsodist who does not understand the whole scope and

[1] *of.* [2] *persons.* [3] *thought.*

intention of the poet, and is not capable of interpreting it to his audience. This he cannot do without a full comprehension of the meaning of the author he undertakes to illustrate; and worthy indeed of envy are those who can fulfil these conditions!

ION.

Thou speakest truth O Socrates, and indeed, I have expended my study particularly on this part of my profession. I flatter myself that no man living[1] excels me in the interpretation of Homer; neither Metrodorus of Lampsacus, nor Stesimbrotus the Thasian, nor Glauco, nor any other rhapsodist of the present times can express so many various and beautiful thoughts upon Homer as I can.

SOCRATES.

I am persuaded of your eminent skill O Ion. You will not, I hope, refuse me a specimen of it.

ION.

And indeed it would be worth your while to hear me declaim upon Homer. I deserve a golden crown from his admirers.[2]

SOCRATES.

And I will find leisure some day or other to request

[1] *and I flatter myself that no human being.*

[2] So in the printed text; but *descendants* in the transcript. Professor Jowett renders *ὥστε οἶμαι ὑπὸ Ὁμηριδῶν, κ.τ.λ.*, thus: "I think that the Homeridae should give me a golden crown," &c.

you to favour me so far; at present I will only trouble you with one question. Do you excel in explaining Homer alone, or are you conscious of a similar power with regard to Hesiod and Archilochus?

ION.

I possess this high degree of skill with regard to Homer alone, and I consider that sufficient.

SOCRATES.

Are there any subjects upon which Homer and Hesiod say the same things?

ION.

Many, as it seems to me.

SOCRATES.

Whether do you demonstrate these things better in Homer or Hesiod?[1]

ION.

In the same manner, doubtless, inasmuch as they say the same words with regard[2] to the same things.

SOCRATES.

But with regard to those things in which they differ. Homer and Hesiod both treat[3] of divination, do they not?

[1] *Whether do you illustrate these subjects better for Homer or in Hesiod?*

[2] *respect.*

[3] *speak.*

ION.

Certainly.

SOCRATES.

Do you think that you or a diviner would make the best exposition, respecting all that these poets say of divination, both as they agree and as they differ?

ION.

A diviner probably.

SOCRATES.

Suppose you were a diviner: do you not think that you could explain the discrepancies of these poets on the subject of your profession, if you understood[1] their agreement?

ION.

Clearly so.

SOCRATES.

How does it happen then that you are possessed of skill to illustrate Homer, and not Hesiod, or any other poet[2] in an equal degree? Is the subject matter of the poetry of Homer different from that of[3] all other poets? Does he not principally treat[4] of war and social intercourse, and of the distinct functions and characters of the brave

[1] So in the transcript, but *understand* in the printed text.

[2] *any of the other poets.*

[3] The words *that of* are not in the printed text, but in the transcript.

[4] *deal.*

man and the coward, the professional and private person, the mutual relations which subsist between the Gods and man[1]; together with the modes of their intercourse, the phænomena of Heaven, the secrets of Hades, and the origin of Gods and heroes? Are not these the materials from which Homer wrought his poem?

ION.

Assuredly O Socrates.

SOCRATES.

And the other poets—do they not treat of the same matter?

ION.

Certainly, but not like Homer.

SOCRATES.

How! worse?

ION.

Oh! far worse.

SOCRATES.

Then Homer treats of them better than they?

ION.

O Jupiter!—how much better!

[1] In former editions *men*.

SOCRATES.

Amongst a number of persons employed in solving a problem of arithmetic, might not a person know, my dear Ion, who[1] had given the right answer?

ION.

Certainly.

SOCRATES.

The same person as[2] had been aware of the false one, or some other?

ION.

The same, clearly.

SOCRATES.

That is, some one who understood arithmetic.

ION.

Certainly.

SOCRATES.

Amongst a number of persons[3] giving their opinions[4] on the wholesomeness of different foods, whether would one person be capable to pronounce upon the rectitude of the opinions of those who judged rightly, and another on the

[1] In previous editions *which*.
[2] In former editions *who*.
[3] *people*.
[4] *opinion*.

erroneousness of those which were incorrect, or would the same person be competent to decide respecting both ?

ION.

The same, evidently.

SOCRATES.

What should you call that person ?

ION.

A physician.

SOCRATES.

We may assert then universally, that the same person who is competent to determine the truth, is competent also to determine the falsehood of whatever assertion is advanced on the same subject; and it is manifest that he who cannot judge respecting the falsehood or unfitness[1] of what is said upon a given subject is equally incompetent to determine upon its truth or beauty.

ION.

Assuredly.

SOCRATES.

The same person then would[2] be competent or incompetent for both ?

[1] *emptiness.*

[2] In former editions *would then.*

ION.

Yes.

SOCRATES.

Do you not say that Homer and the other poets, and among them Hesiod and Archilochus, speak of the same things, but unequally, one better, and the other worse?

ION.

And I speak truth.

SOCRATES.

Yet[1] if you can judge what is well said by the one, you must also be able to judge what is ill said by another, inasmuch as it is expressed less correctly.

ION.

It should seem so.

SOCRATES.

Then my dear friend we should not err if we asserted that Ion possessed a like power of illustration respecting Homer and all other poets, especially since he confesses that the same person must be esteemed a competent judge of all those who speak on the same subjects, inasmuch as those subjects are understood by him when spoken of by one, and[2] the subject-matter of almost all the poets is the same.

[1] In former editions, *But if you can judge of*, and in the next line *judge of* again, and *it expresses* for *it is expressed* in the next line but one.

[2] *if.*

ION.

What can be the reason then O Socrates that when any other poet is the subject of conversation, I cannot compel my attention, and I feel utterly unable to declaim anything worth hearing,[1] and positively[2] go to sleep; but when any one makes mention of Homer, my mind applies itself without effort to the subject; I awaken as it were[3] from a trance, and a profusion of eloquent expressions suggest themselves involuntarily?

SOCRATES.

It is not difficult to suggest[4] the cause of this, my dear friend; you are evidently unable to declaim on Homer according to art or[5] knowledge; for did your art endow you with this faculty, you would be equally capable of exerting it with regard to any other of the poets. Is not poetry, as an art or as a faculty, a thing entire and one?

ION.

Assuredly.

SOCRATES.

The same mode of consideration must be admitted with respect to all arts which are severally one and entire. Do you desire to hear what I understand by this O Ion?

[1] In former editions, *talking of.*
[2] *I instead.*
[3] *as if it were.*
[4] *conjecture.*
[5] In former editions *and.*

ION.

Yes by Jupiter, Socrates; I am delighted with listening to you wise men.

SOCRATES.

It is you who are wise, my dear Ion—you rhapsodists, actors, and the authors of the poems you recite. I, like an unprofessional and private man, can only speak the truth. Observe how common, vulgar, and level to the comprehension of any one, is the question which I now ask relative to the same consideration belonging to one entire art. Is not painting an art whole and entire?

ION.

Yes.

SOCRATES.

Are there not and have there not been many painters both good and bad?[1]

ION.

Certainly.

SOCRATES.

Did you ever know a person competent to judge the merit[2] of the paintings of Polygnotus the son of Aglaophon, and incompetent to judge of any other painter; who, on

[1] This question and the answer preceding it are in their right place in the transcript; but do not appear in former editions.

[2] In former editions, *the merit* is wanting; and we read below *the production of any other painter; who, on the supposition of the works of other painters*, &c.

the compositions of other painters being exhibited to him, was[1] wholly at a loss, and very much inclined to go to sleep, and lost all faculty of reasoning upon the subject; but when his opinion was required of Polygnotus, or any one single painter you please, awoke, paid attention to the subject, and discoursed on it with great eloquence and sagacity?

ION.

Never, by Jupiter!

SOCRATES.

Did you ever know any one very skilful in determining the merits of Dædalus[2] the son of Metion, Epeius the son of Panopeus, Theodorus the Samian, or any other great sculptor, who was immediately[3] at a loss and felt sleepy the moment any other sculptor was mentioned?

ION.

I never met with such a person certainly.

SOCRATES.

Nor do I think that you ever met[4] with a man professing himself a judge of poetry and rhapsody,[5] and competent to criticize either Olympus, Thamyris, Orpheus, or Phemius of Ithaca, the rhapsodist, who the moment he came to Ion the Ephesian felt himself quite at a loss and

[1] *felt.*
[2] *Empedalus.*
[3] *any other one great sculptor, who immediately was.*
[4] *will.*
[5] *melody.*

utterly incompetent to judge[1] whether he rhapsodized well or ill.

ION.

I cannot refute you, Socrates, but of this I am conscious to myself, that I excel all men in the copiousness and beauty of my illustrations of Homer, as all who have heard me will confess; and that with respect to other poets, I am deserted of this power; it is for you to consider what may be the cause of this distinction.

SOCRATES.

I will tell you O Ion what appears to me to be the cause of this inequality of power. It is not that you are master[2] of any art for the illustration of Homer, but it is a divine influence which moves you, like that which resides in the stone called magnet by Euripides, and Heraclea by the people. For not only does this stone itself[3] possess the power of attracting iron rings, but it can communicate to them the power of attracting other rings; so that you may see sometimes a long chain of rings, and other iron substances, attached[4] and suspended one to the other by this influence. And as the power of the stone circulates through all the links of this series, and attaches each to each, so the Muse, communicating through those whom she has first inspired, to all others capable of sharing in the inspiration, the influence of that first enthusiasm, creates a chain and a succession. For the authors of those great poems which we admire, do not attain to

[1] *determine.*

[2] In former editions, *that you are not master.*

[3] Wanting in former editions.

[4] *attracted.*

excellence through the rules of any art, but they utter their beautiful melodies of verse in a state of inspiration, and, as it were, *possessed* by a spirit not their own. Thus the composers of lyrical poetry create those admired[1] songs of theirs in a state of divine insanity, like the Corybantes, who lose all controul over their reason in the enthusiasm of the[2] sacred dance, and during this supernatural possession are excited to the rhythm and harmony which they communicate to men; like the Bacchantes who when possessed by the God, draw honey and milk from the rivers, in which when they come to their senses, they find nothing but simple water.—For the souls of the poets,[3] as poets tell us, have this peculiar ministration in the world. They tell us that these souls, flying like bees from flower to flower, and wandering over the gardens and the meadows, and the honey-flowing fountains of the Muses, return to us laden with the sweetness of melody, and arrayed as they are in the plumes of rapid[4] imagination, they speak truth. For a poet is indeed a thing ætherially light, winged, and sacred, nor can he compose any thing worth calling poetry until he becomes inspired and as it were mad, or whilst any reason remains in him. For whilst a man retains any portion of the thing called reason, he is utterly incompetent to produce poetry, or to vaticinate. Thus those who declaim various and beautiful poetry upon any subject, as for instance upon Homer, are not enabled to do so by art or study; but every rhapsodist or poet, whether dithyrambic, encomiastic, choral, epic, or iambic, is excellent in proportion to the extent of his participation in the divine influence and the degree in which the Muse itself has descended on him. In other respects poets may

[1] *divine.* [2] *their.* [3] *souls of poets.* [4] *vapid.*

be sufficiently ignorant and incapable. For they do not compose according to any art which they have acquired, but from the impulse of the divinity within them; for did they know any rules of criticism, according to which they could compose beautiful verses upon one subject, they would be able to exert the same faculty with respect to all or any other. The God seems purposely to have deprived all poets, prophets, and soothsayers of every particle of reason and understanding, the better to adapt them to their employment as his ministers and interpreters[1]; and that we, their auditors, may acknowledge that those who write so beautifully, are possessed, and address us, inspired by the God. A presumption in favour of this opinion may be drawn from the circumstance of Tynnichus the Chalcidian, having composed no other poem worth mentioning, except the famous poem which is in every body's mouth; perhaps the most beautiful of all lyrical compositions, and which he himself calls a gift of the Muses. I think you will agree with me that examples of this sort are exhibited by the God himself to prove that those beautiful poems are not human nor from

[1] After *interpreters*, the transcript reads thus: "that we their auditors, may acknowledge that such absurd persons cannot possibly be the authors of the excellent and admirable things which they communicate; but that the God himself is he who speaks and that they are merely the organs of his voice." It is immediately after the word *God* in the closer reading of the text that Mrs. Shelley's first bracket occurs, marking the commencement of a passage interpolated to supply a gap found in the MS. in 1839. Although, therefore, I do not doubt that Shelley made the translation just quoted, we must assume that he retranslated the passage, as he doubtless would do in many instances. The following is the passage which the whole evidence points to as the first deficiency made good by Mrs. Shelley:

Tynnicus the Chalcidean, is a manifest proof of this, for he never before composed any poem worthy to be remembered; and yet, was the author of that Pæan which everybody sings, and which excels almost every other hymn, and which he, himself, acknowledges to have been inspired by the Muse. And, thus, it appears to me, that the God proves beyond a doubt, that these transcendent poems are not human as the work of men, but man, but divine and from the Gods, and that poets are only the inspired interpreters of the Gods, each excellent in proportion to the degree of his inspiration. This example of the most beautiful of lyrics having been produced by a poet in other respects the worst seems to have been afforded as a divine evidence of the truth of this opinion.—Do you not think with me Ion?

ION.

By Jupiter I do. You touch as it were my soul with your words, O Socrates. The excellent poets appear to me to be divinely commissioned as interpreters between the Gods and us.

SOCRATES.

Do not you rhapsodists interpret the creations of the poets?

ION.

We do.

SOCRATES.

You are then the interpreters of interpreters?

ION.

Evidently.

divine as coming from the God. Poets then are the interpreters of the divinities—each being possessed by some one deity; and to make this apparent, the God designedly inspires the worst poets with the sublimest verse. Does it seem to you that I am in the right, O Ion?

ION.—Yes, by Jupiter! My mind is enlightened by your words, O Socrates, and it appears to me that great poets interpret to us through some divine election of the God.

SOCRATES.—And do not you rhapsodists interpret poets?

ION.—We do.

SOCRATES.—Thus you interpret the interpreters?

ION.—Evidently.

SOCRATES.

Now confess the truth to me Ion; and conceal not what I ask of you.—When you recite some passage from an epic poem which excites your audience to the highest degree; when for instance you sing of Ulysses leaping upon the threshold of his home, bursting upon the assembled suitors, and pouring forth his arrows before his feet; or of Achilles rushing upon Hector; or when you represent some pathetic scene relating to Andromache, Hecuba, or Priam, do you then feel that you are in your senses, or are you not then, as it were, out of yourself; and is not your soul transported into the midst of the actions which it represents, whether in Ithaca or in Troy, or into whatever other place may be the scene of the passage you recite?

ION.

How justly you conjecture my sensations O Socrates, for I will not conceal from you that when I recite any pathetic passage my eyes overflow with tears, and when I relate anything terrible or fearful, my hair lifts itself upright upon my head and my heart leaps with fear.

SOCRATES.—Remember this, and tell me; and do not conceal that which I ask. When you declaim well, and strike your audience with admiration; whether you sing of Ulysses rushing upon the threshold of his palace, discovering himself to the suitors, and pouring his shafts out at his feet; or of Achilles assailing Hector; or those affecting passages concerning Andromache, or Hecuba, or Priam, are you then self-possessed? or, rather, are you not rapt and filled with such enthusiasm by the deeds you recite, that you fancy yourself in Ithaca or Troy, or wherever else the poem transports you?

ION.—You speak most truly, Socrates, nor will I deny it; for, when I recite of sorrow my eyes fill with tears; and when of fearful or terrible deeds, my hair stands on end, and my heart beats fast.

SOCRATES.—Tell me, Ion, can we call him in his senses, who weeps while dressed in splendid garments, and crowned with a

SOCRATES.

How then O Ion can we call that man anything but mad who arrayed in a many coloured robe, and crowned with a golden crown weeps in the midst of festivity and sacrifice; who surrounded by twenty thousand admiring and friendly persons, and thus secure from all possibility of injury or outrage, trembles with terror?

ION.

No indeed to speak the truth O Socrates.

SOCRATES.

Do you know too that you compel the greater number of your auditors to suffer the same affections with yourself?

ION.

And I know it well. For I see every one of them upon their seats aloft, weeping and looking miserable; indeed it is of importance to me, to observe them anxiously; for whilst I make them weep, I know that my profits will give me occasion to laugh: but if I make them laugh it is then my turn to weep for I shall receive no money.

golden coronal, not losing any of these things? and is filled with fear when surrounded by ten thousand friendly persons, not one among whom desires to despoil or injure him?

ION.—To say the truth, we could not.

SOCRATES.—Do you often perceive your audience moved also?

ION.—Many among them, and frequently. I, standing on the rostrum, see them weeping, with eyes fixed earnestly on me, and overcome by my declamation. I have need so to agitate them; for if they weep, I laugh, taking their money; if they should laugh, I must weep, going without it.

SOCRATES.

Know then that the spectator represents the last of the rings which derive a mutual and successive power from that Heracleotic stone of which I spoke. You, the actor, or rhapsodist, represent the intermediate one, and the poet that attached to the magnet itself. Through all these the God draws the souls of men according to his pleasure, having attached them to one another by the power transmitted from himself. And as from that stone, so a long chain of poets, theatrical performers and subordinate teachers and professors of the musical art, laterally connected with the main series, are suspended from the Muse itself, as from the origin of the influence. We call this inspiration, and our expression indeed comes near to the truth; for the person who is an agent in this universal and reciprocal attraction, is indeed possessed, and some are attracted and suspended by one of the poets who are the first rings in this great chain and some by another. Some are possessed by Orpheus, some by Musæus, and many among whom you may be numbered, my dear friend, by Homer. And so complete is his possession of you, that you doze and are at a loss when any one proposes the verses of any other poet as the subject of recitation; but

SOCRATES.—Do you not perceive that your auditor is the last link of that chain which I have described as held together through the power of the magnet? You rhapsodists and actors are the middle links, of which the poet is the first—and through all these the God influences whichever mind he selects, as they conduct this power one to the other; and thus, as rings from the stone, so hangs a long series of chorus-dancers, teachers, and disciples from the Muse. Some poets are influenced by one Muse, some by another; we call them possessed, and this word really expresses the truth, for they are held. Others, who are interpreters, are inspired by the first links, the poets, and are filled with enthusiasm, some by one, some by another; some by Orpheus, some by Musæus, but the greater number are possessed and inspired by Homer. You, O Ion, are influenced by Homer. If you recite the works of any other poet, you get

no sooner is a single passage of this poet recited than you awaken and your soul dances within you and dictates words at will. For it is not through Art or knowledge that you illustrate Homer, but from a divine influence and election, like the Corybantes who hear no sound except that penetrating melody which proceeds from the Deity by whom they are possessed, and although mad in other respects, are capable of accommodating their words and their dress to the rhythm of that music. Hence O Ion you have a power of speech respecting Homer alone, and this is the cause which you sought why that power is united to Homer; it is by a divine election and not through Art that you have attained so singular an excellence in panegyrizing and illustrating this Poet.

ION.

You speak well O Socrates. Yet I should be surprised if you had eloquence enough to persuade me that when I praise Homer I am mad and possessed. I think you would change your opinion if you once heard me declaim.

SOCRATES.

And indeed I desire to hear you, but first answer me

drowsy, and are at a loss what to say; but when you hear any of the compositions of that poet you are roused, your thoughts are excited, and you grow eloquent;—for what you say of Homer is not derived from any art or knowledge, but from divine inspiration and possession. As the Corybantes feel acutely the melodies of him by whom they are inspired, and abound with verse and gesture for his songs alone, and care for no other; thus, you, O Ion, are eloquent when you expound Homer, and are barren of words with regard to every other poet. And this explains the question you asked, wherefore Homer, and no other poet, inspires you with eloquence. It is that you are thus excellent in your praise, not through science but from divine inspiration.

one question. On what subjects does Homer speak well —not on every one I imagine?

ION.

Be assured O Socrates that he speaks ill on none.

SOCRATES.

And does Homer never speak of anything respecting which you may happen to be ignorant?

ION.

There are indeed subjects spoken of by Homer which I do not understand.

SOCRATES.

Does not Homer speak copiously and in many places of various arts—such for instance as charioteering? If you do not remember the passages I will quote the verses to you.

ION.

Allow me. I remember them well.

ION.—You say the truth, Socrates. Yet, I am surprised that you should be able to persuade me that I am possessed and insane when I praise Homer. I think I shall not appear such to you when you hear me.

SOCRATES.—I desire to hear you, but not before you have answered me this one question. What subject does Homer treat best? for, surely, he does not treat all equally.

ION.—You are aware that he treats of every thing.

SOCRATES.—Does Homer mention subjects on which you are ignorant?

ION.—What can those be?

SOCRATES.—Does not Homer frequently dilate on various arts—on chariot-driving, for instance? if I remember the verses, I will repeat them.

ION.—I will repeat them, for I remember them.

SOCRATES.

Recite me those then in which Nestor warns his son Antilochus to beware of the turn in the course at the horse race given at the funeral of Patroclus.

ION.

Αὐτὸς δὲ κλινθῆναι ἐϋπλέκτῳ ἐνὶ δίφρῳ
Ηκ' ἐπ' ἀριστερὰ τοῖιν, ἀτὰρ τὸν δεξιὸν ἵππον
Κένσαι ὁμοκλήσας, εἶξαί τέ οἱ ἡνία χερσίν.
'Εν νύσσῃ δέ τοι ἵππος ἀριστερὸς ἐγχριμφθήτω,
'Ως ἄν τοι πλήμνη γε δοάσσεται ἄκρον ἱκέσθαι
Κύκλου ποιητοῖο· λίθου δ' ἀλέασθαι ἐπαυρεῖν.

Il. ψ'. 335.

SOCRATES.—Repeat what Nestor says to his son Antilochus, counselling him to be cautious in turning, during the chariot race at the funeral games of Patroclus.

Αὐτὸς δὲ κλινθῆναι ἐϋπλέκτῳ ἐνὶ δίφρῳ
Ηκ' ἐπ' ἀριστερὰ τοῖιν, ἀτὰρ τὸν δεξιὸν ἵππον
Κένσαι ὁμοκλήσας, εἶξαί τέ οἱ ἡνία χερσίν.
'Εν νύσσῃ δέ τοι ἵππος ἀριστερὸς ἐγχριμφθήτω,
'Ως ἄν τοι πλήμνη γε δοάσσεται ἄκρον ἱκέσθαι
Κύκλου ποιητοῖο· λίθου δ' ἀλέασθαι ἐπαυρεῖν.

Il. ψ'. 335.*

SOCRATES.—Enough. Now, O Ion, would a physician or a charioteer be the better judge as to Homer's sagacity on this subject?

ION.—Of course, a charioteer.

SOCRATES.—Because he understands the art—or from what other reason?

ION.—From his knowledge of the art.

SOCRATES.—For one science is not gifted with the power of judging of another—a steersman, for instance, does not understand medicine?

ION.—Without doubt.

SOCRATES. — Nor a physican, architecture?

ION.—Of course not.

SOCRATES.—Is it not thus with every art? If we are adepts in one, we are ignorant of another. But first tell me, do not all arts differ one from the other?

ION.—They do.

SOCRATES.—For you, as well as I, can testify that when we say an art is the knowledge of one thing, we do not mean that it is the knowledge of another.

* —— and warily proceed,
A little bending to the left-hand steed;
But urge the right, and give him all the reins,
While thy strict hand his fellow's head restrains,
And turns him short: till, doubling as they roll,
The wheel's round nave appears to brush the goal.
Yet, not to break the car or lame the horse,
Clear of the stony heap direct the course.
Pope, Book 23.

SOCRATES.

Enough. Now Ion, which would be the best judge of whether Homer had given right directions on this subject or not—a physician or a charioteer?

ION.

A charioteer certainly.

SOCRATES.

For what reason? Because it belongs to his art to determine?

ION.

Because it belongs to his art.

SOCRATES.

For the God has attached to every art the knowledge of the peculiar things which relate to it. The rules for steering a ship would never teach us anything in medicine?

ION.

Certainly not.

SOCRATES.

Nor could we deduce from the art of medicine any rules for architecture.

ION.—Certainly.

SOCRATES.—For, if each art contained the knowledge of all things, why should we call them by different names? we do so that we may distinguish them one from the other. Thus, you as well as I, know that these are five fingers; and if I asked you whether we both meant the same thing or another, when we speak of arithmetic—would you not say the same?

ION.—Yes.

SOCRATES.—And tell me, when we learn one art we must both learn the same things with regard to it; and other things if we learn another?

ION.—Certainly.

SOCRATES.—And he who is not versed in an art, is not a good judge of what is said or done with respect to it?

ION.

We could not.

SOCRATES.

Thus with regard to all arts. We can infer nothing from the rules of one to the subject of another—permit me this one question—you allow a distinction of arts?

ION.

Certainly.

SOCRATES.

Do you understand it in the sense that I do? I say that Arts are distinct one from the other inasmuch as they are the sciences of different things.

ION.

So I understand it.

SOCRATES.

We cannot establish any distinction between sciences the objects of which are the same. For instance we both know that the fingers of our hand are five in number; and if I should ask you whether we acquire this knowledge through the same science, that is arithmetic, or by two different sciences, you would say by the same.

ION.

Certainly.

SOCRATES.

Now answer the question I was just going to propose. Is it not true of all arts that one class of things must be known by one single art, and that the knowledge of other classes belongs to other arts, separately and distinctly considered; so that if the art ceases to be the same the subject must also become different?

ION.

So it should appear O Socrates.

SOCRATES.

No one therefore who is ignorant of any art can be competent to know rightly what to say or to do with respect to it.

ION.

Certainly not.

SOCRATES.

To return to the verses which you just recited.—Do you think that you or a charioteer would be better capable of deciding whether Homer had spoken rightly[1] or not?

ION.

Doubtless a charioteer.

SOCRATES.

For you are a rhapsodist and not a charioteer.

[1] *better able to decide whether Homer had treated this subject correctly.*

ION.

Yes.

SOCRATES.

And the art of reciting verses is different from that of driving chariots?

ION.

Certainly.

SOCRATES.

And if it is different, it supposes[1] a knowledge of different things?

ION.

Certainly.

SOCRATES.[2]

And when Homer introduces Hecamede, the concubine of Nestor, giving Machaon a posset to drink, and he speaks thus:—

> Οἴνῳ πραμνείῳ,—φησίν—ἐπὶ δ' αἴγειον κνῆ τυρὸν
> Κνήστι χαλκείῃ· παρὰ δὲ κρόμιον ποτῷ ὄψον.[3]
>
> *Il.* λ' 639.

[1] *And if the arts which you profess are different they suppose.*

[2] It is with this speech that the gap in Miss Clairmont's transcript mentioned at page 250 begins. The matter omitted embraces fourteen speeches, which are given by Mrs. Shelley without any mark to indicate that they are not of Shelley's translating.

[3] Tempered in this, the nymph of form divine,
Pours a large portion of the Pramnian wine;
With goats'-milk cheese, a flavorous taste bestows,
And last with flour the smiling surface strews.
Pope, Book 11.

Does it belong to the medical or rhapsodical art, to determine whether Homer speaks rightly on this subject?

ION.

The medical.

SOCRATES.

And when he says—

> Ἡ δὲ μολυβδαίνῃ ἰκέλη ἐς βυσσὸν ἵκανεν,
> Ἥ τε κατ' ἀγραύλοιο βοὸς κέρας ἐμμεμαυῖα
> Ερχεται ὠμηστῇσι μετ' ἰχθύσι πῆμα φέρουσα.[1]
>
> *Il.* ω' 80.

Does it belong to the rhapsodical or the piscatorial art, to determine whether he speaks rightly or not?

ION.

Manifestly to the piscatorial art.

SOCRATES.

Consider whether you are not inspired to make some such demand as this to me:—Come, Socrates, since you have found in Homer an accurate description of these arts, assist me also in the inquiry as to his competence on the subject of soothsayers and divination; and how far he speaks well or ill on such subjects; for he often treats of them in the Odyssey, and especially when he

[1] She plunged, and instant shot the dark profound:
As, bearing death in the fallacious bait,
From the bent angle sinks the leaden weight.
Pope, Book 24.

introduces Theoclymenus the Soothsayer of the Melampians, prophesying to the Suitors:—

Δαιμόνιοι, τί κακὸν τόδε πάσχετε; νυκτὶ μὲν ὑμέων
Εἰλύαται κεφαλαί τε προσωπά τε νέρθε τε γυῖα,
Οἰμωγὴ δὲ δέδηε, δεδάκρυνται δὲ παρειαί.
Εἰδώλων τε πλέον πρόθυρον, πλείη δὲ καὶ αὐλὴ
Ἱεμένων ἔρεβόςδε ὑπὸ ζόφον· ἠέλιος δὲ
Οὐρανοῦ ἐξαπόλωλε, κακὴ δ' ἐπιδέδρομεν ἀχλύς.[1]

Odyss. υ'. 351.

Often too in the Iliad, as at the battle at the walls; for he there says—

Ὀρνίς γάρ σφιν ἐπῆλθε περησέμεναι μεμαῶσιν,
Αἰετὸς ὑψιπέτης, ἐπ' ἄριστερὰ λαὸν ἐέργων,
Φοινήεντα δράκοντα φέρων ὀνύχεσσι πέλωρον,
Ζωὸν, ἔτ' ἀσπαίροντα· καὶ οὔπω λήθετο χάρμης.
Κόψε γὰρ αὐτὸν ἔχοντα κατὰ στῆθος παρὰ δειρὴν,
Ἰδνωθεὶς ὀπίσω. ὁ δ' ἀπὸ ἕθεν ἧκε χαμάζε
Ἀλγήσας ὀδύνῃσι, μέσῳ δ' ἐγκάββαλ' ὁμίλῳ·
Αὐτὸς δὲ κλάγξας ἕπετο πνοιῇς ἀνέμοιο.[2]

Il. μ'.

I assert, it belongs to a soothsayer both to observe and to judge respecting such appearances as these.

[1] O race to death devote! with Stygian shade
Each destined peer impending Fates invade;
With tears your wan distorted cheeks are drowned,
With sanguine drops the walls are rubied round;
Thick swarms the spacious hall with howling ghosts,
To people Orcus, and the burning coasts.
Nor gives the sun his golden orb to roll,
But universal night usurps the pole. *Pope*, Book 20.

[2] A signal omen stopped the passing host,
Their martial fury in their wonder lost.
Jove's bird on sounding pinions beats the skies;
A bleeding serpent of enormous size
His talons trussed, alive and curling round,
He stung the bird, whose throat received the wound;
Mad with the smart, he drops the fatal prey,
In airy circles wings his painful way.
Floats on the winds and rends the heaven with cries;
Amidst the host the fallen serpent lies. *Pope*, Book 12.

ION.

And you assert the truth, O Socrates.

SOCRATES.

And you also, my dear Ion. For we have in our turn recited from the Odyssey and the Iliad, passages relating to vaticination, to medicine and the piscatorial art; and as you are more skilled in Homer than I can be, do you now make mention of whatever relates to the rhapsodist and his art; for a rhapsodist is competent above all other men to consider and pronounce on whatever has relation to his art.

ION.

Or with respect to every thing else mentioned by Homer.

SOCRATES.

Do not be so forgetful as to say every thing. A good memory is particularly necessary for a rhapsodist.

ION.

And what do I forget?

SOCRATES.

Do you not remember that you admitted the art of reciting verses was different from that of driving chariots?

ION.

I remember.

SOCRATES.

And did you not admit that being different, the subjects of its knowledge must also be different?

ION.

Certainly.

SOCRATES.[1]

You will not assert that the art of rhapsody is that[2] of universal knowledge; a rhapsodist may be ignorant of some things.[3]

ION.

Except perhaps such things[4] as we now discuss O Socrates.

SOCRATES.

What do you mean by *such* subjects, since you except[5] those which relate to other arts? And with which among these do you profess a competent acquaintance since not with all?

ION.

I imagine that the rhapsodist has a perfect knowledge of what it is becoming for a man to speak—what for a woman; what for a slave, what for a free man; what for the ruler, what for him who is governed.[6]

[1] With the last speech ends the portion omitted from the transcript. From the opening of this speech Miss Clairmont transcribed to the end of the piece only excepting the three final lines.

[2] *the art.*

[3] *There are subjects of which a rhapsodist may be ignorant?*

[4] This word is not in the transcript.

[5] Mrs. Shelley reads *besides* for *since you except*, and in the next line but one *them* for *these*.

[6] In the transcript this speech reads thus: "I imagine that the rhapsodist has a competent knowledge of the varieties of human character and situation and the various expressions of them; he knows what is probable and becoming for a man to say and for a woman, for the slave, for the freeman, for the governor, for the governed." I do not doubt that both readings are Shelley's and that the shorter and closer is the amended version.

SOCRATES.

How! do you think that a[1] rhapsodist knows better than a pilot what the captain of a ship in a tempest[2] ought to say?

ION.

In such a circumstance I allow that the pilot would know best.

SOCRATES.

Has the rhapsodist or the physician the clearest[3] knowledge of what ought to be said to a sick man?

ION.

In that case the physician.

SOCRATES.

But you assert that he knows what a slave ought to say?

ION.

Certainly.[4]

SOCRATES.

To take your example, from cattle-driving[5] a rhapsodist would know much better than the herdsman what ought to be said to a slave engaged in bringing back a herd of oxen run wild?[6]

[1] *assert that the.*
[2] *labouring in a tempest.*
[3] *secret.*
[4] *I do.*
[5] Mrs. Shelley reads *To take for example, in the driving of cattle.*
[6] In the transcript *the rhapsodist*, and *a herdsman*, and *his fellow slave engaged in alluring back a herd of oxen that had run wild.*

ION.

No, indeed.[1]

SOCRATES.[2]

Perhaps you mean that he knows much better than any housewife what ought to be said by a workwoman about the dressing of wool?

ION.

No! No!

[1] *I do not say that.*

[2] With this speech begins Mrs. Shelley's second added passage: it presumably extends to the end of the penultimate speech, or perhaps to the end of the final speech, which does not carry on the surface any positive conviction that it is Shelley's. Indeed I incline to think it is not his. The version supplied by Mrs. Shelley runs thus:—

SOCRATES.—But what a woman should say concerning spinning wool?

ION.—Of course not.

SOCRATES.—He would know, however, what a man, who is a general, should say when exhorting his troops?

ION.—Yes; a rhapsodist would know that.

SOCRATES.—How! is rhapsody and strategy the same art?

ION.—I know what it is fitting for a general to say.

SOCRATES.—Probably because you are learned in war, O Ion. For if you are equally expert in horsemanship and playing on the harp, you would know whether a man rode well or ill. But if I should ask you which understands riding best, a horseman or a harper, what would you answer?

ION.—A horseman, of course.

SOCRATES.—And if you knew a good player on the harp, you would in the same way say that he understood harp-playing and not riding?

ION.—Certainly.

SOCRATES.—Since you understand strategy, you can tell me which is the most excellent, the art of war or rhapsody?

ION.—One does not appear to me to excel the other.

SOCRATES.—One is not better than the other, say you? Do you say that tactics and rhapsody are two arts or one?

ION.—They appear to me to be the same.

SOCRATES.—Then a good rhapsodist is also a good general.

ION.—Of course.

SOCRATES.—And a good general is a good rhapsodist?

ION.—I do not say that.

SOCRATES.—You said that a good rhapsodist was also a good general.

ION.—I did.

SOCRATES.—Are you not the best rhapsodist in Greece?

ION.—By far, O Socrates.

SOCRATES.—And you are also the most excellent general among the Greeks?

SOCRATES.

Or by a general animating his soldiers to battle?

ION.

The rhapsodist is not unacquainted with such matters.

SOCRATES.

What! is rhapsody the military art?

ION.

I should know what it became a general to say.

ION.—I am. I learned the art from Homer.

SOCRATES.—How is it then, by Jupiter, that being both the best general and the best rhapsodist among us, you continually go about Greece rhapsodising, and never lead our armies? Does it seem to you that the Greeks greatly need golden-crowned rhapsodists, and have no want of generals?

ION.—My native town, O Socrates, is ruled by yours, and requires no general for her wars;—and neither will your city nor the Lacedemonians elect me to lead their armies—you think your own generals sufficient.

SOCRATES.—My good Ion, are you acquainted with Apollodorus the Cyzicenian?

ION.—Who do you mean?

SOCRATES.—He whom, though a stranger, the Athenians often elected general; and Phanosthenes the Andrian, and Heraclides the Clazomenian, all foreigners, but whom this city has chosen, as being great men, to lead its armies, and to fill other high offices. Would not, therefore, Ion the Ephesian be elected and honoured if he were esteemed capable? Were not the Ephesians originally from Athens, and is Ephesus the least of cities? But if you spoke true, Ion, and praise Homer according to art and knowledge, you have deceived me,—since you declared that you were learned on the subject of Homer, and would communicate your knowledge to me—but you have disappointed me, and are far from keeping your word. For you will not explain in what you are so excessively clever, though I greatly desire to learn; but, as various as Proteus, you change from one thing to another, and to escape at last, you disappear in the form of a general, without disclosing your Homeric wisdom. If, therefore, you possess the learning which you promised to expound on the subject of Homer, you deceive me and are false. But if you are eloquent on the subject of this Poet, not through knowledge, but by inspiration, being possessed by him, ignorant the while of the wisdom and beauty you display, then I allow that you are no deceiver. Choose then whether you will be considered false or inspired?

ION.—It is far better, O Socrates, to be thought inspired.

SOCRATES.

Very likely, if you have studied tactics. You may be at the same time a musician and horse-breaker, and know whether horses are well or ill broken: now if I asked you, O Ion, by which of these two arts you judged respecting these horses, what would be your reply?

ION.

By that of horse-breaking.

SOCRATES.

And in relation to any judgments you might pronounce upon musical performers, you would profess yourself a musician, not a horse-breaker.

ION.

Certainly.

SOCRATES.

If then you possess any knowledge of military affairs do you possess it in your character of general or rhapsodist?

ION.

I see no difference between a general and a rhapsodist.

SOCRATES.

How! no difference? Are not the arts of generalship and recitation two distinct things.

ION.

No, they are the same.

SOCRATES.

Must he who is a good rhapsodist be also necessarily a good general?

ION.

Infallibly O Socrates.

SOCRATES.

And must a good general be also a good rhapsodist?

ION.

That does not follow.

SOCRATES.

But you are persuaded at least that a good rhapsodist is a good general.

ION.

Assuredly.

SOCRATES.

But you are the first rhapsodist in Greece?

ION.

By far.

SOCRATES.

And consequently best general?

ION.

Be convinced of it O Socrates.

SOCRATES.

Why then, by all the Gods, O Ion, since you are at once the best rhapsodist and the greatest general among the Greeks, do you content yourself with wandering about rhapsodizing from city to city, and never place yourself at the head of your armies? Do you think the Greeks have so great a need of one to recite verses to them in a golden crown, and none whatever of a general?

ION.

Our own city, O Socrates, is subjected to yours, and can give me no employment in that branch of the art; and Athens and Sparta are so strongly persuaded of the competence of their own citizens that I doubt whether they would entrust me with a command.

SOCRATES.

My dear Ion, do you know Apollodorus of Cyzene[1]?

ION.

Which Apollodorus?

[1] So in the transcript,—not *Cyzicus*.

SOCRATES.

Him whom the Athenians entrusted with a command although a foreigner; Phanosthenes the Andrian and Heraclides the Clazomenian, likewise foreigners, were also promoted to many civil and military trusts in Athens on account of their reputation. Why should they not honour and elect Ion the Ephesian as their general, if he should be considered equal to the situation?—you Ephesians were originally Athenians and Ephesus is a city inferior to none.—But you are in the wrong Ion, if you are serious in your pretence of being able to illustrate Homer by Art and Knowledge. For after having promised to explain a multiplicity of subjects mentioned by Homer, and assuring me that you knew them well; you now deceive me; and although I give you every opportunity you are still found wanting even with respect to that very subject of which you profess yourself fully master. Like Proteus, you assume a multiplicity of shapes, until at last escaping through my fingers, that you may avoid giving me any proof of your skill in Homer, you suddenly stand before me in the shape of a general. If now, you have deceived me in your promise of explaining Homer in your quality of a professor in the science of rhapsody you act unjustly by me; but if the various and beautiful expressions which at times you can employ are according to my view of the subject, suggested by the influence of the divine election whilst you are possessed as it were by the spirit of Homer, and you are in yourself ignorant, and incompetent, I absolve you from all blame.—Take your choice—whether you prefer to be considered inspired or unjust:

ION.

There is a great difference between these two imputations, O Socrates, the former is far more honourable.

SOCRATES.

It is better both for you and for us, O Ion, to say that you are the inspired, and not the learned, eulogist of Homer.

A PORTION OF MENEXENUS,

OR

THE FUNERAL ORATION;

TRANSLATED FROM THE GREEK OF PLATO.

[This fragment was first given by Mrs. Shelley in the first volume of the *Essays, Letters* &c. (1840). See the remarks on it at page 153 of the present volume.—H. B. F.]

A PORTION OF MENEXENUS,

OR

THE FUNERAL ORATION;

TRANSLATED FROM PLATO.

PERSONS OF THE DIALOGUE,
SOCRATES *and* MENEXENUS.

SOCRATES.

WHENCE comest thou, O Menexenus? from the forum?

MENEXENUS.

Even so; and from the senate-house.

SOCRATES.

What was thy business with the senate? Art thou persuaded that thou hast attained to that perfection of discipline and philosophy, from which thou mayest aspire to undertake greater matters? Wouldst thou, at thine age, my wonderful friend, assume to thyself the government of us who are thine elders, lest thy family should at any time fail in affording us a protector?

U 2

MENEXENUS.

If thou, O Socrates, shouldst permit and counsel me to enter into public life, I would earnestly endeavour to fit myself for the attempt. If otherwise, I would abstain. On the present occasion, I went to the senate-house, merely from having heard that the senate was about to elect one to speak concerning those who are dead. Thou knowest that the celebration of their funeral approaches?

SOCRATES.

Assuredly. But whom have they chosen?

MENEXENUS.

The election is deferred until to-morrow; I imagine that either Dion or Archinus will be chosen?

SOCRATES.

In truth, Menexenus, the condition of him who dies in battle is, in every respect, fortunate and glorious. If he is poor, he is conducted to his tomb with a magnificent and honourable funeral, amidst the praises of all; if even he were a coward, his name is included in a panegyric pronounced by the most learned men; from which all the vulgar expressions, which unpremeditated composition might admit, have been excluded by the careful labour of leisure; who praise so admirably, enlarging upon every topic remotely or immediately connected with the subject, and blending so eloquent a variety of expressions, that, praising in every manner the state of which we are citizens, and those who have perished in battle, and the ancestors who preceded our generation, and ourselves who yet live, they steal away our spirits as with inchantment. Whilst I listen to their praises, O Menexenus, I am penetrated with a very lofty conception of myself, and overcome by their flatteries. I appear to myself immeasurably more honourable and generous than before, and many of the strangers who are accustomed to accompany me, regard me with additional veneration, after having heard these relations; they seem to consider the whole state, including me, much more worthy of admiration, after they have been soothed into persuasion by the orator. The opinion thus inspired of my own majesty will last me more than three days sometimes, and the penetrating melody of the words descends through the ears into the mind, and clings to it; so that it is often three or four days before I come to my senses sufficiently to perceive in what part of the world I am, or succeed in persuading myself that I do not inhabit one of the islands of the blessed. So skilful are these orators of ours.

MENEXENUS.

Thou always laughest at the orators, O Socrates. On the present occasion, however, the unforeseen election will preclude the person chosen from the advantages of a preconcerted speech; the speaker will probably be reduced to the necessity of extemporizing.

SOCRATES.

How so, my good friend? Every one of the candidates has, without doubt, his oration prepared; and if not, there were little difficulty, on this occasion, of inventing an unpremeditated speech. If, indeed, the question were of Athenians, who should speak in the Peloponnesus; or of Peloponnesians, who should speak at Athens, an orator who would persuade and be applauded, must employ all the resources of his skill. But to the orator who contends for the approbation of those whom he praises, success will be little difficult.

MENEXENUS.

Is that thy opinion, O Socrates?

SOCRATES.

In truth it is.

MENEXENUS.

Shouldst thou consider thyself competent to pronounce this oration, if thou shouldst be chosen by the senate?

SOCRATES.

There would be nothing astonishing if I should consider myself equal to such an undertaking. My mistress in oratory was perfect in the science which she taught, and had formed many other excellent orators, and one of the most eminent among the Greeks, Pericles, the son of Xantippus.

MENEXENUS.

Who is she? Assuredly thou meanest Aspasia.

SOCRATES.

Aspasia, and Connus the son of Metrobius, the two

instructors. From the former of these I learned rhetoric, and from the latter music. There would be nothing wonderful if a man so educated should be capable of great energy of speech. A person who should have been instructed in a manner totally different from me; who should have learned rhetoric from Antiphon the son of Rhamnusius, and music from Lampses, would be competent to succeed in such an attempt as praising the Athenians to the Athenians.

MENEXENUS.

And what shouldst thou have to say, if thou wert chosen to pronounce the oration?

SOCRATES.

Of my own, probably nothing. But yesterday I heard Aspasia declaim a funeral oration over these same persons. She had heard, as thou sayest, that the Athenians were about to choose an orator, and she took the occasion of suggesting a series of topics proper for such an orator to select; in part extemporaneously, and in part such as she had already prepared. I think it probable that she composed the oration by interweaving such fragments of oratory as Pericles might have left.

MENEXENUS.

Rememberest thou what Aspasia said?

SOCRATES.

Unless I am greatly mistaken. I learned it from her; and she is so good a school-mistress, that I should have been beaten if I had not been perfect in my lesson.

MENEXENUS.

Why not repeat it to me?

SOCRATES.

I fear lest my mistress be angry, should I publish her discourse.

MENEXENUS.

O, fear not. At least deliver a discourse; you will do what is exceedingly delightful to me, whether it be of Aspasia or any other. I intreat you to do me this pleasure.

SOCRATES.

But you will laugh at me, who, being old, attempt to repeat a pleasant discourse.

MENEXENUS.

O no, Socrates; I intreat you to speak, however it may be.

SOCRATES.

I see that I must do what you require. In a little while, if you should ask me to strip naked and dance, I shall be unable to refuse you, at least, if we are alone. Now, listen. She spoke thus, if I recollect, beginning with the dead, in whose honour the oration is supposed to have been delivered.

FRAGMENTS OF THE REPUBLIC,

TRANSLATED FROM THE GREEK OF PLATO;

WITH NOTES.

[The Fragments from the Republic also were first given by Mrs. Shelley in the *Essays, Letters* &c. (1840). See remarks at page 153 of the present volume. Shelley's Notes on these passages are printed in Italics, in order to distinguish them readily from the translations.—H. B. F.]

FRAGMENTS OF THE REPUBLIC,

TRANSLATED FROM PLATO;

WITH NOTES.

I.

But it would be almost impossible to build your city in such a situation that it would need no imports.—Impossible.—Other persons would then be required, who might undertake to conduct from another city those things of which they stood in need.—Certainly.—But the merchant who should return to his own city, without any of those articles which it needed, would return empty-handed. It will be necessary, therefore, not only to produce a sufficient supply, but such articles, both in quantity and in kind, as may be required to remunerate those who conduct the imports. There will be needed then more husbandmen, and other artificers in our city. There will be needed also other persons who will undertake the conveyance of the imports and the exports, and these persons are called merchants. If the commerce which these necessities produce is carried on by sea, other persons will be required who are accustomed to nautical affairs. And, in the city itself, how shall the products of each man's labour be transported from one to another; those products, for the sake of the enjoyment and the ready distribution of which, they were first induced to institute a civil society?—By selling and buying, surely.—A market and money, as a symbol of exchange, arises out of this necessity.—Evidently.—When the husbandman, or any other artificer, brings the produce of his labours to the public place, and those who desire to barter their produce for it do not happen to arrive exactly at the same time, would he not lose his time, and the profit of it, if he were to sit in the market waiting for them?—Assuredly.—But, there are persons, who, perceiving this, will take upon themselves the arrangement between the buyer and the seller. In constituted civil societies, those who are employed on this service, ought to be the infirm, and unable to perform any other; but, exchanging on one hand for money, what any person comes to sell, and giving the articles thus bought for a similar equivalent to those who might wish to buy.

II.

Description of a frugal enjoyment of the goods of the world.

III.

But with this system of life some are not contented. They must have beds and tables, and other furniture. They must have scarce ointments and perfumes, women, and a thousand superfluities of the same character. The things which we mentioned as sufficient, houses, and clothes, and food, are not enough. Painting and mosaic-work must be cultivated, and works in gold and ivory. The society must be enlarged in consequence. This city, which is of a healthy proportion, will not suffice, but it must be replenished with a multitude of persons, whose occupations are by no means indispensable. Huntsmen and mimics, persons whose occupation it is to arrange forms and colours, persons whose trade is the cultivation of the more delicate arts, poets and their ministers, rhapsodists, actors, dancers, manufacturers of all kinds of instruments and schemes of female dress, and an immense crowd of other ministers to pleasure and necessity. Do you not think we should want schoolmasters, tutors, nurses, hair-dressers, barbers, manufacturers, and cooks? Should we not want pig-drivers, which were not wanted in our more modest city, in this one, and a multitude of others to administer to other animals, which would then become necessary articles of food,—or should we not?—Certainly we should.—Should we not want physicians much more, living in this manner than before? The same tract of country would no longer provide sustenance for the state. Must we then not usurp from the territory of our neighbours, and then we should make aggressions, and so we have discovered the origin of war; which is the principal cause of the greatest public and private calamities.—C. xi.

IV.

And first, we must improve upon the composers of fabulous histories in verse, to compose them according to the rules of moral beauty; and those not composed according to the rules must be rejected; and we must persuade mothers and nurses to teach those which we approve to their children, and to form their minds by moral fables, far more than their bodies by their hands. —Lib. ii.

V.

ON THE DANGER OF THE STUDY OF ALLEGORICAL COMPOSITION (IN A LARGE SENSE) FOR YOUNG PEOPLE.

For a young person is not competent to judge what portions of a fabulous composition are allegorical and what literal; but the opinions produced by a literal acceptation of that which has no meaning, or a bad one, except in an allegorical sense, are often irradicable. —Lib. ii.

VI.

God then, since he is good, cannot be, as is vulgarly supposed, the cause of all things; he is the cause, indeed, of very few things. Among the great variety of events which happen in the course of human affairs, evil prodigiously overbalances good in everything which regards men. Of all that is good there can be no other cause than God; but some other cause ought to be discovered for evil, which should never be imputed as an effect to God.—L. ii.

VII.

Plato's doctrine of punishment as laid down, p. 146, *is refuted by his previous reasonings.—P.* 26.

VIII.

THE UNCHANGEABLE NATURE OF GOD.

Do you think that God is like a vulgar conjuror, and

that he is capable for the sake of effect, of assuming, at one time, one form, and at another time, another? Now, in his own character, converting his proper form into a multitude of shapes, now deceiving us, and offering vain images of himself to our imagination? Or do you think that God is single and one, and least of all things capable of departing from his permanent nature and appearance?

IX.

THE PERMANENCY OF WHAT IS EXCELLENT.

But everything, in proportion as it is excellent, either in art or nature, or in both, is least susceptible of receiving change from any external influence.

X.

AGAINST SUPERSTITIOUS TALES.

Nor should mothers terrify their children by these fables, that Gods go about in the night-time, resembling strangers, in all sorts of forms: at once blaspheming the Gods and rendering their children cowardly.

XI.

THE TRUE ESSENCE OF FALSEHOOD AND ITS ORIGIN.

Know you not, that that which is truly false, if it may be permitted me so to speak, all, both gods and men, detest?—How do you mean?—Thus: No person is willing to falsify in matters of the highest concern to himself concerning those matters, but fears, above all things, lest he should accept falsehood.—Yet, I understand you not.—You think that I mean something profound. I say that no person is willing in his own mind to receive or to assert a falsehood, to be ignorant, to be in error, to possess that which is not true. This is truly to be called falsehood, this ignorance and error in the mind itself. What is usually called falsehood, or deceit in words, is but a voluntary imitation of what the mind itself suffers in the involuntary possession of that falsehood, an image of later birth, and scarcely, in a strict and complete sense, deserving the name of falsehood.—Lib. ii.

XII.

AGAINST A BELIEF IN HELL.

If they are to possess courage, are not those doctrines alone to be taught, which render death least terrible? Or do you conceive that any man can be brave who is subjected to a fear of death? that he who believes the things that are related of hell, and thinks that they are truth, will prefer in battle, death to slavery, or defeat?—Lib. iii.—*Then follows a criticism on the poetical accounts of hell.*

XIII.

ON GRIEF.

We must then abolish the custom of lamenting and commiserating the deaths of illustrious men. Do we assert that an excellent man will consider it anything dreadful that his intimate friend, who is also an excellent man, should die?—By no means. (*an excessive refinement*). He will abstain then from lamenting over his loss, as if he had suffered some great evil?—Surely.—May we not assert in addition, that such a person as we have described suffices to himself for all purposes of living well and happily, and in no manner needs the assistance or society of another? that he would endure with resignation the destitution of a son, or a brother, or possessions, or whatever external adjuncts of life might have been attached to him? and that, on the occurrence of such contingencies, he would support them with moderation and mildness, by no means bursting into lamentations, or resigning himself to despondence?—Lib. iii.

Then he proceeds to allege passages of the poets in which opposite examples were held up to approbation and imitation.

XIV.

THE INFLUENCE OF EARLY CONSTANT IMITATION.

Do you not apprehend that imitations, if they shall have been practised and persevered in from early youth, become established in the habits and nature, in the gestures of the body, and the tones of the voice, and lastly, in the intellect itself?—C. iii.

XV.

ON THE EFFECT OF BAD TASTE IN ART.

Nor must we restrict the poets alone to an exhibition of the example of virtuous manners in their compositions, but all other artists must be forbidden, either in sculpture, or painting, or architecture, to employ their skill upon forms of an immoral, unchastened, monstrous, or illiberal type, either in the forms of living beings, or in architectural arrangements. And the artist capable of this employment of his art, must not be suffered in our community, lest those destined to be guardians of the society, nourished upon images of deformity and vice, like cattle upon bad grass, gradually gathering and depasturing every day a little, may ignorantly establish one great evil composed of these many evil things, in their minds. —C. iii.

The monstrous figures called Arabesques, however in some of them is to be found a mixture of a truer and simpler taste, which are found in the ruined palaces of the Roman Emperors, bear, nevertheless, the same relation to the brutal profligacy and killing luxury which required them, as the majestic figures of Castor and Pollux, and the simple beauty of the sculpture of the frieze of the Parthenon, bear to the more beautiful and simple manners of the Greeks of that period. With a liberal interpretation, a similar analogy might be extended into literary composition.

XVI.

AGAINST THE LEARNED PROFESSIONS.

What better evidence can you require of a corrupt and pernicious system of discipline in a state, than that not merely persons of base habits and plebeian employments, but men who pretend to have received a liberal education, require the assistance of lawyers and physicians, and those too who have attained to a singular degree (so desperate are these diseases of body and mind) of skill? Do you not consider it an abject necessity, a proof of the deepest degradation, to need to be instructed in what is just or what is needful, as by a master and a judge, with regard to your personal knowledge and suffering?—C. iii.

What would Plato have said to a priest, such as his office is, in modern times?

XVII.

ON MEDICINE.

Do you not think it an abject thing to require the assistance of the medicinal art, not for the cure of wounds, or such external diseases as result from the accidents of the seasons (ἐπετείην), but on account of sloth and the superfluous indulgences which we have already condemned; this being filled with wind and water, like holes in earth, and compelling the elegant successors of Æsculapius to invent new names, flatulences, and catarrhs, &c., for the new diseases which are the progeny of your luxury and sloth?—L. iii.

XVIII.

THE EFFECT OF THE DIETETIC SYSTEM.

Herodicus being pædotribe (παιδοτρίβης, *Magister palæstræ*), and his health becoming weak, united the gymnastic with the medical art, and having condemned himself to a life of weariness, afterwards extended the same pernicious system to others. He made his life a long death. For humouring the disease, mortal in its own nature, to which he was subject, without being able to cure it, he postponed all other purposes to the care of medicating himself, and through his whole life was subject to an access of his malady, if he departed in any degree from his accustomed diet, and by the employment of this skill, dying by degrees, he arrived at an old age. —L. iii.

Æsculapius never pursued these systems, nor Machaon or Podalirius. They never undertook the treatment of those whose frames were inwardly and thoroughly diseased, so to prolong a worthless existence, and bestow on a man a long and wretched being, during which they might generate children in every respect the inheritors of their infirmity.—L. iii.

XIX.

AGAINST WHAT IS FALSELY CALLED "KNOWLEDGE OF THE WORLD."

A man ought not to be a good judge until he be old; because he ought not to have acquired a knowledge of what injustice is, until his understanding has arrived at maturity: not apprehending its nature from a consideration of its existence in himself; but having contemplated it distinct from his own nature in that of others, for a long time, until he shall perceive what an evil it is, not from his own experience and its effects within himself, but from his observations of them as resulting in others. Such a one were indeed an honourable judge, and a good; for he who has a good mind, is good. But that judge who is considered so wise, who having himself committed great injustices, is supposed to be qualified for the detection of it in others, and who is quick to suspect, appears keen, indeed, as long as he associates with those who resemble him; because, deriving experience from the example afforded by a consideration of his own conduct and character, he acts with caution; but when he associates with men of universal experience and real virtue, he exposes the defects resulting from such experience as he possesses, by distrusting men unreasonably and mistaking true virtue, having no example of it within himself with which to compare the appearances manifested in others: yet, such a one finding more associates who are virtuous than such as are wise, necessarily appears, both to himself and others, rather to be wise than foolish. —But we ought rather to search for a wise and good judge; one who has examples within himself of that upon which he is to pronounce.—C. iii.

XX.

Those who use gymnastics unmingled with music become too savage, whilst those who use music unmingled with gymnastics, become more delicate than is befitting.

ON A PASSAGE IN CRITO,[1]

WHEREIN SOCRATES REFUSES TO ESCAPE FROM PRISON AND DEATH, ALLEGING THAT A GOOD CITIZEN OUGHT TO OBEY HIS COUNTRY'S LAWS.

THE reply is simple.

Indeed, your city cannot subsist, because the laws are no longer of avail. For how can the laws be said to exist, when those who deserve to be nourished in the Prytanea at the public expense, are condemned to suffer the penalties only dne to the most atrocious criminals; whilst those against, and to protect from, whose injustice, the laws were framed, live in honour and security? I neither overthrow your state, nor infringe your laws. Although you have inflicted an injustice on me, which is sufficient, according to the opinions of the multitude, to authorize me to consider you and me as in a state of warfare; yet, had I the power, so far from inflicting any revenge, I would endeavour to overcome you by benefits. All that I do at present is, that which the peaceful traveller would do, who, caught by robbers in a forest, escapes from them whilst they are engaged in the division of the spoil. And this I do, when it would not only be

[1] Mrs. Shelley published this Note in the *Essays, Letters,* &c. (1840), with the other Platonic translations and notes.

indifferent, but delightful to me to die, surrounded by my friends, secure of the inheritance of glory, and escaping, after such a life as mine, from the decay of mind and body which must soon begin to be my portion should I live. But, I prefer the good, which I have it in my power yet to perform.

Such are the arguments, which overturn the sophism placed in the mouth of Socrates by Plato. But there are others which prove that he did well to die.

ON THE DÆMON OF SOCRATES.[1]

Socrates' dæmon a form of Augury.

Socrates made a distinction between things subject to divination and those not subject to it. He said—a supernatural force has sway over the greatest things in all human undertakings (p. 5.) and that the uncertainty belonging to them all, is the introduction of that power, or rather that all events except those which the human will modifies, are modified by the divine will.

[1] This is the memorandum referred to at p. 50 as being made among the Notes on Sculptures. At the beginning is written, indistinctly, what seems to read thus,—*Mem. on. L. I.*

ON PROPHECY.

AN EXCERPT FROM THE TRACTATUS THEOLOGICO-POLITICUS.

TRANSLATED FROM THE LATIN OF SPINOZA.

[The following translation was printed in Middleton's *Shelley and his Writings* as an original work of the poet's, and assigned to the period of *Zastrozzi* and *St. Irvyne*, on "internal evidence"! Two pages of the MS. were reproduced in fac-simile: as far as I can judge from this, which is not well executed, the MS. seems to be of about the year 1815, or perhaps later. Middleton does not profess to give the whole fragment, which he describes as "too crude for publication entire"; but I suspect that, either as it stood, or in the way of quotation and paraphrase, he gave nearly all he had. Mr. Garnett subsequently identified this fragment as a translation from the *Tractatus Theologico-Politicus.* Mr. Rossetti (Poetical Works, 1878, Vol. I, page 150) records that, in March 1820, "Shelley was dictating to his wife a translation of Spinoza." From the part of Williams's journal published by Mr. Garnett in *The Fortnightly Review* for June 1878, we learn that, on the evening of the 11th of November 1821, Shelley proposed to Williams "to assist him in a continuation of the translation of Spinoza's Theologico-political tract, to which Lord B. has consented to put his name, and to give it greater currency, will write the life of that celebrated Jew to preface the work." On the 12th of November, Williams records, "S. and I commence Spinoza, that is to say, I write while he dictates. Write from page 178 to page 188." The following day's entry is "Write fifteen pages. S. talks of printing here"—and the record of the 14th is "Four and a half pages." Mr. Garnett says that "the abortive translation must have progressed at least as far as Spinoza's sixth definition"; but he does not lead us to suppose that the work is known to be extant. Perhaps the rest of it will be found some day; and it would certainly be well worth recovering.—H. B. F.]

ON PROPHECY.

TRANSLATED FROM SPINOZA.

All considerations which relate to this question must be drawn from Scripture alone; for what conclusions can we establish with respect to matters which exceed the limits of our own understanding, besides the doctrines delivered in the writing or traditions of the Prophets? and, since in our own times we acknowledge no prophets, nothing is left to us but the contemplation of those sacred volumes which have been handed down from those whom we do acknowledge, with this caution, indeed, that we determine nothing on the subjects of which they treat, or attribute anything to the Prophets themselves, which does not flow directly from their own words. Here we should observe that the Jews never acknowledge secondary or intermediate causes; but from a sense of religion, or (as the vulgar would allege) from a desire of rendering homage to God, refer everything to divine interference. If, for instance, they have made a successful adventure in commerce, they say that God gave it them. If they desire anything, it is their phrase to say, "God has disposed my heart thus." If any imagination suggests itself to their thoughts, they say that God has told it them. Everything, therefore, that Scripture asserts God to have communicated to any one, is not to be considered prophetic and supernatural, but only that which Scripture expressly affirms.[1]

* * * * * *

It is the opinion of many of the Jews that the words of the Decalogue were not promulgated by God; but that at the time of its delivery nothing but an obscure tumult was heard by the Israelites, in which no words were to be distinguished, but that the laws of the Decalogue were then communicated to their minds,

[1] At this point Middleton breaks into a mixture of quotation and paraphrase, thus:

"He commences by attempting to explain prophecy, as differing only in degree from human foresight, which he calls 'natural knowledge'; the former being nothing more than a much clearer perception, and more far-seeing vision, than enjoyed by mankind in general; but singularly enough he proceeds immediately to 'a more elaborate consideration of other causes and means through which God reveals those things *which exceed the limits of natural knowledge.*'

"Of these 'causes and means' he says Scripture affords three examples, namely: 'By words, by signs, and by a combination of both'; but inspiration is always a necessary adjunct, which he speaks of as 'a peculiar disposition of the imagination,' making it appear that the words and signs may be actual or imaginary.

"Here, too, there is full scope for his favourite theory of dreams, for the revelations made to the Prophets are often spoken of as conveyed in visions; and speaking of sleep, he calls it 'a condition of body and mind when the imagination is best prepared to the shaping out those things which are not.'

"Under this last medium of communication, he classes many things which are not given as visions. Such as God's command to Abraham to sacrifice his son. God's first making himself known to Samuel, who at first mistook his voice for that of Eli. One he seems to consider a kind of day-dream, the other inspiration, as just defined, which would make it appear that visions and the peculiar disposition of the imagination are in many respects the same thing."

without the intervention of language. This opinion has so much foundation, as the circumstance of the variations of the Decalogue of Exodus from that of Deuteronomy may afford; whence it should seem to follow (inasmuch as God never spoke but once) that the Decalogue assumes to teach, not the very words, but only the *opinions* of God.

The sacred Scriptures announce no other means besides these, through which God reveals himself to man, none are therefore to be admitted into our conception of his nature; and although we distinctly apprehend that God may communicate immediately with the mind of man without the intervention of material means, yet that intellect must necessarily be of a nature more elevated and excellent than the intellect of man, which can perceive within itself anything not comprised under the original elements of human knowledge, whence I am induced to believe that no person ever arrived at so great an eminence above mankind except Christ, to whom the decrees of God, conducive to human salvation, were immediately revealed, without either words or visions, God manifesting himself through the mind of Christ to the Apostles as formerly to Moses through the mediation of an aërial voice.

Therefore[1] the voice of Christ, like that which Moses heard, may be called the voice of God. And thus it may be said that the Wisdom of God, that is superhuman wisdom, assumed human nature in Christ. And that Christ was the way of salvation.

[1] The portion of the MS. given by Middleton in fac-simile extends from here to the end.

But I must warn the reader that I here avoid the consideration of certain doctrines established by some Churches concerning Christ, which utterly unable to comprehend, I neither affirm, nor deny.

That which I have affirmed, I infer from Scripture. For it is nowhere stated that God appeared, or spoke to Christ, but only that God revealed himself through Christ to the Apostles, and that he was the way of salvation, and lastly that the old law was immediately delivered through an Angel, and not by God himself. Therefore, if Moses spoke with God face to face as one man with[1] his friend (that is through the intermediation of two bodies) Christ communicated with God mind to mind.

We may assume, therefore, that, with the exception of Christ, none ever apprehended the revelations of God without the assistance of the imagination, that is of words or forms imaged forth in the mind, and that therefore, as shall be shewn more clearly in the following chapter, the qualification to prophecy is rather a more vivid imagination than a profounder understanding than other men.

[1] In the fac-simile MS. *was* stands in the place of *with*, of course through a slip of the pen. In printing the line before, Middleton substituted *if God spoke to Moses* for *if Moses spoke with God*, which is very clearly shewn by the fac-simile to be the right reading.

PASSAGES FROM FAUST.

TRANSLATED, AS AN EXERCISE, FROM THE GERMAN OF GOETHE.

[Mr. Rossetti records in a note (see his edition of the Poetical Works, 1878, Vol. III, page 436) that he had seen in Mr. Garnett's hands "a literal translation made by the poet, when he began learning German in 1815, from the opening portion of *Faust*, up to where the infernal dog first makes his appearance. It is done as a mere exercise in acquiring the language, . . . but has its interest as showing . . . the way he went to work in studying." Mr. Rossetti gave three specimens of this exercise; and I am content to repeat them here. The whole translation described is in Sir Percy Shelley's possession; and it is not thought worth while to publish it entire.—H. B. F.]

PASSAGES FROM FAUST;

TRANSLATED, AS AN EXERCISE, FROM GOETHE.

I.

The Spirit appears in the flame.

SPIRIT.

Who calls me?

FAUST (*turning away*).

Horrible sight!

SPIRIT.

Thou hast me mighty drawn forth from my sphere long: and now . . .

FAUST.

Alas! I cannot endure thee!

SPIRIT.

Thou didst implore earnestly me to see, my voice to hear, my countenance to behold. Me bent thy mighty soul-prayer: here am I. What pitiful terror seizes superhuman you? Where is of thy soul the flame? Where is the breast which a world in itself contains, and . . . and possesses, which, with joy trembling, swelled as us the spirits' like to rise? What art thou, Faust? That voice to me resounds which itself to me with all its powers urged. Art thou he? who, by my breath round-thundered, in all thy life's depth shook—a cowardly crooked worm!

FAUST.

Shall I thee, Image of Fire, propitiate? I am, I am Faust—I am thy likeness!

SPIRIT.

In the flux of life, in the storm of things, proceed I to and fro, move here and there. Birth and the grave, an eternal sea, a changeful web, a burning life—thus provide I for the rushing alternation of time, and work of Deity the living robe.

FAUST.

Who thou the immense world wanderest around, active spirit, how near feel I thee to me!

SPIRIT.

Thou resemblest a spirit; then thou comprehendest nothing to me. (*Disappears.*)

II.

Scholar.

Lightning-like the vigorous maidens stride. Mr. brother, come! We must them accompany. A strong beer, a macerated tobacco, and a maid in dress—that is now my taste.

Town Girl.

There see to me now handsome lads! It is really a shame! Company can they the all-best have, and run these maidens to.

Second Scholar.

Not so quick! Far behind come two who are enough pretty to attract. It is my neighbour thereby: I am maidens to see fond. They go with their still step, and draw us yet from to the end with.

III.

Faust.

Seest thou that black dog, the corn and stubble near?

Wagner.

I have seen him long already: nothing important he to me seems.

FAUST.

Consider him well: for what holdest thou the beast?

WAGNER.

For a shock-dog which, to his manner, himself at the heels of his master plagues.

FAUST.

Mark you how in far circles he round us here and ever nearer hunts? And err I not—so draws he a whirlpool of fire to his path behind him.

WAGNER.

I see nothing but a black shock-dog; it may by you well a deception of sight be.

FAUST.

To me appears it that he magic low snares to the fifth band round our feet draws.

WAGNER.

I see him uncertain and timorous to us upspring, while he near his master two unknown sees.

FAUST.

The circle will close: already is it near.

WAGNER.

Thou seest, a dog and no spectre is there. He knarls, and hesitating lays himself on his belly: he wags his tail—of all dogs the custom.

FAUST.

Accompany thyself to us—come here!

WAGNER.

It is a blundering foolish beast. Thou standest still—he waits too: thou speakest him to—he struggles to thee only on: loose what—he would it bring, after thy stick in the water would spring.

FAUST.

Thou hast well: I find not the step of a ghost, and all is . . .

WAGNER.

With a dog, when he well pulls, will himself a wise man weigh. Yes, thy affection desires he quite and entirely; he of students the most excellent scholar.

LETTERS WRITTEN BEFORE THE FINAL DEPARTURE FROM ENGLAND.

[The following letters are given either for their interest in connexion with Shelley's literary career, or as having some strong independent interest. Some are gathered from outlying publications which have but little of Shelley's *ipsissima verba* in them; and others are published from the original manuscripts. The first in the series, from an autograph letter in the possession of Mr. Frederick Locker, is chiefly valuable on account of its evidence of Shelley's early engagement in literary projects. When Mr. Garnett discovered the letters in *Stockdale's Budget*, he pointed out (*Macmillan's Magazine*, June, 1860, article, "Shelley in Pall Mall") that the one about the *Victor and Cazire* Poems, dated the 6th of September, 1810, was the earliest extant except "the childish note printed by Medwin." The letter to Messrs. Longman and Co., now placed first in the series, is dated sixteen months earlier than the first to Stockdale, and must take its place as the opening of Shelley's literary correspondence, until superseded by further discovery. Mr. Garnett explained to his readers that *Stockdale's Budget* was "a periodical issued in 1827; a sort of appendix to the more celebrated 'Memoirs of Harriet Wilson;'" and such an explanation is still more or less necessary; for though Shelley's letters to Stockdale have been more than once reprinted, Stockdale's memoirs of his connexion with the youthful author have never been republished *in extenso*. Indeed, though they might form a proper appendix to an exhaustive biography, they have no literary value whatever, and only a mediocre biographic value. All the letters given in the *Budget* Series are here reprinted. Their genuineness is beyond question; and of one of them I have seen the original in Shelley's writing. The letter to Sir James Lawrence has been unduly left out of sight, because the obscurity of the book in which it first appeared seems to have emboldened the forger of the spurious letters of 1852 to copy it out in a *quasi*-Shelleyan hand and sell it as an original; but there is no possibility of doubt that the composition is Shelley's. The same may be said of all the twenty-one given in this group.—H. B. F.]

LETTERS WRITTEN BEFORE THE FINAL DEPARTURE FROM ENGLAND.

LETTER I.

To Messrs. LONGMAN & Co.

Eton College, May 7th, 1809.

Gentlemen,

It is my intention to complete and publish a Romance[1] of which I have already written a large portion, before the end of July.—My object in writing it was not pecuniary, as I am independent, being the heir of a gentleman of large fortune in the county of Sussex, and prosecuting my studies as an Oppidan at Eton; from the many leisure hours I have, I have taken an opportunity of indulging my favourite propensity in writing. Should it produce any pecuniary advantages, so much the better for me, I do not expect it. If you would be so kind as to answer this, direct it to me at the Rev. George Bethell's.

[1] We need not doubt that the reference is to *Zastrozzi*. Messrs. Longman & Co's memorandum on the letter is "We shall be happy to see the MS. when finished." If they ever saw it, it would seem it did not suit them, as it was published elsewhere.

Might I likewise request the favour of secresy until the Romance is published.

I am,

Your very humble servant,

PERCY SHELLEY.

Be so good as to tell me, whether I shall send you the original manuscript when I have completed it or one corrected, &c.

LETTER II.

To MR. J. J. STOCKDALE.

Field Place, September 6th, 1810.

SIR,

I have to return you my thankful acknowledgment for the receipt of the books, which arrived as soon as I had any reason to expect,[1] the superfluity shall be balanced

[1] Mr. Garnett gives in *Macmillan's Magazine* the following account of Shelley's first acquaintance with Stockdale,—an account derived from that in *Stockdale's Budget*:—"Shelley's first introduction to Stockdale was verbal, and occurred under singularly characteristic circumstances. In the autumn of 1810 he presented himself at the publisher's place of business, and requested his aid in extricating him from a dilemma in which he had involved himself by commissioning a printer at Horsham to strike off fourteen hundred and eighty copies of a volume of poems, without having the wherewithal to discharge his account. He could hardly have expected Stockdale to do it for him, and the latter's silence is conclusive testimony that he contributed no pecuniary assistance, liberal as he doubtless was with good advice. By some means, however, the mute inglorious Aldus of Horsham was appeased, and the copies of the work transferred to Stockdale, who proceeded to advertise them, and take the other usual steps to promote their sale. An advertisement of 'Original Poetry, by Victor and Cazire,' will be found in the *Morning Chronicle* of September 18, 1810, and the assumed duality of authorship was not, like the particular names employed, fictitious. The poems were principally—Shelley thought entirely—the production of himself and a friend, and it becomes a matter of no small interest to ascertain who this friend was. It was not Mr.

as soon as I pay for some books which I shall trouble you to bind for me.

I inclose you the title-page of the Poems which as you will see, you have mistaken on account of the illegibility of my hand-writing. I have had the last proof impression from my printer this morning, and I suppose the execution of the work will not be long delayed. As soon as it possibly can, it shall reach you, and believe me, Sir, grateful for the interest you take in it.

I am, Sir,

Your obedient, humble servant,

PERCY B. SHELLEY.

Hogg, whose acquaintance Shelley had not yet made, nor Captain Medwin, or the circumstance would have been long since made public.

"A more likely coadjutor would be Harriet Grove, Shelley's cousin, and the object of his first attachment, who is said to have aided him in the composition of his first romance, 'Zastrozzi.' Indeed, 'Cazire' seems to be intended for a female name; perhaps it was adopted from some novel. However this may be, the little book had evidently been ushered into the world under an unlucky star; few and evil were its days. It had hardly been published a week when Stockdale, inspecting it with more attention than he had previously had leisure to bestow, recognised one of the pieces as an old acquaintance in the pages of M. G. Lewis, author of "The Monk." It was but too clear that Shelley's colleague, doubtless under the compulsion of the poet's impetuous solicitations for more verses, had appropriated whatever came first to hand, with slight respect for pedantic considerations of *meum* and *tuum*. Stockdale lost no time in communicating his discovery to his employer, whose mortification may be imagined, and his directions for the instant suppression of the edition anticipated. By this time, however, nearly a hundred copies had been put into circulation, so that we will not altogether resign the hope of yet recovering this interesting volume, hitherto totally unknown to, or at least unnoticed by all Shelley's biographers. Only one of the letters relating to it remains."

LETTER III.

To Mr. J. J. STOCKDALE.

Field Place, September 28th, 1810.

Sir,

I sent, before I had the pleasure of knowing you, the MS. of a poem to Messieurs Ballantyne & Co. Edinburgh; they have declined publishing it, with the inclosed letter.[1] I now offer it to you, and depend upon your honour as a gentleman for a fair price for the copyright. It will be sent to you from Edinburgh. The subject is "The Wandering Jew."[2] As to its containing Atheistical principles, I assure you, I was wholly unaware of the fact hinted at. Your good sense will point out to you the impossibility of inculcating pernicious doctrines in a poem, which as you will see is so totally abstract from any circumstances which occur under the possible view of mankind.

I am, Sir,

Your obliged and humble servant,

Percy B. Shelley.

[1] The enclosure will be found in the Appendix.

[2] See Poetical Works, Vol. IV, pp. 317 and 318.

LETTER IV.

To Mr. J. J. STOCKDALE.

University Coll., Oxford, Sunday, 11 *November*, 1810.

Sir,

I wish you to obtain for me a book which answers to the following description. It is an Hebrew essay, demonstrating that the Christian religion is false, and is mentioned in one of the numbers of the Christian Observer of last spring, by a clergyman, as an unanswerable, yet sophistical argument.[1]—If it is translated in Greek, Latin, or any of the European languages, I would thank you to send it to me.

I am, Sir, your humble servant,

Percy B. Shelley.

LETTER V.

To Mr. J. J. STOCKDALE.

University Coll., Nov. 14th, 1810.

Dear Sir,

I return you the Romance by this day's coach. I am much obligated[2] by the trouble you have taken to fit it for the press.

I am, myself, by no means a good hand at correction, but I think I have obviated the principal objections which you allege.

[1] Mr. Garnett "searched the *Observer* in vain for the notice referred to."

[2] The Romance was of course *St. Irvyne*. Mr. Garnett points out that *obligated* was "not a vulgarism in Shelley's day, any more than 'ruinated.' Both may be found in good writers of the 18th century."

Ginotti, as you will see did *not* die by Wolfstein's hand, but by the influence of that natural magic which when the secret was imparted to the latter, destroyed him.—Mountfort being a character of inferior import, I did not think it necessary to state the catastrophe of *him*, as at best it could be but uninteresting.—Eloise and Fitzeustace, are married and happy I suppose, and Megalena dies by the same means as Wolfstein.—I do not myself see any other explanation that is required.—As to the method of publishing it, I think as it is a thing which almost *mechanically* sells to circulating libraries, &c., I would wish it to be published on my *own* account.

I am surprised that you have not received the Wandering Jew, and in consequence write to Mr. Ballantyne to mention it; you will doubtlessly therefore, receive it soon.—Should you still perceive in the romance any error of flagrant incoherency, &c., it must be altered, but I should conceive it will (being wholly so abrupt) not require it.

I am your sincere humble servant,

PERCY B. SHELLEY.

Shall you make this in one or two volumes? Mr. Robinson, of Paternoster Row, published Zastrozzi.

LETTER VI.

To Mr. J. J. STOCKDALE.

University Coll., Monday, 19 *November,* 1810.

My dear Sir,

I did not think it possible that the romance would make but one small volume, it will at all events be larger than Zastrozzi. What I mean as " Rosicrucian " is the elixir of eternal life which Ginotti had obtained, Mr. Godwin's romance of St. Leon turns upon that superstition ; I enveloped it in mystery for the greater excitement of interest, and on a re-examination, you will perceive that Mountfort physically did kill Ginotti, which must appear from the latter's paleness.—

Will you have the goodness to send me Mr. Godwin's Political Justice ?

When do you suppose " St. Irvyne " will be out ? If you have not yet got the Wandering Jew from Mr. B., I will send you a MS. copy which I possess.[1]

Yours sincerely,

P. B. Shelley.

[1] Mr. Garnett notes—"It appears from the next note that this copy was sent, but it miscarried."

LETTER VII.

To Mr. J. J. STOCKDALE.

Oxford, December 2nd, 1810.

Dear Sir,

Will you, if you have got two copies of the Wandering Jew send one of them to me, as I have thought of some corrections which I wish to make,—your opinion on it will likewise much oblige me.

When do you suppose that Southey's Curse of Kehama will come out? I am curious to see it, and

When *does* St. Irvyne come out?

I shall be in London, the middle of this month, when I will do myself the pleasure of calling on you.

Yours sincerely,

P. B. Shelley.

LETTER VIII.

To Mr. J. J. STOCKDALE.

F. P.[1] *December* 18, 1810.

My dear Sir,

I saw your advertisement of the Romance, and approve of it highly; it is likely to excite curiosity.—I would thank you to send copies directed as follows:—

Miss Marshall, Horsham, Sussex.

T. Medwin, Esq., Horsham, Sussex.

T. J. Hogg, Esq., Rev.—Dayrell's, Lynnington Dayrell, Buckingham,

and six copies to myself.—In case the 'Curse of Kehama' has yet appeared, I would thank you for that

[1] *Field Place.*

likewise.—I have in preparation a novel; it is principally constructed to convey metaphysical and political opinions by way of conversation, it shall be sent to you as soon as completed, but it shall receive more correction than I trouble myself to give to wild Romance and Poetry.—

Mr. Munday of Oxford will take some Romances; I do not know whether he sends directly to you, or through the medium of some other Bookseller. I will inclose the Printer's account for your inspection in a future letter.

Dear sir,

Yours sincerely,

PERCY B. SHELLEY.

LETTER IX.

To MR. J. J. STOCKDALE.

January 11*th*, 1811.

DEAR SIR,

I would thank you to send a copy of St. Irvyne, to Miss Harriet Westbrook, 10, Chapel Street, Grosvenor Square. In the course of a fortnight I shall do myself the pleasure of calling on you: with respect to the printer's bill, I made him explain the distinction of the costs, which I hope are intelligible.

Do you find that the public are captivated by the title-page of St. Irvyne ?[1]

Your sincere

P. B. SHELLEY.

[1] Mr. Garnett's note on this letter is particularly valuable:

"This is interesting, in so far as it assists us in determining the date of Shelley's first acquaintance with Harriet Westbrook. Had he known her on December 18th, he would probably have included

LETTER X.

To Mr. J. J. STOCKDALE.

Oxford, 28th of January, 1811.

Sir,

On my arrival at Oxford my friend Mr. Hogg communicated to me the letters which passed in consequence of your misrepresentations of his character, the abuse of that confidence which he invariably reposed in you. I now, Sir, desire to know whether you mean the evasions in your first letter to Mr. Hogg, your insulting *attempt* at coolness in your second, as a method of escaping *safely* from the opprobrium naturally attached to so ungentlemanlike an abuse of confidence (to say nothing of misrepresentations) as that which my father communicated

her among those to whom he on that day desired that copies of his novel should be sent. It may then be inferred with confidence, that he first became interested in her between December 18th, and January 11th, and as there appears no trace of his having visited town during that period, his knowledge of her, when he wrote the second of these letters, was most likely merely derived from the accounts of his sisters, her schoolfellows. This accords with the assertion, made in an interesting but unpublished document in the writer's possession, that he first saw her in January, 1811. Whenever this and similar MSS. are made public, it will for the first time be clearly understood how slight was the acquaintance of Shelley with Harriet, previous to their marriage; what advantage was taken of his chivalry of sentiment, and her compliant disposition, and the inexperience of both; and how little entitled or disposed she felt herself to complain of his behaviour.

"This was the last friendly communication between Shelley and his publisher. Three days later we find him writing thus to his friend Hogg (Hogg's 'Life of Shelley,' vol. I. page 171):—

"'S—— [Stockdale] has behaved infamously to me: he has abused the confidence I reposed in him in sending him my work; and he has made very free with your character, of which he knows nothing, with my father. I shall call on S—— on my way [to Oxford], that he may explain.'

"The work alluded to was either the unlucky pamphlet which occasioned Shelley's expulsion from Oxford, or something of a very similar description."

Sir Timothy's letters to Stockdale as well as those of Hogg, will be found in the Appendix.

to me; or as a *denial* of the fact of having acted in this unprecedented, this *scandalous* manner. If the former be your intention I will compassionate your cowardice, and my friend pitying your *weakness* will take no further notice of your contemptible *attempts* at calumny. If the latter is your intention, I feel it my duty to declare, as my veracity and that of my father is thereby called in question, that I will never be satisfied, despicable as I may consider the author of that affront, until my friend has ample apology for the injury which you have *attempted* to do him. I expect an immediate, and *demand* a satisfactory letter.

Sir, I am,

Your obedient humble servant,

PERCY B. SHELLEY.

LETTER XI.

To LEIGH HUNT.

AS EDITOR OF THE EXAMINER.[1]

University College, Oxford, March 2nd, 1811.

SIR,

Permit me, although a stranger, to offer my sincerest congratulations on the occasion of that triumph so highly to be prized by men of liberality; permit me also to submit to your consideration, as one of the most fearless

[1] This letter was originally published in Mr. Lewes's article in *The Westminster Review* (No. LXIX, April, 1841), together with the letter to Keats dated the 27th of July, 1820. Like that, it was afterwards made the basis of a forgery: see note on the letter to Keats. In this case the letter had appeared meanwhile in Hogg's *Life*, and was too well known to be simply copied. The forgery was therefore not identical throughout. and was addressed to another Editor—the Editor of *The Statesman*. It appears in the spurious

enlighteners of the public mind at the present time, a scheme of mutual safety and mutual indemnification for men of public spirit and principle, which, if carried into effect, would evidently be productive of incalculable advantages. Of the scheme, the inclosed is an address to the public, the proposal for a meeting, and shall be modified according to your judgment, if you will do me the honour to consider the point.

The ultimate intention of my aim is to induce a meeting of such enlightened unprejudiced members of the community, whose independent principles expose them to evils which might thus become alleviated; and to form a methodical society which should be organized so as to resist the coalition of the enemies of liberty, which at present renders any expression of opinion on matters of policy dangerous to individuals. It has been for the want of societies of this nature that corruption has attained the height at which we behold it; nor can any of us bear in mind the very great influence which, some years since, was gained by *Illuminism*, without considering that a society of equal extent might establish *rational liberty* on as firm a basis as that which would have supported the visionary schemes of a completely equalized community.

Although perfectly unacquainted with you privately, I address you as a common friend to liberty, thinking that, in cases of this urgency and importance, etiquette ought not to stand in the way of usefulness.

My father is in Parliament, and on attaining twenty-

volume of 1852, and was reprinted in *Shelley's Early Life* (pp. 64–5) by Mr. MacCarthy, who thought it might be genuine. In my opinion this was a case in which matter as well as writing was forged; but it is conceivable that the forger copied an unpublished letter of Shelley's.

one I shall, in all probability, fill his vacant seat. On account of the responsibility to which my residence in this University subjects me, I, of course, dare not publicly avow all that I think; but the time will come when I hope that my every endeavour, insufficient as they may be, will be directed to the advancement of liberty.

Your most obedient servant,

P. B. Shelley.

LETTER XII.

To Mr. J. J. STOCKDALE.

15, *Poland Street, Oxford Street* [11 *April*, 1811].

Sir,

Will you have the goodness to inform me of the number of copies which you have sold of St. Irvyne. Circumstances may occur which will oblige me, in case of their event, to wish for my accounts suddenly, perhaps you had better make them out.

Sir,

Your obedient humble servant,

P. B. Shelley.

LETTER XIII.

To Mr. J. J. STOCKDALE.

Cwmelan, Rhayader, Radnorshire, August 1st, 1811.

Sir,

Your letter has at length reached me: the remoteness of my present situation must apologize for my apparent neglect. I am sorry to say, in answer to your requisition, that the state of my finances render immediate payment perfectly impossible. It is my intention at the earliest period in my power to do so, to discharge your account. I am aware of the imprudence of publishing a book so ill-digested as St. Irvyne; but are there no expectations on the profits of its sale?[1] My studies have since my writing it been of a more serious nature. I am at present engaged in completing a series of moral and metaphysical essays—perhaps their copy-right would be accepted in lieu of part of my debt?

Sir, I have the honour to be,

Your very humble servant,

Percy B. Shelley.

[1] It will be remembered that the edition was still unsold in 1822, so that the "profits" in 1811 were probably very difficult to find.

LETTER XIV.

To HAMILTON ROWAN.

7, Lower Sackville Street, [Dublin,] Feb. 25th, 1812.

SIR,

Although I have not the pleasure of being personally known to you, I consider the motives which actuated me in writing the inclosed[1] sufficiently introductory to authorize me in sending you some copies, and waiving ceremonials in a case where public benefit is concerned. Sir, although an Englishman, I feel for Ireland; and I have left the country in which the chance of birth placed me for the sole purpose of adding my little stock of usefulness to the fund which I hope that Ireland possesses to aid me in the unequal yet sacred combat in which she is engaged. In the course of a few days more I shall print another small pamphlet, which shall be sent to you. I have intentionally vulgarized the language of the inclosed. I have printed 1500 copies, and am now distributing them throughout Dublin.

Sir, with respect,

I am your obedient humble servant,

P. B. SHELLEY.

[1] The *Address to the Irish People.*

LETTER XV.

To T. C. MEDWIN

(HORSHAM).

Dublin, No. 17, *Grafton Street, March* 20*th*, 1812.

MY DEAR SIR,

The tumult of business and travelling has prevented my addressing you before.

I am now engaged with a literary friend in the publication of a voluminous History of Ireland,[1] of which two hundred and fifty pages are already printed, and for the completion of which, I wish to raise two hundred and fifty pounds. I could obtain undeniable security for its payment at the expiration of eighteen months. Can you tell me how I ought to proceed? *The work* will produce great profits. As you will see by the Lewes paper, I am in the midst of overwhelming engagements. My kindest regards to all your family. Be assured I shall not forget you or them.

My dear Sir,

Yours very truly,

P. B. SHELLEY.

[1] The reference is to *A Compendium of the History of Ireland, from the Earliest Period to the Reign of George I.*, by John Lawless. It has been assumed that some of this book was *written* by Shelley. It does not seem certain from the letter that he *wrote* anything intended for it: he may have done so; but equally his task may have been to raise the money and forward the publication. Even if he wrote anything towards it, there is no evidence that Lawless used it; and I find no unmistakeable trace of Shelley's hand in the book; though there are passages that he might equally well have written,—or have had in mind when he wrote some of his prose effusions of 1812–13.

LETTER XVI.

To Sir JAMES LAWRENCE,[1]

KNIGHT OF MALTA.

Lymouth, Barnstaple, Devon, August 17, 1812.

Sir,

I feel peculiar satisfaction in seizing the opportunity which your politeness places in my power, of expressing to you personally (as I may say) a high acknowledgment of my sense of your talents and principles, which, before I conceived it possible that I should ever know you, I sincerely entertained. Your "Empire of the Nairs," which I read this spring, succeeded in making me a perfect convert to its doctrines. I then retained no doubts of the evils of marriage,—Mrs. Wollstonecraft reasons too well for that; but I had been dull enough not to perceive the greatest argument against it, until developed in the "Nairs," viz. prostitution both legal and illegal.

[1] Sir James Lawrence, or the Chevalier de Laurence, as he sometimes called himself, printed this letter in *The Etonian out of Bounds* (John Brooks, 1834), Vol. I, Appendix, p. xxiii, with the following remarks :—

"My acquaintance with Shelley having originated in the 'Allegory of Love,' inserted in this volume, I take this opportunity of noticing the following passage in Captain Medwin's interesting Memoir of our lost friend (p. 43)—'That he continued to think with Plato on the subject of Wedlock, is clear from a letter addressed to Sir James Lawrence, who had sent to him his "History of the Nairs." Shelley says, "I abhor seduction as much as I adore love,"' &c.

"Here I must remark that, though I was several years younger than Shelley, when I first conceived my present opinions, and still a minor studying at Brunswick, when in 1793, the celebrated Wieland, then the patriarch of German literature, published in his Mercury, my Essay on the Nair System of Gallantry and Inheritance; yet I, however con-

I am a young man, not yet of age, and have now been married a year to a woman younger than myself. Love seems inclined to stay in the prison, and my only reason for putting him in chains, whilst convinced of the unholiness of the act, was, a knowledge that, in the present state of society, if love is not thus villainously treated, she, who is most loved, will be treated worse by a misjudging world. In short, seduction, which term could have no meaning in a rational society, has now a most tremendous one; the fictitious merit attached to chastity has made that a forerunner of the most terrible of ruins, which, in Malabar, would be a pledge of honour and homage. If there is any enormous and desolating crime, of which I should shudder to be accused, it is seduction.[1] I need not say how much I admire "Love;" and

vinced of its morality, would have scrupled to send my 'Empire of the Nairs' to any minor, however promising his talents. In fact, I knew not of Shelley's existence, before he wrote for 'Love, an Allegory;' when this poem being out of print, Mr. Hookham applied to me, and I lent him, for Shelley, my only remaining copy. Not long afterward, I received the following letter, of which Captain Medwin seems to have discovered the intended original amongst Shelley's papers.

"During the following winter, I knew not which most to admire in him, his talents, his enthusiasm, his angelic goodness, his manly character, or his youthful appearance. He showed me what he had finished of his 'Queen Mab,' and the sketch of the remainder. I frequently objected to him that he went too far, and we discussed several points. We subsequently exchanged letters, but I never saw him after Buonaparte's overthrow, in 1814, when I returned to the Continent, from which the atrocities of the Corsican had driven me."

[1] In the foregoing passage, Lawrence refers, of course, to Medwin's Memoir in *The Shelley Papers*, first published in *The Athenæum* in 1832, and then in a separate form in 1833, the year before the issue of *The Etonian out of Bounds;* and the whole passage which he considers Medwin to have taken from the intended original is—

"I abhor seduction as much as I adore love; and if I have conformed to the usages of the world on the score of matrimony, it is that disgrace always attaches to the weaker sex."

Whether this passage really stood in the draft that would seem to have come into Medwin's hands appears to me questionable enough: it may have so stood; but it is quite as likely that finding so cold a word as *admire* applied to *Love*, and not knowing that *Love* was the title of a book, Medwin saw fit to trim the phrase a little.

little as a British public seems to appreciate its merit, in never permitting it to emerge from a first edition, it is with satisfaction I find, that justice has conceded abroad what bigotry has denied at home.

I shall take the liberty of sending you any little publication I may give to the world. Mrs. S. joins with myself in hoping, if we come to London this winter, we may be favoured with the personal friendship of one whose writings we have learned to esteem.

Yours very truly,

PERCY BYSSHE SHELLEY.

LETTER XVII.

To THOMAS JEFFERSON HOGG.

Bishopgate, September, 1815.

MY DEAR FRIEND,

Your letter has lain by me for the last week, reproaching me every day. I found it on my return from a water excursion on the Thames, the particulars of which will have been recounted in another letter. The exercise and dissipation of mind attached to such an expedition have produced so favourable an effect on my health, that my habitual dejection and irritability have almost deserted me, and I can devote six hours in the day to study without difficulty. I have been engaged lately in the commencement of several literary plans, which if my present temper of mind endures, I shall probably complete in the winter. I have consequently deserted Cicero or proceed but slowly with his philosophic dialogues. I have read the Oration for the poet Archias, and am only disappointed with its brevity.

I have been induced by one of the subjects which I am now pursuing to consult Bayle. I think he betrays great obliquity of understanding and coarseness of feeling. I have also read the four first books of Lucan's Pharsalia, a poem as it appears to me of wonderful genius and transcending Virgil. Mary has finished the 5th book of the Æneid and her progress in Latin is such as to satisfy my best expectations.

The East wind—the wind of autumn—is abroad, and even now the leaves of the forest are shattered at every gust. When may we expect you? September is almost passed and October the month of your promised return is at hand, when we shall be happy to welcome you again to our fireside.

No events, as you know, disturb our tranquillity.

Adieu.

Ever affectionately yours,

PERCY B. SHELLEY.[1]

[1] This letter, which as far as I know has not appeared in print till now, represents a most important period of Shelley's life, and one of which but few letters are known. Those readers who have observed how many unfinished prose works have been conjecturally assigned to the year 1815 will know how to appreciate the statement in the text as to "the commencement of several literary plans."

LETTER XVIII.

To THOMAS LOVE PEACOCK.[1]

Hotel de Sécheron, Geneva, May 15th, 1816.

After a journey of ten days, we arrived at Geneva. The journey, like that of life, was variegated with intermingled rain and sunshine, though these many showers were to me, as you know, April showers, quickly passing away, and foretelling the calm brightness of summer.

The journey was in some respects exceedingly delightful, but the prudential considerations arising out of the necessity of preventing delay, and the continual attention to pecuniary disbursements, detract terribly from the pleasure of all travelling schemes.

* * * * * *

You live by the shores of a tranquil stream, among low and woody hills. You live in a free country, where you may act without restraint, and possess that which you possess in security; and so long as the name of

[1] This is a portion of the "very little original matter, curiously obtained," which Peacock refers to in speaking of Middleton's *Shelley and his Writings*, in *Fraser's Magazine* for June, 1858 (p. 644). In the same magazine for January, 1860, Peacock says (p. 99) that copies of two unpublished letters from Shelley to him were obtained by Middleton, who published "portions of them:" this and No. XIX are the portions. It is explained that the copies were made by Mrs. Shelley, and, being left accidentally at Marlow, "fell into unscrupulous hands." The originals were sold among the rest at the sale of Peacock's books, &c., in June, 1866. The present letter I identify by means of the extract given in the auctioneer's catalogue, and am thus enabled to insert the date. The fact that Mrs. Shelley had kept a copy of this letter accounts for the occurrence of some of the finest passages from it in the *Six Weeks' Tour*, where they will be found incorporated in Letter No I, a letter dated two days later than this one.

country and the selfish conceptions it includes shall subsist, England I am persuaded, is the most free and the most refined.

Perhaps you have chosen wisely, but if I return and follow your example, it will be no subject of regret to me that I have seen other things. Surely there is much of bad and much of good, there is much to disgust, and much to elevate, which he cannot have felt or known who has never passed the limits of his native land.

So long as man is such as he now is, the experience of which I speak will never teach him to despise the country of his birth—far otherwise, like Wordsworth, he will never know what love subsists between that and him until absence shall have made its beauty more heartfelt; our poets and our philosophers, our mountains and our lakes, the rural lanes and fields which are so especially our own, are ties which, until I become utterly senseless, can never be broken asunder.

These, and the memory of them, if I never should return, these and the affections of the mind, with which, having been once united, are[1] inseparable, will make the name of England dear to me for ever, even if I should permanently return to it no more.

But I suppose you did not pay the postage of this, expecting nothing but sentimental gossip, and I fear it will be long before I play the tourist properly. I will, however, tell you that to come to Geneva we crossed the Jura branch of the Alps.

The mere difficulties of horses, high bills, postilions, and cheating, lying *aubergistes*, you can easily conceive;

[1] There seems to be something wanting here,—perhaps the word *we* before *are*; but I am not sure that that is the right reading, and therefore leave the text as Middleton left it.

fill up that part of the picture according to your own experience, and it cannot fail to resemble.

The mountains of Jura exhibit scenery of wonderful sublimity. Pine forests of impenetrable thickness, and untrodden, nay, inaccessible expanse, spreading on every side. Sometimes descending they follow the route into the valleys clothing the precipitous rocks, and struggling with knotted roots between the most barren clefts. Sometimes the road winds high into the regions of frost, and there these forests become scattered, and loaded with snow.

The trees in these regions are incredibly large, and stand in scattered clumps over the white wilderness. Never was scene more awfully desolate than that which we passed on the evening of our last day's journey.

The natural silence of that uninhabited desert contrasted strangely with the voices of the people who conducted us, for it was necessary in this part of the mountain to take a number of persons, who should assist the horses to force the chaise through the snow, and prevent it from falling down the precipice.

We are now at Geneva, where, or in the neighbourhood, we shall remain probably until the autumn. I may return in a fortnight or three weeks, to attend to the last exertions which L——[1] is to make for the settlement of my affairs; of course I shall then see you; in the meantime it will interest me to hear all that you have to tell of yourself.

* * * * * *

P. B. SHELLEY.

[1] Longdill, Shelley's solicitor, I presume.

LETTER XIX.

To THOMAS LOVE PEACOCK.[1]

Geneva, July 17th, 1816.

MY opinion of turning to one spot of earth and calling it our home, and of the excellencies and usefulness of the sentiments arising out of this attachment, has at length produced in me the resolution of acquiring this possession.

You are the only man who has sufficient regard for me to take an interest in the fulfilment of this design, and whose tastes conform sufficiently to mine to engage me to confide the execution of it to your discretion.

I do not trouble you with apologies for giving you this commission. I require only rural exertions, walks, and circuitous wanderings, some slight negotiations about the letting of a house—the superintendence of a disorderly garden, some palings to be mended, some books to be removed and set up.

I wish you would get all my books and all my furniture from Bishopgate, and all other effects appertaining to me. I have written to * * * to secure all that belongs to me there to you. I have written also to L—— to give up possession of the house on the third of August.

When you have possessed yourself of all my affairs, I wish you to look out for a home for me and Mary and

[1] This is the complement of the diary of Shelley's excursion with Byron round the Lake of Geneva. See notes at pages 160 and 185 of Vol. II, and the note on the preceding letter (No. XVIII).

William, and the kitten who is now *en pension*. I wish you to get an unfurnished house, with as good a garden as may be, near Windsor Forest, and take a lease of it for fourteen or twenty-one years. The house must not be too small. I wish the situation to resemble as nearly as possible that of Bishopgate, and should think that Sunning Hill or Winkfield Plain, or the neighbourhood of Virginia Waters, would afford some possibilities.

Houses are now exceedingly cheap and plentiful; but I entrust the whole of this affair entirely to your own discretion.

I shall hear from you of course, as to what you have done on this subject, and shall not delay to remit you whatever expenses you may find it necessary to incur. Perhaps, however, you had better sell the useless part of the Bishopgate furniture—I mean those odious curtains, &c.

Will you write to L—— to tell him that you are authorized on my part to go over the inventory with Lady L——'s people on the third of August, if they please, and to make whatever arrangements may be requisite. I should be content with the Bishopgate house, dear as it is, if Lady L—— would make the sale of it a post obit transaction. I merely suggest this, that if you see any possibility of proposing such an arrangement with effect, you might do it.

My present intention is to return to England, and to make that most excellent of nations my perpetual resting place. I think it is extremely probable that we shall return next spring—perhaps before, perhaps after, but certainly we shall return.

On the motives and on the consequences of this journey, I reserve much explanation for some future winter walk or summer expedition. This much alone is certain, that before we return we shall have seen, and felt, and heard, a multiplicity of things which will haunt our talk and make us a little better worth knowing than we were before our departure.

If possible, we think of descending the Danube in a boat, of visiting Constantinople and Athens, then Rome and the Tuscan cities, and returning by the south of France, always following great rivers. The Danube, the Po, the Rhone, and the Garonne; rivers are not like roads, the work of the hands of man; they imitate mind, which wanders at will over pathless deserts, and flows through nature's loveliest recesses, which are inaccessible to anything besides. They have the viler advantage also of affording a cheaper mode of conveyance.

This eastern scheme is one which has just seized on our imaginations. I fear that the detail of execution will destroy it, as all other wild and beautiful visions; but at all events you will hear from us wherever we are, and to whatever adventures destiny enforces us.

Tell me in return all English news. What has become of my poem?[1] I hope it has already sheltered itself in the bosom of its mother, Oblivion, from whose embraces no one could have been so barbarous as to tear it except me.

Tell me of the political state of England. Its literature, of which when I speak Coleridge is in my thoughts;—yourself, lastly your own employments, your historical labours.

I had written thus far when your letter to Mary dated the 8th, arrived. What you say of Bishopgate of course modifies that part of this letter which relates to

[1] Presumably *Alastor*.

it. I confess I did not learn the destined ruin without some pain, but it is well for me perhaps that a situation requiring so large an expense should be placed beyond our hopes.

You must shelter my roofless Penates, dedicate some new temple to them, and perform the functions of a priest in my absence. They are innocent deities, and their worship neither sanguinary nor absurd.

Leave Mammon and Jehovah to those who delight in wickedness and slavery—their altars are stained with blood, or polluted with gold, the price of blood. But the shrines of the Penates are good wood fires, or window frames intertwined with creeping plants; their hymns are the purring of kittens, the hissing of kettles; the long talks over the past and dead; the laugh of children; the warm wind of summer filling the quiet house, and the pelting storm of winter struggling in vain for entrance. In talking of the Penates, will you not liken me to Julius Cæsar dedicating a temple to Liberty?

As I have said in the former part of my letter, I trust entirely to your discretion on the subject of a house. Certainly the Forest engages my preference, because of the sylvan nature of the place, and the beasts with which it is filled. But I am not insensible to the beauties of the Thames, and any extraordinary eligibility of situation you mention in your letter would overbalance our habitual affection for the neighbourhood of Bishopgate.

Its proximity to the spot you have chosen is an argument with us in favour of the Thames. Recollect, however, we are now choosing a fixed, settled, eternal home, and as such its internal qualities will affect us more constantly than those which consist in the surrounding scenery, which whatever it may be at first, will shortly be no more than the colours with which our own habits shall invest it.

I am glad that circumstances do not permit the choice to be my own. I shall abide by yours as others abide by the necessity of their birth.

*　　*　　*　　*　　*　　*

P. B. S.

LETTER XX.

APPARENTLY TO MR. MURRAY.[1]

Bath, No. 5 Abbey Church Yard, Oct. 2, 1816.

DEAR SIR,

Be so kind as to address the proofs of Childe Harold, when you print it, to me according to the above address. I shall remain here probably during the whole winter, and you may depend on no attention being spared on my part to render the proofs as correct as possible.

I imagine that Lord Byron is anxious that the poem should be committed to the press as soon as possible; the time of publication of course depends upon your own discretion.—For myself, I cannot but confess the anxiety I feel that the public should have an early opportunity of confirming—I will not say by a more extensive; but by a profounder species of approbation—the superior merit which private judgment has already assigned to it.

I have the honour to be, Dear Sir,

Your very obliged obedient servant,

PERCY B. SHELLEY.

[1] The outer leaf, bearing the address, has been detached from the original, formerly in the Addington Collection, and now in that of Mr. C. W. Frederickson, of New York, who has kindly furnished me with a copy. I have examined the original, and can answer for its genuineness.

LETTER XXI.

To Mr. and Mrs. LEIGH HUNT.

Great Marlow, 29th June, 1817.

My dear Friends,

I performed my promise, and arrived here the night after I set off. Everybody up to this minute has been and continues well. I ought to have written yesterday, for to-day, I know not how, I have so constant a pain in my side, and such a depression of strength and spirits, as to make my holding the pen whilst I write to you an almost intolerable exertion. This, you know, with me is transitory. Do not mention that I am unwell to your nephew; for the advocate of a new system of diet is held bound to be invulnerable by disease, in the same manner as the sectaries of a new system of religion are held to be more moral than other people, or as a reformed parliament must at least be assumed as the remedy of all political evils. No one will change the diet, adopt the religion, or reform the parliament else.

Well, I am very anxious to hear how you get on, and I intreat Marianne to excite Hunt not to delay a minute in writing the necessary letters, and in informing me of the result. Kings are only to be approached through their ministers; who indeed as Marianne shall know to her cost, if she don't take care, are responsible not only for all their commissions, but, a more dreadful responsibility, for all their *omissions.* And I know not who has a right to the title of king, if not according to the Stoics, he to whom the King of kings had delegated the prerogative of lord of the creation.

Let me know how Henry gets on, and make my best respects to your brother and Mrs. Hunt. Adieu.

Always most affectionately yours,

P. B. S.

APPENDIX TO PROSE WORKS,

VOLS. I, II, AND III.

CONTENTS OF THE APPENDIX.

APPENDIX.

I.

Letter to the Editor of "The Morning Chronicle," on the Candidature of Lord Grenville for the Chancellorship of the University of Oxford.[1]

Sir,—It has been truly said, that a silly friend is frequently more injurious than a decided enemy. This observation recurred to me while reading in the Courier, a letter from an injudicious opponent of Lord Grenville, in which the attention of the University of Oxford is called to the personal pretensions of the three Candidates, for the vacant Chancellorship. Now, it is only by keeping out of sight the personal inferiority of the Duke of Beaufort and Lord Eldon, by the artful introduction of extraneous

[1] Medwin, in his Life of Shelley (Vol. I, p. 146), says that Shelley "was by no means in good odour with the authorities of the college, from the side he took in the election of Lord Grenville, as chancellor, against his competitor, a member of the University." He adds, "Plain and loud was the avowal of his sentiments, nor were they confined to words, for he published, I think in the *Morning Chronicle*, under the signature of A Master of Arts of Oxford, a letter advocating the claims of Lord Grenville. . ." At the bottom of this puddle of inaccuracies one would look to find a basis of solid fact. Mr. MacCarthy (*Shelley's Early Life*, p. 24) found in *The Morning Chronicle* for the 15th of November, 1809, a date long before Shelley went to Oxford, a letter on this subject signed "A. M. Oxon." There is some reason to think this letter was written by Sir Timothy Shelley, with his son's assistance. It is therefore included in the Appendix to Shelley's Prose Works.

topics, that any Member of the Convocation can have the hardihood to propose either of them in opposition to Lord Grenville.

That Lord Eldon has been a successful man—that he is a moral man and a prudent man nobody will deny, but that he is distinguished by the talents of his predecessors on the Woolsack, that he is celebrated as a scholar or as a statesman, that he possesses a large and enlightened mind will be asserted by few, who are not in expectation of the good things he has to give, and believed by none, who are not, through his favour, in the actual enjoyment of a snug living, a comfortable commissionership of bankrupts, or a warm mastership in Chancery. By the bye his Lordship very opportunely, a short time since, made the nephew of the Master of one of the most numerous Colleges a Commissioner of Bankrupts. In fact, Lord Eldon's life is chiefly remarkable for an inordinate love of the *profits* of place. He has never shewn himself animated with a laudable political ambition. He has been seen Chancellor under Mr. Pitt's Administration, Chancellor under Mr. Addington's, still Chancellor when Mr. Pitt turned out Mr. Addington, now Chancellor with Mr. Perceval, and ready to have been Chancellor under Lords Grey and Grenville, had they listened to the proposal lately, so impudently made to them ; to enable the rump of the No Popery Junta to continue in office—Lord Eldon deprived of the seals would be personally as insignificant as the Duke of Beaufort.

As to his Grace, it would be unfair towards him not to state, that from some supposed *littlenesses*, which are said to deform Lord Eldon's character, he is understood to be entirely free. He is admitted to be an hospitable, correct, and generally respectable man, and if the question were, whether he should be appointed Chairman of Quarter Sessions in one of his dependent Counties, Monmouth or Gloucester, it might perhaps, be thought, that his mediocrity of understanding did not render him incompetent for such a situation. But as Chancellor of Oxford—to preside in the seat of learning, I do assert, that he has no qualification whatever. Is his rank to carry it? If his Dukedom is to recommend him, why does not the University present its honours to a Royal Duke—the Duke of York, for instance, has now leisure to attend to the concerns of *Alma mater*. In truth, the Duke of Beaufort would not have been named, if his influence in a certain House had not made him a powerful patron. —Believe me, Sir, my brethren here are not inattentive to the disposition of Church patronage, looking in vain for superior merit in those who are put over their heads, they have searched for the recommendations they have been fortunate enough to procure. In this inquiry they have discovered, that the Duke of Beaufort is one of the few whose wishes upon such subjects are in the nature of commands. They have seen him make Dr. Luxmore a Bishop of a valuable See, and before his Lordship was enthroned, they saw him obtain for Mr. Talbot, who married a daughter of the Duke; and who is a very young man, the rich Deanery of Salisbury—besides, in other departments of the State, he is accounted lucky in obtaining for his friends the most desirable appointments. But these sordid considerations, however they may have influenced persons who have proposed the Duke, will, I trust, have no effect upon the great body of electors, who ought to have, and I am convinced, will have, no other views in the choice they may make, than the honour of their University, and the interests of learning.

Lord Grenville between his pigmy rivals rises with a colossal grandeur of character—with all the private worth that belongs to both of his competitors, and without the infirmities that are imputed to one of them, he unites the accomplished scholar with the eminent statesman. As a parliamentary orator, he is considered by a celebrated author, whose works now lie before me, since the extinction of the great luminary, Mr. Fox, without an equal. But Lord Grenville not only possesses appropriate excellence for the Chair of an University, but is also particularly recommended to the admiration of the country by his manly political career. Twice has he given up place and power, and lately refused them, solely upon *public principle.* These are facts which confer real dignity, and constitute a great man. In these times, when independence is so rare, and when place is generally sought alone for the *profit* it produces, it is the duty of those with whom the expression of any part of the national voice is entrusted, to honour with all the distinction they can bestow, him who is almost a solitary exception to the opprobrium cast upon public men; a contrary course of conduct must induce a suspicion, especially if it be seen on the present occasion, that if public virtue be seldom found in the Statesmen of the present day, it is because the public itself is degraded.

I am, Sir, your obedient servant,

A. M. OXON.

Oxford, Nov. 13, 1809.[1]

P. S.—I am happy to say, that the Colleges most in repute among us, Christ Church, Brazenose, and Oriel, are decidedly in favour of Lord Grenville.

[1] Misprinted "1808" in the newspaper.

II.

SHELLEY'S SPEECH IN FISHAMBLE STREET THEATRE, DUBLIN, ON THE 28TH OF FEBRUARY, 1812.[1]

From *The Freeman's Journal*, Dublin, 29 February, 1812, and other papers.

On the fifth[2] resolution being proposed, Mr. Shelley, an English gentleman (very young), the son of a Member of Parliament, rose to address the meeting. He was received with great kindness, and declared that the greatest misery this country endured was the Union Law, the Penal Code, and the state of the representation. He drew a lively picture of the misery of the country, which he attributed to the unfortunate Act of Legislative Union.

[1] Mr. MacCarthy (*Shelley's Early Life*, p. 226) records that on the 28th of February, 1812, the poet attended an Aggregate Meeting of the Catholics of Ireland, at the Theatre in Fishamble Street, Dublin, and spoke for an hour. The precise words of the speech we shall probably never recover; but in their absence we cannot do better than repeat the three reports of it which Mr. MacCarthy's indefatigable industry has disinterred from the contemporary newspaper press. Of the first, Mr. MacCarthy says:

"This brief report appeared on the morning after the meeting in *The Freeman's Journal* of Saturday, Feb. 29th, 1812. It was repeated in *The Hibernian Journal, or Daily Chronicle of Liberty*, Dublin, Monday, March 2nd, 1812. And again in a more accessible shape in *Walker's Hibernian Magazine* for February, 1812, p. 83."

[2] Mr. MacCarthy says we should read *sixth*. The resolution was as follows:

"RESOLVED, That the grateful thanks of this Meeting are due, and hereby returned to Lord Glentworth, the Right Hon. Maurice Fitzgerald, and the other DISTINGUISHED PROTESTANTS who have this day honoured us with their presence."

From *The Dublin Evening Post*, Saturday, 29 February, 1812.

Mr. Shelley requested a hearing. He was an Englishman, and when he reflected on *the crimes committed by his nation on Ireland,* he could not but blush for his countrymen, did he not know that arbitrary power never failed to corrupt the heart of man. (Loud applause for several minutes.)

He had come to Ireland for the sole purpose of interesting himself in her misfortunes. He was deeply impressed with a sense of the evils which Ireland endured, and he considered them to be truly ascribed to the fatal effects of the legislative union with Great Britain.

He walked through the streets, and he saw the *fane of liberty converted into a temple of Mammon.* (Loud applause.) He beheld beggary and famine in the country, and he could lay his hand on his heart and say that the cause of such sights was the union with Great Britain. (Hear, hear.) He was resolved to do his utmost to promote a Repeal of the Union. Catholic Emancipation would do a great deal towards the amelioration of the condition of the people, but he was convinced that the Repeal of the Union was of more importance. He considered that the victims whose members were vibrating on gibbets were driven to the commission of the crimes which they expiated by their lives by the effects of the Union.

From *Saunders's News Letter*, Saturday, 29 February, 1812, and *The Patriot*, 2 March, 1812.

Mr. Shelley then addressed the Chair. He hoped he should not be accounted a transgressor on the time of the meeting. He felt inadequate to the task he had undertaken, but he hoped the feelings which urged him forward would plead his pardon. He was an Englishman; when he reflected on the outrages that his countrymen had committed here for the last twenty years he confessed that he blushed for them. He had come to Ireland for the sole purpose of interesting himself in the misfortunes of this country, and impressed with a full conviction of the necessity of Catholic Emancipation, and of the baneful effects which the union with Great Britain had entailed upon Ireland. He had walked through the fields of the country and the streets of the city, and he had in both seen the miserable effects of that fatal step. He had seen that edifice which ought to have been the fane of their liberties converted to a temple of Mammon. Many of the crimes which are daily committed he could not avoid attributing to the effect of that measure, which had thrown numbers of people out of the employment they had in manufacture, and induced them to commit acts of the greatest desperation for the support of their existence.

He could not imagine that the religious opinion of a man should exclude him from the rights of society. The original founder of our religion taught no such doctrine. Equality in this respect was general in the American States, and why not here? Did a change of place change the nature of man? He would beg those in power to recollect the French Revolution: the suddenness, the violence with which it burst forth, and the causes which gave rise to it.

Both the measures of Emancipation and a Repeal of the Union should meet his decided support, but he hoped many years would not pass over his head when he would make himself conspicuous at least by his zeal for them.[1]

III.

ARTICLE FROM "THE WEEKLY MESSENGER," DUBLIN, SATURDAY, 7 MARCH, 1812, RELATING TO SHELLEY'S SPEECH, AND HEADED "PIERCE BYSHE SHELLY, ESQ."[2]

The highly interesting appearance of this young gentleman at the late Aggregate Meeting of the Catholics of Ireland, has naturally excited a spirit of enquiry, as to his objects and views, in coming forward at *such* a meeting; and the publications which he has circulated with such uncommon industry, through the Metropolis, has set curiosity on the wing to ascertain who he is, from whence he comes, and what his pretensions are to the confidence he solicits, and the character he assumes. To those who have read the productions we have alluded to, we need bring forward no evidence of the cultivation of his mind—the benignity of his principles—or the peculiar fascination with which he seems able to recommend them.

Of this gentleman's family we can say but little, but we can set down what we have heard from respectable authority. That his father is a member of the Imperial Parliament, and that this young gentleman, whom we

[1] Mr. MacCarthy says that in an unpublished letter, dated "17, Grafton Street, Dublin, March 14, 1812." Shelley writes thus :—

"My speech was misinterpreted. I spoke for more than an hour. The hisses with which they greeted me when I spoke of *religion*, though in terms of respect, were mixed with applause when I avowed my mission. The newspapers have only noted that which did not excite disapprobation."

[2] Given by Mr. MacCarthy as "the first public notice of Shelley."

have seen, is the *immediate* heir of one of the *first* fortunes in England. Of his principles and his manners we can say more, because we can collect from conversation, as well as from reading, that he seems devoted to the propagation of those divine and Christian feelings which purify the human heart, give shelter to the poor, and consolation to the unfortunate. That he is the *bold* and *intrepid* advocate of those principles which are calculated to give energy to truth, and to depose from their guilty eminence the bad and vicious passions of a corrupt community;—that a universality of charity is *his* object, and a perfectibility of human society *his* end, which cannot be attained by the *conflicting* dogmas of religious sects, *each* priding itself on the extinction of the *other*, and *all* existing by the mutual misfortunes which flow from polemical warfare. The principles of this young gentleman embrace *all* sects and all persuasions. His doctrines, *political* and *religious*, may be accommodated to *all*; every friend to true Christianity will be his religious friend, and every enemy to the liberties of Ireland will be his *political* enemy. The weapons he wields are those of reason, and the most *social benevolence.* He deprecates violence in the accomplishment of his views, and relies upon the mild and merciful spirit of toleration for the completion of all his designs, and the consummation of all his wishes. To the religious bigot such a *missionary of truth* is a formidable opponent, by the political monopolist he will be considered the child of Chimera, the creature of fancy, an imaginary legislator who presumes to make laws without reflecting upon his *materials*, and despises those considerations which have baffled the hopes of the most philanthropic and the efforts of the most wise. It is true. human nature may be too depraved for such a hand as

Mr. Shelly's to form to anything that is good, or liberal, or beneficent. Let him but take down *one* of the rotten pillars by which society is *now* propped, and substitute the purity of his own principles, and Mr. Shelly shall have done a great and lasting service to human nature. To this gentleman Ireland is much indebted, for selecting *her* as the theatre of his first attempts in this holy work of human regeneration; the Catholics of Ireland should listen to him with respect, because they will find that an enlightened Englishman has interposed between the treason of their own countrymen and the almost conquered spirit of their country; that Mr. Shelly has come to Ireland to demonstrate in his person that there are hearts in his own country not rendered callous by six hundred years of injustice; and that the genius of freedom, which has communicated comfort and content to the cottage of the Englishman, has found its way to the humble roof of the Irish peasant, and promises by its presence to dissipate the sorrows of past ages, to obliterate the remembrance of persecution, and close the long and wearisome scene of centuries of human depression. We extract from Mr. Shelly's last production, which he calls "PROPOSALS FOR AN ASSOCIATION, &c."[1]

* * * * * *

We have but one word more to add. Mr. Shelly, commiserating the sufferings of our distinguished countryman Mr. Finerty, whose exertions in the cause of political freedom he much admired, wrote a very beautiful poem,[2]

[1] It is not necessary to give the extract. The whole pamphlet is given in Vol. I.

[2] Mr. MacCarthy's volume, *Shelley's Early Life*, deals very minutely with the evidence of Shelley's having written such a poem and put the proceeds of its sale to such a purpose. Peter Finnerty (not Finerty) was one of the victims of the libel prosecutions of the early part of this century; and there is much reason for believing that Shelley wrote, and

the profits of which we understand, from *undoubted* authority, Mr. Shelly remitted to Mr. Finerty; we have heard they amounted to nearly an hundred pounds. This fact speaks a volume in favour of our new friend.

IV.

LETTER OF "AN ENGLISHMAN" TO THE EDITOR OF "THE DUBLIN JOURNAL," RELATING TO SHELLEY'S SPEECH.[1]

Saturday, March 7th, 1812.

SIR,

Our public meetings now-a-days, instead of exhibiting the deliberations of men of acknowledged wisdom and experience, resemble mere debating societies, where unfledged candidates for national distinction rant out a few trite and commonplace observations with as much exultation and self-applause as if they possessed the talents or eloquence of a Saurin or a Burke. This remark is particularly applicable to almost the whole of the meetings which have been assembled within the last twelve months by the Catholics; at which young gentlemen of this description have constantly intruded themselves upon the public notice, and by the unseasonable and injudicious violence of their language, have not a little prejudiced the cause they attempted to support. Curiosity and the expected gratification of hearing a display of oratory by some of the leading members of the Catholic body led

published for Finnerty's benefit, a small book, *A Poetical Essay on the Existing State of Things*, whereof no copy is known to be extant.

[1] This is another result of Mr. MacCarthy's researches, and helps somewhat in forming a notion of the speech.

me on Friday, for the first time, to the Aggregate Meeting in Fishamble Street. Being rather late I missed the orations of Mr. Connell [*sic*] and the leading orators, and only heard a dry monotonous effusion from Counsellor ——, and, to me, a most disgusting harangue from a stripling, with whom I am unacquainted, but who, I am sorry to say, styled himself my countryman—an Englishman. This young gentleman, after stating that he had been only a fortnight in Ireland, expatiated on the miseries which this country endured in consequence of its connexion with his own, and asserted (from the knowledge, I presume, which his peculiar sagacity enabled him to acquire in so short a period) that its cities were depopulated, its fields laid waste, and its inhabitants degraded and enslaved; and all this by its union with England. If it revolted against my principles, Mr. Editor, to hear such language from one of my own countrymen, you will readily conceive that my disgust was infinitely heightened to observe with what transport the invectives of this renegade Englishman against his native country were *hailed* by the assembly he addressed. Joy beamed in every countenance and rapture glistened in every eye at the aggravated detail: the delirium of ecstasy got the better of prudential control; the veil was for a moment withdrawn. I thought I saw the *purpose*, in spite of the *pretence*, written in legible characters in each of their faces, and though emancipation *alone* flowed from the tongue, separation and ascendancy were rooted in the heart.

As for the young gentleman alluded to, I congratulate the Catholics of Ireland on the acquisition of so *patriotic* and *enlightened* an advocate; and England, I dare say, will spare him without regret. I must, however, remark that as the love of his country is one of the strongest principles implanted in the breast of man by his Maker, and as the affections are more ardent in youth than in maturer years, that this young gentleman should at so early an age have overcome the strongest impulses of nature, seems to me a complete refutation of the hitherto supposed infallible maxim that *Nemo fuit repente turpissimus.*

AN ENGLISHMAN.

V.

LETTER OF "A DISSENTER" TO THE EDITOR OF "THE DUBLIN JOURNAL," RELATING TO SHELLEY'S SPEECH AND "PROPOSALS FOR AN ASSOCIATION."[1]

Saturday, March 21st, 1812.

SIR,

I question the propriety of contributing to the public introduction of those literary nondescripts and political adventurers who figure occasionally on the Catholic stage. Men there are who, preferring distinction procured by infamy to inglorious obscurity, do not hesitate at the violation of any law, civil or sacred, in order to attain it: swimming at the surface by their own putrescence, these merit not our attention; silence and contempt are all we owe to the individual whose sole ambition is to become the idol of a mob, and who like Herostratus, could fire a temple the wonder of the world, merely for the sake of

[1] This also was unearthed by Mr. MacCarthy, from *Faulkner's Dublin Journal* (21 March, 1812).

transmitting to posterity a name which might otherwise rot.

Through the medium of your paper, however, the attention of the public has been called to another of the Catholic performers, and a late worthy correspondent has obliged you with some deserved and judicious animadversions upon his début. In a weekly paper, the appearance of this "very interesting" personage is announced with as much parade as if Dogberry, Verges, and the Watch graced the scene. "Oh, a stool and a cushion for the sexton." "An two men ride of a horse, one must ride behind." "The ewe that will not hear her lamb when it baes, will never answer a calf when he bleats." His panegyrist has described him with the minuteness of an interested biographer; the prospects and the talents of the "stranger" and his generosity, his amazing generosity to an incarcerated individual whose crime was not loyalty, are made the subjects of commendation; and in illustration of the excellence of this modern Apollonius, who travels but for the improvement of the human race, a specimen of his composition is printed and circulated. I do not find that he, like the Cappadocian, has laid claims to miraculous powers, but he is a poet, and his very prose is so full of poetic fire, so vivid, so redundant with words, which, like those often used by a celebrated female novelist, were probably never intended to represent any specific idea—one is tempted to think he must now and then compose under the influence of the moon. Now, sir, though I really can neither "make occasions," nor "improve those that offer," for perusing the whole of a production which is scarcely to be paralleled in the ravings of Diderot, the rhapsodies of Rousseau, or the soft sentimental stuff of the Prebend of York, I have read enough of this specimen to confirm me in the old-fashioned but honest and conscientious prejudices which it is evidently the wish of its author to eradicate. He proposes to "exterminate the eyeless monster Bigotry," and "make the teeth of the palsied beldame Superstition chatter." This, which is doubtless designed as an allegorical allusion to the Romish Church, must, if actually accomplished, be its death; and when "the teeth of the beldame chatter," her brats may go beg; he proposes to make us all "kneel at the altar of the common God," and to "hang upon that altar the garland of devotion," figures which Deism borrows from the old Heathen mythology, which are mere poetic smoke, and resemble most the steams of a perfumer's shop, or the smock of an Eastern bride smelling of "myrrh, aloes, and cassia."

In a style less elevated and Heliconian this modern annihilator of moral and political evil roundly proposes an association throughout Ireland for the attainment of "Catholic Emancipation and the repeal of the Union Act." That the abolition of the aristocracy of the country is a feature in his picture of Utopian amelioration, though, for reasons obvious, but lightly touched, and as yet kept in the shade, is evident from the manner and connexion in which he disapproves "of other distinctions than those of virtue and talent"—a disapproval specious indeed, worthy the head of him who expects a new Jerusalem on earth, or seeks divine perfection among created beings. But ignorant, shamefully ignorant, must they be of human nature, and of the awful events which have taken place in Europe of late years, who can be gulled by such a pretext now. It is "*Vox èt prœterca nihil,*" the very cant of republicans. I would suspect the cause which recommends itself by such a pretext, as I would the chastity of a wanton assuming the dress of a nun—the loyalty of a friar or a presbyter armed with a pike, or the honesty of a beggar with a casquet of jewels. "No distinctions but those of virtue and talent" was the pretext of Monsieur Egalité, of Legendre the butcher, of the bloody Roland, and of that monster in human shape Marat, who proposed, and was applauded by a banditti of ruffians calling themselves a National Convention for professing, the cutting off one hundred and fifty thousand heads as a sovereign specific for the disorders of France.

It is said in a book to whose pages the "very interesting" Philanthropist seems not to be a stranger, that "burning lips and a wicked heart" are "like a potsherd covered with silver;" the man I mean has himself quoted the phrase "a tree is known by its fruits," and if I mistake not, such expressions warrant the opinion that from certain noisy but worthless characters nothing but what is noxious can be expected. Men whose private life and known habits make them the refuse of the political, and the terror or the stain of the moral world, would make but sorry reformers of public abuse. I need not whisper "whence I steal the waters" when I say, "Physician, heal thyself." It is usual to commend the Catholic body for their loyalty; that they are generally loyal is sometimes acknowledged even by those who, in their official situations, reprobate the proceedings of the Catholic Committee. That there are loyal Catholics, both lay and clerical, is, I believe, probable, but it would puzzle a conjuror to reconcile with loyalty, as it is by loyalists understood, some of the Catholic measures.[1]

* * * * * *

[1] The omitted portion does not relate to Shelley.

Leaving this "interesting stranger" to amuse the admirers of the Catholic Drama by puffing at "the meteors" of his own creation, "which play over the loathsome pool" of his own pantomimic invention, I will ask you, sir, what has the Protestant cause, and what has that consummation of political wisdom the British constitution, to fear from a party which has to shelter in the shade of such paltry and unmeaning bombast? The Philanthropist talks bigly of "blossoms to be matured by the summer sun of improved intellect and progressive virtue,"—but if his root be rotten his blossoms will be dust. . . . From such corrections and such apologists, and from the machinations of all pseudo-philanthropists, may the good Lord deliver us!

I have the honour to be, Sir,

Yours, &c.,

A DISSENTER.

VI.

Official Papers connected with Shelley's Visit to Ireland.[1]

1. Letter from Harriet Shelley to Eliza Hitchener, seized at Holyhead among copies of the Irish Pamphlets.
2. Letter from the Surveyor of Customs, Holyhead, to the Home Secretary, enclosing Harriet's letter.
3. Two Letters from the Post Office Agent at Holyhead to the Secretary of the Post Office.
4. Letter from the Postmaster General to the Secretary of the Post Office.

1. *Letter from Harriet Shelley to Eliza Hitchener.*[2]

Dublin, March 18th [1812.]

My dear Portia,

As Percy has sent you such a large Box so full of inflammable matter, I think I may be allowed to send a little but not such a nature as his. I sent you two letters in a newspaper, which I hope you received safe from the intrusion of Post masters. I sent one of the Pamphlets to my Father in a newspaper, which was opened and charged, but which was very trifling when compared to what you and Godwin paid.

I believe I have mentioned a new acquaintance of

[1] These have appeared in *Shelley's Early Life.*

[2] The original letter and that from the Surveyor of Customs in which it was forwarded to the Home Secretary, are in the Public Record Office, marked "Ireland, January to April, 1812, No. 655." One of the three known copies of the Broadside *Declaration of Rights* is in these papers. Miss Hitchener is the lady who figures in Hogg's Life of Shelley as "the brown demon."

ours, a Mrs. Nugent, who is sitting in the room now and talking to Percy about Virtue. You see how little I stand upon ceremony. I have seen her but twice before, and I find her a very greeable, sensible woman. She has felt most severely the miseries of her country in which she has been a very active member. She visited all the Prisons in the time of the Rebellion to exhort the people to have courage and hope. She says it was a most dreadful task; but it was her duty, and she would not shrink from the performance of it. This excellent woman, with all her notions of Philanthropy and justice, is obliged to work for her subsistence—to work in a shop which is a furrier's; there she is every day confined to her needle. Is it not a thousand pities that such a woman should be so dependent upon others? She has visited us this evening for about three hours, and is now returned home. The evening is the only time she can get out in the week; but Sunday is her own, and then we are to see her. She told Percy that her country was her only love, when he asked her if she was married. She called herself *Mrs.* I suppose on account of her age, as she looks rather old for a *Miss.* She has never been out of her own country, and has no wish to leave it.

This is St. Patrick's night, and the Irish always get very tipsy on such a night as this. The Horse Guards are pacing the streets and will be so all the night, so fearful are they of disturbances, the poor people being very much that way inclined, as Provisions are very scarce in the southern counties. Poor Irish People, how much I feel for them. Do you know, such is their ignorance that when there is a drawing-room held they go from some distance to see the people who keep them starving to get their luxuries; they will crowd round the state carriages in great glee to see those within who have stripped them of their rights, and who wantonly revel in a profusion of ill-gotten luxury whilst so many of those harmless people are wanting Bread for their wives and children. What a spectacle! People talk of the fiery spirit of these distressed creatures, but that spirit is very much broken and ground down by the oppressors of this poor country. I may with truth say there are more Beggars in this city than any other in the world. They are so poor they have hardly a rag to cover their naked limbs, and such is their passion for drink that when you relieve them one day you see them in the same deplorable situation the next. Poor creatures, they live more on whiskey than anything, for meat is so dear they cannot afford to purchase any. If they had the means I do not know that they would, whiskey being so much cheaper and to their palates so much more desirable. Yet how often do we hear people say that Poverty is no evil. I think if they had experienced it they would soon alter their tone. To my idea it is the worst of all evils, as the miseries that flow from it are certainly very great; the many crimes we hear of daily are the consequences of Poverty, and that, to a very great degree; I think, the Laws are extremely unjust—they condemn a person to Death for stealing 13 shillings and 4 pence.

Disperse the Declarations. Percy says the farmers are very fond of having something posted upon their walls.

Percy has sent you all his Pamphlets with the Declaration of Rights, which you will disperse to advantage. He has not many of his first Address, having taken great pains to circulate them through this city.

All thoughts of an Association are given up as impracticable. We shall leave this noisy town on the 7th of April, unless the Habeas Corpus Act should be suspended, and then we shall be obliged to leave here *as soon as possible.* Adieu.

2. *Letter from the Surveyor of Customs, Holyhead, to the Home Secretary, enclosing Harriet's letter.*

Confidential.

Holyhead, March 30th, 1812.

SIR,

The important contents of the enclosed letter, with a Pamphlet and a Declaration of rights (forming part of the contents of a box detained by me), which I feel it my duty to transmit to you, will, I trust, be a sufficient apology for addressing myself to you in the first instance. Holding as I do an official situation under the Board of Customs, it would perhaps have been more strictly regular to have first communicated them to my own Board, and if the not having done it should appear to you to be informal, I must trust to your candour in not implicating me for my zealous intentions. Some days since a large deal box, directed to Miss Hitchener, Hurstpierpoint, Brighton, England, was landed from on board one of the Holyhead Packets, and brought to the Custom House, where, as Surveyor and Searcher of the Customs, I opened it, and found the enclosed open letter —the tendency of which at this moment I need not point out; and it still remains in my custody. If it should be your desire to have them transmitted to

London, and withheld from the person to whom they are addressed, I should be glad to be honoured with your confidential opinion and commands in what way I ought to forward it, consistent with my public duty as an officer of the Customs, and the respect due to my Board.

I have the honour to be,

Your very obedient servant,

PIERCE THOMAS.

Private.

The Right Honble. R. Ryder, Secretary.

3. *Two Letters from the Post Office Agent at Holyhead, to the Secretary of the Post Office.*[1]

Most Private.

***Holyhead, March 31st*, 1812.**

MY DEAR SIR,

The Surveyor of the Customs consulted me yesterday on having discovered in the Custom House, a few days since, a Large deal box, directed to "Miss Hitchener Hurst per pier, Brighton Sussex England," which had been landed from one of the Packets from Ireland.—It contained, besides a great quantity of Pamphlets and printed papers, an *open letter*, of a tendency so dangerous to Government, that I urged him to write without further loss of time, a confidential letter, either to the Secretary of State, or to Mr. Percival, [*sic*] and enclose the

[1] These two letters and that from the Postmaster General which follows them are in the possession of Lord Carlingford, attached to a copy of the *Proposals for an Association* and one of the *Declaration of Rights*. Mr. Fellowes's letters were forwarded by Mr. Freeling to the Earl of Chichester, then joint Postmaster General with the Earl of Sandwich.

letter, and one of each of the Pamphlets and printed Declarations (as they are styled), which he accordingly did by yesterday's Post, to Mr. Percival.

As the Letter in question, which the Surveyor gave me to read, contained a paragraph injurious to the revenue of the P. Office—I think it my duty to make you acquainted with it—it is as follows :—

" Percy has sent you a box full of inflammable matter, therefore I think I may send this."

" I sent you two *letters in news Papers,* which I hope you received safe from the Intrusion of the Post Masters. —I sent a Pamphlet to my Father some time since in the same way."

" *Disperse the Declarations, Percy says the Farmers are fond of having them stuck on their walls.*"

Mr. Thomas, the gentleman who gave me this information, having acted by my advice, in order to avoid the delay of reporting to the Custom House and the possibility of its being considered as a common seizure, of which there are a great many every year—has requested that I would not mention it—and I therefore request you to consider this as confidential.—I will send you a Pamphlet in the course of a day or two. But I trust in the mean time this communication may enable the office to detect any future correspondence between the parties under the cover of a News Paper.

I have the honour to remain, Dear Sir,

Your faithful Humble Servant,

William Douce Fellowes.

Francis Freeling, Esq.

It is a very common custom with the people in Ireland

to write in News Papers, I open all that come through my hands, and have charged many from being written in.

The Person whose letter I have quoted from, appears to be English, and to have lately gone to Ireland, I have no doubt but an extensive correspondence will be attempted in the way mentioned—there is no signature to the letter—or address.

April 1*st*, 1812.

MY DEAR SIR,

I send you the Pamphlet, and *Declaration of Rights*, which I mentioned in my letter of yesterday, and remain yours faithfully,

WILLIAM DOUCE FELLOWES.

Francis Freeling, Esq.

4. *Letter from the Postmaster General, to the Secretary of the Post Office.*

Stanmer, *April* 5, 1812.

DEAR FREELING,

I return the Pamphlet and Declaration the writer of the first is son of Mr. Shelley member for the Rape of Bramber,[1] and is by all accounts a most extraordinary Man. . . . . He has been in Ireland some time, and I heard of his speaking at the Catholic Convention.

Miss Hichener of Hurstperpoint keeps a school there, and is well spoken of: her Father keeps a Publick

[1] This is a mistake. Shelley's father was Member for Shoreham.

House in the neighbourhood, he was originally a Smugler, and changed his Name from Yorke to Tichener, before he took the publick House.

I shall have a watch upon the Daughter and discover whether there is any connection between her and Shelley.

I shall come to Town on Wednesday.

As I am to see Mr. Scott tomorrow, I shall keep the Brighton Papers untill I have seen him.

Your's most sincerely

CHICHESTER.

I send my Receipt enclosed, you will be so good as to pay the Salary to Messrs. Hoare's.[1]

[1] The foregoing papers, forming Appendix VI, have not been corrected or amended, as far as this edition is concerned. Harriet's letter to Miss Hitchener I have left just as I found it; and the letters of Mr. Fellowes and the Earl of Chichester I have given *verbatim et literatim* from the originals, kindly lent to me by Lord Carlingford. The Earl of Chichester's spelling and punctuation are not altogether beyond reproach; and his Lordship cannot be regarded as in any sense an accurate letter-writer. I have omitted an unpleasant inaccuracy from his first paragraph.

VII.

THE FOUR AGES OF POETRY.

By Thomas Love Peacock.[1]

Qui inter hæc nutriuntur non magis sapere possunt, quam bene olere qui in culinâ habitant.—Petronius.

Poetry, like the world, may be said to have four ages, but in a different order: the first age of poetry being the age of iron; the second, of gold; the third of silver; and the fourth of brass.

The first, or iron age of poetry, is that in which rude bards celebrate in rough numbers the exploits of ruder chiefs, in days when every man is a warrior, and when the great practical maxim of every form of society, "to keep what we have and to catch what we can," is not yet disguised under names of justice and forms of law, but is the naked motto of the naked sword, which is the only judge and jury in every question of *meum* and *tuum*. In these days, the only three trades flourishing (besides that of priest, which flourishes always) are those of king, thief, and beggar: the beggar being, for the most part, a king deject, and the thief a king expectant. The first question asked of a stranger is, whether he is a beggar or a thief:[2] the stranger, in reply, usually assumes the first, and awaits

[1] Published in *Ollier's Literary Miscellany*, 1820. See Note to *Defence of Poetry*, Vol. III, p. 98.

[2] See the Odyssey, passim: and Thucydides, I. 5. [Peacock's Note.]

a convenient opportunity to prove his claim to the second appellation.

The natural desire of every man to engross to himself as much power and property as he can acquire by any of the means which might makes right, is accompanied by the no less natural desire of making known to as many people as possible the extent to which he has been a winner in this universal game. The successful warrior becomes a chief; the successful chief becomes a king: his next want is an organ to disseminate the fame of his achievements and the extent of his possessions; and this organ he finds in a bard, who is always ready to celebrate the strength of his arm, being first duly inspired by that of his liquor. This is the origin of poetry, which, like all other trades, takes its rise in the demand for the commodity, and flourishes in proportion to the extent of the market.

Poetry is thus in its origin panegyrical. The first rude songs of all nations appear to be a sort of brief historical notices, in a strain of tumid hyperbole, of the exploits and possessions of a few pre-eminent individuals. They tell us how many battles such an one has fought, how many helmets he has cleft, how many breastplates he has pierced, how many widows he has made, how much land he has appropriated, how many houses he has demolished for other people, what a large one he has built for himself, how much gold he has stowed away in it, and how liberally and plentifully he pays, feeds, and intoxicates the divine and immortal bards, the sons of Jupiter, but for whose everlasting songs the names of heroes would perish.

This is the first stage of poetry before the invention of written letters. The numerical modulation is at once useful as a help to memory, and pleasant to the ears of uncultured men, who are easily caught by sound: and, from the exceeding flexibility of the yet unformed language, the poet does no violence to his ideas in subjecting them to the fetters of number. The savage, indeed, lisps in numbers, and all rude and uncivilized people express themselves in the manner which we call poetical.

The scenery by which he is surrounded, and the superstitions which are the creed of his age, form the poet's mind. Rocks, mountains, seas, unsubdued forests, unnavigable rivers, surround him with forms of power and mystery, which ignorance and fear have peopled with spirits, under multifarious names of gods, goddesses, nymphs, genii, and dæmons. Of all these personages marvellous tales are in existence: the nymphs are not indifferent to handsome young men, and the gentlemen-genii are much troubled and very troublesome with a propensity to be rude to pretty maidens: the bard, therefore, finds no difficulty in tracing the genealogy of his chief to any of the deities in his neighbourhood with whom the said chief may be most desirous of claiming relationship.

In this pursuit, as in all others, some, of course, will attain a very marked pre-eminence; and these will be held in high honour, like Demodocus in the Odyssey, and will be consequently inflated with boundless vanity, like Thamyris in the Iliad. Poets are as yet the only historians and chroniclers of their time, and the sole depositories of all the knowledge of their age; and though this knowledge is rather a crude congeries of traditional phantasies than a collection of useful truths, yet, such as it is, they have it to themselves. They are observing and thinking, while others are robbing and fighting: and though their object be nothing more than to secure a share of the spoil, yet they accomplish this end by intellectual, not by physical power: their success excites emulation to the attainment of intellectual eminence: thus they sharpen their own wits and awaken those of others, at the same time that they gratify vanity and amuse curiosity. A skilful display of the little knowledge they have gains them credit for the possession of much more which they have not. Their familiarity with the secret history of gods and genii obtains for them, without much difficulty, the reputation of inspiration; thus they are not only historians, but theologians, moralists, and legislators: delivering their oracles *ex cathedrâ*, and being indeed often themselves (as Orpheus and Amphion) regarded as portions and emanations of divinity: building cities with a song, and leading brutes with a symphony; which are only metaphors for the faculty of leading multitudes by the nose.

The golden age of poetry finds its materials in the age of iron. This age begins when poetry begins to be retrospective; when something like a more extended system of civil polity is established; when personal strength and courage avail less to the aggrandizing of their possessor, and to the making and marring of kings and kingdoms, and are checked by organized bodies, social institutions, and hereditary successions. Men also live more in the light of truth and within the interchange of observation; and thus perceive that the agency of gods and genii is not so frequent among themselves as, to judge from the songs and legends of the past time, it was among their ancestors. From these two circumstances, really diminished personal power, and apparently diminished familiarity with gods and genii, they very easily and naturally deduce two conclusions: 1st, That men are degenerated, and 2nd, That they are less in favour with the gods. The people of the petty states and colonies, which have now acquired stability and form, which owed their origin and first prosperity to the talents and courage of a single chief, magnify their founder through the mists of distance and tradition, and perceive him achieving wonders with a god or goddess always at his elbow. They find his name and his exploits thus magnified and accompanied in their traditionary songs, which are their only memorials. All that is said of him is in this character. There is nothing to contradict it. The man and his exploits and his tutelary deities are mixed and blended in one invariable association. The marvellous, too, is very much like a snow-ball: it grows as it rolls downward, till the little nucleus of truth, which began its descent from the summit, is hidden in the accumulation of superinduced hyperbole.

When tradition, thus adorned and exaggerated, has surrounded the founders of families and states with so much adventitious power and magnificence, there is no praise which a living poet can, without fear of being kicked for clumsy flattery, address to a living chief, that will not still leave the impression that the latter is not so great a man as his ancestors. The man must, in this case, be praised through his ancestors. Their greatness must be established, and he must be shown to be their worthy descendant. All the people of a state are interested in the founder of their state. All states that have harmonized into a common form of society, are interested in their respective founders. All men are interested in their ancestors. All men love to look back into the days that are past. In these circumstances traditional national poetry is reconstructed and brought, like chaos, into order and form. The interest is more universal: understanding is enlarged: passion still has scope and play: character is still various and strong: nature is still unsubdued and existing in all her beauty and magnificence, and men are not yet excluded from her observation by the magnitude of cities, or the daily confinement of civic life: poetry is more an art: it requires greater skill in numbers, greater command of language, more extensive and various knowledge, and greater comprehensiveness of mind. It still exists without rivals in any other department of literature; and even the arts, painting and sculpture certainly, and music probably, are comparatively rude and imperfect. The whole field of intellect is its own. It has no rivals in history, nor in philosophy, nor in science. It is cultivated by the greatest intellects of the age, and listened to by all the rest. This is the age of Homer, the golden age of poetry. Poetry has now attained its perfection: it has attained the point which it cannot pass: genius therefore seeks new forms for the treatment of the same subjects: hence the lyric poetry of Pindar and Alcæus, and the tragic poetry of Æschylus and Sophocles. The favour of kings, the honour of the Olympic crown, the applause of present multitudes, all that can feed vanity and stimulate rivalry, await the successful cultivator of this art, till its forms become exhausted, and new rivals arise around it in new fields of literature, which gradually acquire more influence as, with the progress of reason and civilization, facts become more interesting than fiction: indeed, the maturity of poetry may be considered the infancy of history. The transition from Homer to Herodotus is scarcely more remarkable than that from Herodotus to Thucydides in the gradual dereliction of fabulous incident and ornamented language. Herodotus is as much a poet in relation to Thucydides as Homer is in relation to Herodotus. The history of Herodotus is half a poem: it was written while the whole field of literature yet belonged to the Muses, and the nine books of which it was composed were therefore of right, as well as of courtesy, superinscribed with their nine names.

Speculations, too, and disputes, on the nature of man and of mind; on moral duties and on good and evil; on the animate and inanimate components of the visible world; begin to share attention with the eggs of Leda and the horns of Io, and to draw off from poetry a portion of its once undivided audience.

Then comes the silver age, or the poetry of civilized life. This poetry is of two kinds, imitative and original. The imitative consists in recasting, and giving an exquisite polish to the poetry of the age of gold: of this Virgil is the most obvious and striking example. The original is chiefly comic, didactic, or satiric: as in Menander, Aristophanes, Horace, and Juvenal. The poetry of this age is characterized by an exquisite and fastidious selection of words, and a laboured and somewhat monotonous harmony of expression: but its monotony consists in this, that experience having exhausted all the varieties of modulation, the civilized poetry selects the most beautiful, and prefers the repetition of these to ranging through the variety of all. But the best expression being that into which the idea naturally falls, it requires the utmost labour and care so to reconcile the inflexibility of civilized language and the laboured polish of versification with the idea intended to be expressed, that sense may not appear to be sacrificed to sound. Hence numerous efforts and rare success.

This state of poetry is, however, a step towards its extinction. Feeling and passion are best painted in, and roused by, ornamental and figurative language; but the reason and the understanding are best addressed in the simplest and most unvarnished phrase. Pure reason and dispassionate truth would be perfectly ridiculous in verse, as we may judge by versifying one of Euclid's demonstrations. This will be found true of all dispassionate reasoning whatever, and of all reasoning that requires comprehensive views and enlarged combinations. It is only the more tangible points of morality, those which command assent at once, those which have a mirror in every mind, and in which the severity of reason is warmed and rendered palatable by being mixed up with feeling and imagination, that are applicable even to what is called moral poetry: and as the sciences of morals and of mind advance towards perfection, as they become more enlarged and comprehensive in their views, as reason gains the ascendancy in them over imagination and feeling, poetry can no longer accompany them in their progress, but drops into the background, and leaves them to advance alone.

Thus the empire of thought is withdrawn from poetry, as the empire of facts had been before. In respect of the latter, the poet of the age of iron celebrates the achievements of his contemporaries; the poet of the age of gold celebrates the heroes of the age of iron; the poet of the age of silver re-casts the poems of the age of gold: we may here see how very slight a ray of historical truth is sufficient to dissipate all the illusions of poetry. We know no more of the men than of the gods of the Iliad; no more of Achilles than we do of Thetis; no more of Hector and Andromache than we do of Vulcan and

Venus: these belong altogether to poetry; history has no share in them: but Virgil knew better than to write an epic about Cæsar; he left him to Livy; and travelled out of the confines of truth and history into the old regions of poetry and fiction.

Good sense and elegant learning, conveyed in polished and somewhat monotonous verse, are the perfection of the original and imitative poetry of civilized life. Its range is limited, and when exhausted, nothing remains but the *crambe repetita* of commonplace, which at length becomes thoroughly wearisome, even to the most indefatigable readers of the newest new nothings.

It is now evident that poetry must either cease to be cultivated, or strike into a new path. The poets of the age of gold have been imitated and repeated till no new imitation will attract notice: the limited range of ethical and didactic poetry is exhausted: the associations of daily life in an advanced state of society are of very dry, methodical, unpoetical matters-of-fact: but there is always a multitude of listless idlers, yawning for amusement, and gaping for novelty: and the poet makes it his glory to be foremost among their purveyors.

Then comes the age of brass, which, by rejecting the polish and the learning of the age of silver, and taking a retrograde stride to the barbarisms and crude traditions of the age of iron, professes to return to nature and revive the age of gold. This is the second childhood of poetry. To the comprehensive energy of the Homeric Muse, which, by giving at once the grand outline of things, presented to the mind a vivid picture in one or two verses, inimitable alike in simplicity and magnificence, is substituted a verbose and minutely-detailed description of thoughts, passions, actions, persons, and things, in that loose rambling style of verse, which any one may write, *stans pede in uno*, at the rate of two hundred lines in an hour. To this age may be referred all the poets who flourished in the decline of the Roman Empire. The best specimen of it, though not the most generally known, is the Dionysiaca of Nonnus, which contains many passages of exceeding beauty in the midst of masses of amplification and repetition.

The iron age of classical poetry may be called the bardic; the golden, the Homeric; the silver, the Virgilian; and the brass, the Nonnic.

Modern poetry has also its four ages: but "it wears its rue with a difference."

To the age of brass in the ancient world succeeded the dark ages, in which the light of the Gospel began to spread over Europe, and in which, by a mysterious and inscrutable dispensation, the darkness thickened with the progress of the light. The tribes that overran the Roman Empire brought back the days of barbarism, but with this difference, that there were many books in the world, many places in which they were preserved, and occasionally some one by whom they were read, who indeed (if he escaped being burned *pour l'amour de Dieu*) generally lived an object of mysterious fear, with the reputation of magician, alchymist, and astrologer. The emerging of the nations of Europe from this superinduced barbarism, and their settling into new forms of polity, was accompanied, as the first ages of Greece had been, with a wild spirit of adventure, which, co-operating with new manners and new superstitions, raised up a fresh crop of chimæras, not less fruitful, though far less beautiful, than those of Greece. The semi-deification of women by the maxims of the age of chivalry, combining with these new fables, produced the romance of the middle ages. The founders of the new line of heroes took the place of the demi-gods of Grecian poetry. Charlemagne and his Paladins, Arthur and his knights of the round table, the heroes of the iron age of chivalrous poetry, were seen through the same magnifying mist of distance, and their exploits were celebrated with even more extravagant hyperbole. These legends, combined with the exaggerated love that pervades the songs of the troubadours, the reputation of magic that attached to learned men, the infant wonders of natural philosophy, the crazy fanaticism of the crusades, the power and privileges of the great feudal chiefs, and the holy mysteries of monks and nuns, formed a state of society in which no two laymen could meet without fighting, and in which the three staple ingredients of lover, prize-fighter, and fanatic, that composed the basis of the character of every true man, were mixed up and diversified, in different individuals and classes, with so many distinctive excellences, and under such an infinite motley variety of costume, as gave the range of a most extensive and picturesque field to the two great constituents of poetry, love and battle.

From these ingredients of the iron age of modern poetry, dispersed in the rhymes of ministrels and the songs of the troubadours, arose the golden age, in which the scattered materials were harmonized and blended about the time of the revival of learning; but with this peculiar difference, that Greek and Roman literature pervaded all the poetry of the golden age of modern poetry, and hence resulted a heterogeneous compound of all ages and nations in one picture; an infinite licence, which gave to the poet the free range of the whole field of imagination and memory. This was carried very far by Ariosto, but farthest of all by Shakespeare and his contemporaries, who used time and locality merely because they could not do without them, because every action must have its when and where: but they made no scruple of deposing a Roman Emperor by an Italian Count, and sending him off in the disguise of a French pilgrim to be shot with a blunderbuss by an English archer. This makes the old English drama very picturesque, at any rate, in the variety of costume, and very diversified in action and character; though it is a picture of nothing that ever was seen on earth except a Venetian carnival.

The greatest of English poets, Milton, may be said to stand alone between the ages of gold and silver, combining the excellences of both; for with all the energy, and power, and freshness of the first, he united all the studied and elaborate magnificence of the second.

The silver age succeeded; beginning with Dryden, coming to perfection with Pope, and ending with Goldsmith, Collins, and Gray.

Cowper divested verse of its exquisite polish; he thought in metre, but paid more attention to his thoughts than his verse. It would be difficult to draw the boundary of prose and blank verse between his letters and his poetry.

The silver age was the reign of authority; but authority now began to be shaken, not only in poetry but in the whole sphere of its dominion. The contemporaries of Gray and Cowper were deep and elaborate thinkers. The subtle scepticism of Hume, the solemn irony of Gibbon, the daring paradoxes of Rousseau, and the biting ridicule of Voltaire, directed the energies of four extraordinary minds to shake every portion of the reign of authority. Inquiry was roused, the activity of intellect was excited, and poetry came in for its share of the general result. The changes had been rung on lovely maid and sylvan shade, summer heat and green retreat, waving trees and sighing breeze, gentle swains and amorous pains, by versifiers who took them on trust, as meaning something very soft and tender, without much caring what: but with this general activity of intellect came a necessity for even poets to appear to know something of what they professed to talk of. Thomson and Cowper looked at the trees and hills which so many ingenious gentlemen had rhymed about so long without looking at them at all, and the effect of the operation on poetry was like the discovery of a new world. Painting shared the influence, and the principles of picturesque beauty were explored by adventurous essayists with indefatigable pertinacity. The success which attended these experiments, and the pleasure which resulted from them, had the usual effect of all new enthusiasms, that of turning the heads of a few unfortunate persons, the patriarchs of the age of brass, who, mistaking the prominent novelty for the all-important totality, seem to have ratiocinated much in the following manner: "Poetical genius is the finest of all things, and we feel that we have more of it than any one ever had. The way to bring it to perfection is to cultivate poetical impressions exclusively. Poetical impressions can be received only among natural scenes: for all that is artificial is anti-poetical. Society is artificial, therefore we will live out of society. The mountains are natural, therefore we will live in the mountains. There we shall be shining models of purity and virtue, passing the whole day in the innocent and amiable occupation of going up and down hill, receiving poetical impressions, and communicating them in immortal verse to admiring generations." To some such perversion of intellect we owe that egregious confraternity of rhymesters, known by the name of the Lake Poets; who certainly did receive and communicate to the world some of the most extraordinary poetical impressions that ever were heard of, and ripened into models of public virtue, too splendid to need illustration. They wrote verses on a new principle; saw rocks and rivers in a new light; and remaining studiously ignorant of history, society, and human nature, cultivated the phantasy only at the expense of the memory and the reason; and contrived, though they had retreated from the world for the express purpose of seeing nature as she was, to see her only as she was not, converting the land they lived in into a sort of fairy-land, which they peopled with mysticisms and chimæras. This gave what is called a new tone to poetry, and conjured up a herd of desperate imitators, who have brought the age of brass prematurely to its dotage.

The descriptive poetry of the present day has been called by its cultivators a return to nature. Nothing is more impertinent than this pretension. Poetry cannot travel out of the regions of its birth, the uncultivated lands of semi-civilized men. Mr. Wordsworth, the great leader of the returners to nature, cannot describe a scene under his own eyes without putting into it the shadow of a Danish boy or the living ghost of Lucy Gray, or some similar phantastical parturition of the moods of his own mind.

In the origin and perfection of poetry, all the associations of life were composed of poetical materials. With us it is decidedly the reverse. We know too that there are no Dryads in Hyde-park nor Naiads in the

Regent's-canal. But barbaric manners and supernatural interventions are essential to poetry. Either in the scene, or in the time, or in both, it must be remote from our ordinary perceptions. While the historian and the philosopher are advancing in, and accelerating, the progress of knowledge, the poet is wallowing in the rubbish of departed ignorance, and raking up the ashes of dead savages to find gewgaws and rattles for the grown babies of the age. Mr. Scott digs up the poachers and cattle-stealers of the ancient border. Lord Byron cruises for thieves and pirates on the shores of the Morea and among the Greek islands. Mr. Southey wades through ponderous volumes of travels and old chronicles, from which he carefully selects all that is false, useless, and absurd, as being essentially poetical; and when he has a commonplace book full of monstrosities, strings them into an epic. Mr. Wordsworth picks up village legends from old women and sextons; and Mr. Coleridge, to the valuable information acquired from similar sources, superadds the dreams of crazy theologians and the mysticisms of German metaphysics, and favours the world with visions in verse, in which the quadruple elements of sexton, old woman, Jeremy Taylor, and Emanuel Kant are harmonized into a delicious poetical compound. Mr. Moore presents us with a Persian, and Mr. Campbell with a Pennsylvanian tale, both formed on the same principle as Mr. Southey's epics, by extracting from a perfunctory and desultory perusal of a collection of voyages and travels, all that useful investigation would not seek for and that common sense would reject.

These disjointed relics of tradition and fragments of second-hand observation, being woven into a tissue of verse, constructed on what Mr. Coleridge calls a new principle (that is, no principle at all), compose a modern-antique compound of frippery and barbarism, in which the puling sentimentality of the present time is grafted on the misrepresented ruggedness of the past into a heterogeneous congeries of unamalgamating manners, sufficient to impose on the common readers of poetry, over whose understandings the poet of this class possesses that commanding advantage, which, in all circumstances and conditions of life, a man who knows something, however little, always possesses over one who knows nothing.

A poet in our times is a semi-barbarian in a civilized community. He lives in the days that are past. His ideas, thoughts, feelings, associations, are all with barbarous manners, obsolete customs, and exploded superstitions. The march of his intellect is like that of a crab, backward. The brighter the light diffused around him by the progress of reason, the thicker is the darkness of antiquated barbarism, in which he buries himself like a mole, to throw up the barren hillocks of his Cimmerian labours. The philosophic mental tranquillity which looks round with an equal eye on all external things, collects a store of ideas, discriminates their relative value, assigns to all their proper place, and from the materials of useful knowledge thus collected, appreciated, and arranged, forms new combinations that impress the stamp of their power and utility on the real business of life, is diametrically the reverse of that frame of mind which poetry inspires, or from which poetry can emanate. The highest inspirations of poetry are resolvable into three ingredients: the rant of unregulated passion, the whining of exaggerated feeling, and the cant of factitious sentiment: and can therefore serve only to ripen a splendid lunatic like Alexander, a puling driveller like Werter, or a morbid dreamer like Wordsworth. It can never make a philosopher, nor a statesman, nor in any class of life an useful or rational man. It cannot claim the slightest share in any one of the comforts and utilities of life of which we have witnessed so many and so rapid advances. But though not useful, it may be said it is highly ornamental, and deserves to be cultivated for the pleasure it yields. Even if this be granted, it does not follow that a writer of poetry in the present state of society is not a waster of his own time, and a robber of that of others. Poetry is not one of those arts which, like painting, require repetition and multiplication, in order to be diffused among society. There are more good poems already existing than are sufficient to employ that portion of life which any mere reader and recipient of poetical impressions should devote to them, and these having been produced in poetical times, are far superior in all the characteristics of poetry to the artificial reconstructions of a few morbid ascetics in unpoetical times. To read the promiscuous rubbish of the present time to the exclusion of the select treasures of the past, is to substitute the worse for the better variety of the same mode of enjoyment.

But in whatever degree poetry is cultivated, it must necessarily be to the neglect of some branch of useful study: and it is a lamentable spectacle to see minds, capable of better things, running to seed in the specious indolence of these empty aimless mockeries of intellectual exertion. Poetry was the mental rattle that awakened the attention of intellect in the infancy of civil society: but for the maturity of mind to make a serious business of the playthings of its childhood, is as absurd as for a full-grown man to rub his gums with coral, and cry to be charmed to sleep by the jingle of silver bells.

As to that small portion of our contemporary poetry, which is neither descriptive, nor narrative, nor dramatic, and which, for want of a better name, may be called ethical, the most distinguished portion of it, consisting merely of querulous, egotistical rhapsodies, to express the writer's high dissatisfaction with the world and everything in it, serves only to confirm what has been said of the semi-barbarous character of poets, who from singing dithyrambics and "Io Triumphe," while society was savage, grow rabid, and out of their element, as it becomes polished and enlightened.

Now when we consider that it is not to the thinking and studious, and scientific and philosophical part of the community, not to those whose minds are bent on the pursuit and promotion of permanently useful ends and aims, that poets must address their minstrelsy, but to that much larger portion of the reading public, whose minds are not awakened to the desire of valuable knowledge, and who are indifferent to anything beyond being charmed, moved, excited, affected, and exalted; charmed by harmony, moved by sentiment, excited by passion, affected by pathos, and exalted by sublimity; harmony, which is language on the rack of Procrustes; sentiment, which is canting egotism in the mask of refined feeling; passion, which is the commotion of a weak and selfish mind; pathos, which is the whining of an unmanly spirit; and sublimity, which is the inflation of an empty head: when we consider that the great and permanent interests of human society become more and more the main-spring of intellectual pursuit; that in proportion as they become so, the subordinacy of the ornamental to the useful will be more and more seen and acknowledged, and that therefore the progress of useful art and science, and of moral and political knowledge, will continue more and more to withdraw attention from frivolous and unconducive, to solid and conducive studies: that therefore the poetical audience will not only continually diminish in the proportion of its number to that of the rest of the reading public, but will also sink lower and lower in the comparison of intellectual acquirement: when we consider that the poet must still please his audience, and must therefore continue to sink to their level, while the rest of the community is rising above it: we may easily conceive that the day is not distant, when the degraded state of every species of poetry will be as generally recognized as that of dramatic poetry has long been: and this not from any decrease either of intellectual power, or intellectual acquisition, but because intellectual power and intellectual acquisition have turned themselves into other and better channels, and have abandoned the cultivation and the fate of poetry to the degenerate fry of modern rhymesters, and their olympic judges, the magazine critics, who continue to debate and promulgate oracles about poetry, as if it were still what it was in the Homeric age, the all-in-all of intellectual progression, and as if there were no such things in existence as mathematicians, astronomers, chemists, moralists, metaphysicians, historians, politicians, and political economists, who have built into the upper air of intelligence a pyramid, from the summit of which they see the modern Parnassus far beneath them, and, knowing how small a place it occupies in the comprehensiveness of their prospect, smile at the little ambition and the circumscribed perceptions with which the drivellers and mountebanks upon it are contending for the poetical palm and the critical chair.

VIII.

LETTER OF MESSRS. JOHN BALLANTYNE & CO. CONCERNING "THE WANDERING JEW."[1]

Edinburgh, September 24th, 1810.

SIR,

The delay which occurred in our reply to you, respecting the poem you have obligingly offered us for publication, has arisen from our literary friends and advisers (at least such as we have confidence in) being in the country at this season, as is usual, and the time they have bestowed on its perusal.

We are extremely sorry at length, after the most mature deliberation, to be under the necessity of declining the honour of being the publishers of the present poem; —not that we doubt its success, but that it is perhaps, better suited to the character, and liberal feelings of the English, than the bigoted spirit, which yet pervades

[1] This is the letter referred to in Shelley's letter to Stockdale, dated the 28th of September, 1810, and printed at p. 332 of the present volume. Mr. Garnett makes the following very pertinent remarks on this letter (*Macmillan's Magazine*, June, 1860, pp. 103–4):—

"Now, had Shelley told any of his friends that the 'Lady of the Lake' had been assailed in Scotland on the ground of atheism, and professed to have derived his information from the Ballantynes, the circumstance would ere this have made its appearance in print as a proof of his irresistible tendency to 'hallucinations,' and his 'inability to relate anything exactly as it happened.' Here, however, we see that he would not have spoken without authority. It is, of course, quite possible that the Ballantynes may themselves have been mystified or mystificators—otherwise it would appear that it had, in that fortunate age, been vouchsafed to certain Scotch clergymen to attain the *ne plus ultra* of absurdity—

'Topmost stars of unascended heaven,
Pinnacled dim in the intense inane'—

or insane, whichever may be the

many cultivated minds in this country. Even Walter Scott, is assailed on all hands at present by our Scotch spiritual, and Evangelical magazines, and instructors, for having promulgated atheistical doctrines in the Lady of the Lake.

We beg you will have the goodness to advise us how it should be returned, and we think its being consigned to the care of some person in London, would be more likely to ensure its safety than addressing it to Horsham.

We are, sir,

Your most obedient humble servants,

JOHN BALLANTYNE & CO.

correct reading. It is needless to add that the 'Wandering Jew' is quite guiltless of atheism, or any 'ism' but an occasional solecism. Whatever precautions may have been taken to ensure the safety of the MS., they failed to bring it into Stockdale's hands. He never received it, and it seems to have remained peaceably at Edinburgh till its discovery in 1831, when a portion of it appeared in *Fraser's Magazine*, and has since been reprinted in one of the many unauthorised editions of Shelley's works. According to Captain Medwin, indeed, Shelley left it at his lodgings in Edinburgh in 1811. But the Captain evidently knew nothing of the negotiation with the Ballantynes, which affords a much more plausible explanation of the discovery of the MS. in the Scotch metropolis. He adds, indeed, that the young authors were induced to lay aside all thoughts of publication by the adverse judgment of Campbell, who returned the MS. submitted for his inspection with the remark that there were only two good lines in the whole, naming a pair of exceedingly commonplace ones. Whatever the effect on his coadjutor, it is now clear that Shelley was not to be daunted by the condemnation even of a poet he admired, though, doubtless, he would have himself admitted in after life that the quest after tolerable lines in the 'Wandering Jew' might scarcely be more hopeful than that undertaken of old after righteous men in the Cities of the Plain."

IX.

Letters to Stockdale from Sir Timothy Shelley and Thomas Jefferson Hogg.[1]

1. *Letter from Sir Timothy Shelley.*

Field Place, 23rd December, 1810.

Sir,

I take the earliest opportunity of expressing to you my best thanks for the very liberal and handsome manner in which you imparted to me the sentiments you hold towards my son, and the open and friendly communication. I shall ever esteem it, and hold it in remembrance. I will take an opportunity of calling on you again, when the call at St. Stephen's Chapel enforces my attendance by a call of the House.

My son begs to make his compliments to you.

I have the honour to be, sir,

Your very obedient humble servant,

T. Shelley.

[1] These letters are from *Stockdale's Budget* (See note at p. 328 of the present volume). Stockdale printed them in connexion with his Memoirs of Shelley's relations with him as a publisher. The publisher affects to have been alarmed at the heterodox views of the young poet, and to have communicated his alarm to Shelley's father. Mr. Garnett's notes on this subject (*Macmillan's Magazine*, June, 1860, pp. 106 *et seq.*) are indispensable; and I make no apology for extracting them :—

"Sir (then Mr.) Timothy Shelley, the poet's uncongenial father, now appears upon the scene. At the date

2. *Letter from Thomas Jefferson Hogg.*

Univ. Coll., Oxford, Jan. 21st, 1811.

SIR,

I have just heard from a friend to my great surprize that you have made very free with my character to Mr. Shelley. I feel it my duty as a gentleman closely to investigate this extraordinary conduct. I ask what there was in my behaviour to you contrary to the strictest politeness, what there was to justify such an infamous proceeding ?

I insist Sir upon knowing the precise nature the very words of your conversation with Mr. S——.

I insist upon being informed upon what authority you spoke thus of me. I demand a full, a perfect apology from yourself. I desire that you should immediately write in order to contradict whatever you may have told Mr. Shelley or any one else.

When I am informed of the exact nature of the offence I can judge of the necessary apology.——

The bare mention of the MS. with which I entrusted

of the next letter, he had already several times called at Stockdale's shop in the company of his son, and thus afforded the publisher an opportunity of contributing the result of his own observation to the universal testimony respecting the dispositions of the two, and the relation in which they stood to each other. Percy Shelley captivated all hearts; the roughest were subdued by his sweetness, the most reserved won by his affectionate candour. No man ever made more strange or unsympathetic friends, and they who may seem to have dealt most hardly with his memory since his death are chiefly the well-meaning people whose error it has been

you to any one was an unparallelled breach of confidence. —There have been instances of booksellers who have honourably refused to betray the authors whose works they have published altho actions were brought against them. I believe that one gentleman had honor enough to submit to the pillory rather than disgrace himself by giving up the name of one who had confided in him however unworthy he might be of such generous treatment. Altho I might be disposed to pardon this offence against myself I feel it my duty to caution the world against such flagrant violation of principle.

I shall consequently insert in the public newspapers an anonymous advertisement containing a plain statement of the manner in which you have acted. An immediate answer to this letter is desired by Sir

Yours, &c., &c.,

T. JEFFERSON HOGG.

to mistake an accidental intimacy with a remarkable character for the power of appreciating it. Among these, Stockdale cannot be refused a place, for it would be unjust not to recognise, amid all his pomposity and blundering, traces of a sincere affection for the young author whose acquaintance was certainly anything but advantageous to him in a pecuniary point of view. An equal unanimity of sentiment prevails respecting Sir Timothy; he undoubtedly meant well, but had scarcely a single prominent trait of character which would not of itself have unfitted him to be the father of such a son. Stockdale had frequent opportunities of observing the uneasy terms on which the two stood towards each other, and unhesitatingly throws the entire blame upon the father, whom he represents as narrow-minded and wrong-headed, behaving with extreme niggardliness in money matters, and at the same time continually fretting Shelley by harsh and unnecessary interference with his most indifferent actions. According to the bookseller, he ineffectually tried his best at once to dispose Sir Timothy to a more judicious line of conduct, and to put him on his guard against his son's speculative rashness. The following note [that of the 23rd of December, 1810], is probably in answer to some communication of this character."

Stockdale appears to have represented to Shelley's father that Hogg was at the bottom of the young poet's heterodoxy; and the publisher's wife (I follow Mr. Garnett's narrative) "chancing to have relations in the part of Buckinghamshire where Mr. Hogg

3. *Letter from Thomas Jefferson Hogg.*

Univ. Coll. Oxford, Jan. 23rd, 1811.

SIR,

I have just received from you a very evasive letter which I assure you is very far from being satisfactory. When you have recovered from your astonishment I must request that you will be a little more explicit. Make my case your own Sir; place yourself in my situation. Suppose that you had heard from a friend, of whose truth upon every occasion you were as perfectly convinced as of your own existence, that "your character had been made very free with that you had been infamously treated that no other bookseller would have abused your confidence in that manner?" Let me ask you Sir, if under such circumstances you would not have immediately written to the person who had behaved thus to you? Would you not have made precisely the same demands as I did? Let me enquire if under such circumstances an answer similar to the one I have just received would satisfy you? An answer which informed

had been residing, he availed himself of the circumstance to make inquiries. In those days Mr. Hogg's 'Life of Shelley' was not, and the world had not learned on his own authority that not only 'he would not walk across Chancery Lane in the narrowest part to redress all the wrongs of Ireland, past, present, and to come,' but, which is even more to the purpose, that 'he has always been totally ignorant respecting all the varieties of religious dissent.' It was therefore easier for Mrs. Stockdale to collect, with incredible celerity, full materials for such a representation of Shelley's honest but unspeculative friend as suited the views of her husband, who immediately transmitted the account to Sir Timothy. Sir Timothy naturally informed his son, who informed Mr. Hogg, who imyou that your letter was indecent, your conduct was not that of a gentleman. That the addresses, the epithets you had made use of were unusual, in consequence of which the correspondence could not be continued.

Would not this last circumstance have had a very suspicious appearance? A person is astonished that an explanation should be demanded, he refuses to comply because he never gave one before! Instead of any direct statement of facts the improbability of any ill will is urged. A feeling of the greatest respect for a gentleman who has no concern in the affair is brought upon the tapis together with a vague and futile caution. Now Sir if you received the same information from as unquestionable authority, if you had in consequence requested an explanation, would they not rather increase your conviction of the improper manner in which you had been treated when no better apology than the trite feint of astonishment was produced? I am convinced Sir that you would demand a further explanation. I Sir, do the same; I must request to hear again from you as soon as possible.

I am, Sir,

Yours, &c., &c.,

T. JEFFERSON HOGG.

mediately visited the delinquent publisher with two most indignant letters, which that pachydermatous personage has very composedly reproduced in his journal exactly as they were written. Shelley does not appear to have fulfilled his intention of calling upon Stockdale in London; but, the latter's replies to Mr. Hogg proving eminently unsatisfactory, with his wonted chivalry of feeling he addressed him the following letter from Oxford [that given at pp. 338–9 of this volume].

"On receiving this, Stockdale wrote Sir Timothy a letter, which the baronet, like Dr. Folliott, in 'Crotchet Castle,' appears to have considered 'deficient in the two great requisites of head and tail.'"

Sir Timothy sent in reply the brief note of the 30th of January 1811, given in the text, and

4. *Letter from Sir Timothy Shelley.*

Field Place, 30th of January, 1811.

SIR,

I am so surprised at the receipt of your letter of this morning, that I cannot comprehend the meaning of the language you use. I shall be in London next week, and will then call on you.

I am, sir,

Your obedient humble servant,

T. SHELLEY.

afterwards called on Stockdale, who says that he gave the anxious parent "such particulars as the urgency of the case required," and that, in consequence, "all concerned became inimical to" him (Stockdale).

END OF VOL. III.

www.ingramcontent.com/pod-product-compliance
Lightning Source LLC
Chambersburg PA
CBHW032308280326
41932CB00009B/747

* 9 7 8 3 7 4 4 6 8 5 9 5 5 *